Social Identities across the Life Course

Social Identities across the Life Course

Jenny Hockey and Allison James

palgrave
macmillan

First published 2003 by
PALGRAVE MACMILLAN
Houndmills, Basingstoke, Hampshire RG21 6XS and
175 Fifth Avenue, New York, N.Y. 10010
Companies and representatives throughout the world

PALGRAVE MACMILLAN is the global academic imprint of the Palgrave Macmillan division of St. Martin's Press, LLC and of Palgrave Macmillan Ltd. Macmillan® is a registered trademark in the United States, United Kingdom and other countries. Palgrave is a registered trademark in the European Union and other countries.

ISBN 0–333–91283–7 hardback
ISBN 0–333–91284–5 paperback

This book is printed on paper suitable for recycling and made from fully managed and sustained forest sources.

A catalogue record for this book is available from the British Library.

Library of Congress Cataloging-in-Publication Data
Hockey, Jennifer Lorna.
    Social identities across the life course / Jenny Hockey and Allison James.
        p.   cm.
    Includes bibliographical references and index.
    ISBN 0–333–91283–7 (cloth) — ISBN 0–333–91284–5 (paper)
    1. Aging—Social aspects.   2. Aging—Psychological aspects.   3. Group identity.   I. James, Allison.   II. Title.

HQ1061 .H556 2002
305.26—dc21   2002026752

10   9   8   7   6   5   4   3   2   1
12   11   10   09   08   07   06   05   04   03

Printed in China

For all our sources and our successors,
especially Joan (b. 1922) and Blue (b. 2001)

Contents

PART I

Structure, Agency and the Life Course

1

Problematising Ageing and Identity

Introduction

The title of this book *Social Identities across the Life Course* stems from a question which is implicit in theories of the life course: how do we come to know that we are ageing? In asking this question we recognise that, though our bodies change over time, those changes are imperceptible on a day-to-day basis. And yet we are, nonetheless, aware that we are ageing and we know that being of a certain age brings with it social obligations and expectations. The task of the social sciences, and one we set ourselves in this book, is to explain such processes and their impact on people's everyday lives. Just as gender and 'race' shape people's identities, so does the ageing process. In this book, we assess the extent to which social science has provided a satisfactory account of how it is we come to know that we are ageing.

We ask what the terms 'age' and 'ageing' might mean, both now and in the past. They are often taken for granted as biologically-grounded givens. That is, age is thought of simply as a measure of the passage of time between birth and death. Yet, in the West, our age impacts very powerfully on the way we see ourselves – and are seen by others. Indeed, here we argue that it has become one of the key bases for the production of social identity, acting as a way to classify and order the passing of time in an individual's life. It is not only a pervasive focus for interest, birthdays of the famous being announced daily in national newspapers with details of their age, but additionally, years since birth bear a culturally specific, ideological and symbolic load. Age, for example, implies social and moral obligations. Individuals who overstep or step outside the expectations

3

of their age become newsworthy. Thus, in 1997, Sufiah Yusof made the headlines when, at twelve years of age, she entered Oxford University to become one of Britain's youngest university students. The case of Pauline Lyon who, at 55-years old, became Britain's oldest test-tube mother, was similarly brought to our attention because of actions that appeared to transgress the norms of age-related behaviour when she gave birth to a boy in March 1999. Age therefore has a powerful effect on what is expected of us and also what is refused us.

If we consider the idea that our age is integral to our identity, then we need to recognise that it is also frequently in potential tension with it. As we shall argue, the meaning of 'age' and 'ageing' has varied in different societies and points in history. In addition, identity is itself not a unitary aspect of selfhood. More accurately, we can think of it as a negotiated, unstable assemblage of ideas and perceptions within which 'age' competes with other imperatives such as gender, class and ethnicity. These both delimit and afford opportunities for the practices which make up everyday social life. Thus, in its 'Where are they now?' column, the Saturday *Guardian* retrieved ephemeral television personalities of the 1960s and 1970s and set their photos of 'then' and 'now' alongside one another. Its intent was to assess, implicitly, the extent to which, as they grow older, such people have been able to sustain their identity as a 'famous person'. Similarly, film and pop stars, who continue to live out their screen personae, are scrutinised carefully for the humiliating marks of 'old age' upon once lithe bodies and sexually alluring faces. On the other hand, those stars who succeed in reinventing themselves during middle age are regarded with suspicion, as if, by masking their 'true' age, the authenticity of their professional identity becomes suddenly questionable. Age and ageing are therefore very central features of our social identities, but not in any straightfor-ward way.

Ageing, it would seem, thus legitimates access to certain social experiences, while denying access to others, and also embraces sets of implicit expectations about behaviour in relation to aged identities. As Berkeman (1999) points out, for example, to be a lottery jackpot winner at 85 is a rather different experience from that of a younger person. In his poignant account of the five pensioners living in a Lincolnshire old people's home, who became millionaires one Saturday night, he argues that 'the multiplicity of potential lives made possible by their win serves only to throw into sharp relief the one they already have' (*Guardian*, 15 December 1999). It underscores the irony of amassing great wealth at the end of one's life when, rather than personal jets, foreign holidays or Ferraris, it is help just to move around the house which is needed most.

Together with young scholars and elderly mothers, such transgressive examples highlight, therefore, our common, everyday recourse to the stereotypes of ageing through which we place and locate people's identities. These reveal that, perhaps, we know only relatively little about the variety of age-based identities which individuals *actually* take on across the course of their lives; and even less about how these identities are, *in practice*, made sense of by individuals in relation to the wider social and cultural norms of ageing. As we shall argue in this book, therefore, though identity has been addressed within the social sciences, there have been relatively few attempts to account theoretically for the contribution of age to social identity, and those that have largely fail to explain this as both an experiential *and* a situated process. Thus, while we know something about what it is like to *be* a child, to be middle aged or elderly, the complex social processes and experiences involved in *becoming* a school-child, a grown-up or an old-age pensioner, and making the shift from one identity to another, still remain largely uncharted and certainly undertheorised (Craib, 1998: 9). Our starting point in this book, therefore, is to bring together two rather separate areas within the social sciences – work on social identity and work on ageing and the life course. Without *both* these literatures it is difficult to provide, we argue, an adequate account of how we come to know we are ageing.

Age and the life course

If, as already suggested, we begin by thinking of both ageing and identity as social processes, we find ourselves in line with the developing trend in social theory which challenges static accounts of the 'life cycle' as a fixed and repetitive sequence of ages and stages within human life and experience. In its place we find a notion of ageing as a social as well as a physical process which is infinitely varied and variable (Spencer, 1990; Featherstone and Wernick, 1995). The term 'life course' has, therefore, been adopted as a way of envisaging the passage of a lifetime less as the mechanical turning of a wheel and more as the unpredictable flow of river. Similarly, the notion of identity has recently come to be seen as not fixed or ascribed, but as emerging out of and through people's social relationships. This perspective focuses attention, then, on the relationship between the 'self' and 'society' and acknowledges the temporal framework of the changes and movements which have and will continue to shape the context of particular cultures and historical periods (Rapport, 1993; Cohen, 1994; Hall, 1996). However, an approach which specifically seeks to address the experience of changing *age*-based identities across the life course has yet to be fully developed, despite age being one of the key bases for the production of identity. As we shall show through this volume, age is a significant resource through which individual selves construct their biographical narratives across the life course, both in terms of the past, looking back from old age and the future, looking forward from childhood. Bringing together recent attempts to reframe the life course *and* theoretical developments in the study of identity and the body, this book builds on their insights and seeks to engage with the ways in which both individuals and societies change over time and how, within particular societies, processes of physical ageing are represented and configured. In this very broad sense, then, ours is a concern with the identity politics of ageing across the life course.

In unravelling the complexities of this issue, we investigate a wide range of material and symbolic forms, making Europe and North America our primary case study areas. In these settings, we explore the cultural mores which reflect particular conceptions of children as 'incompetent' social actors and compare this classificatory process with the later sequestration of older people from mainstream economic activity on the grounds that age is thought to involve a loss of social or physical competence. We examine the valuation and promotion of young, healthy bodies in the media hype of advertising and television and explore the stigmatising power of the linguistic devaluation and degradation of those who are elderly and infirm. In a society where what we do defines who we are, it is also important to examine the changing relationship between age and work. If work has long been seen as central to social identity, what has been the effect of a now more flexible and often attenuated work-based social identity? Retirement from paid employment may no longer necessarily mark a symbolic retreat into old age and social exclusion but may, instead, register the beginning of thirty years of a new and rather different kind of life. Do increasing divorce rates in Europe and North America signal a change in the continuities which once lent coherence to an individual's life course? Do land, local community, marriage and family trades, inheritance, cross-generational oral history and family names still confer a sense of belonging? Or are these no longer important, having been superseded by new ways of understanding the self and identity across the life course? In summary: this book asks about the ideological and practical consequences of such reconfigurations of the life course and whether age, any longer, offers us firm reassurance about the developing path of identity in relation to our changing social experiences.

Sontag's interpretation of the popularisation of photography is revealing in this regard. She argues that 'as that claustrophobic unit, the nuclear family, was being carved out of a much larger family aggregate, photography came along to memorialise, to restate symbolically, the imperilled continuity and vanishing extendedness of family life' (1978: 9). The camera in this sense provided a technological fix for the diminished experience of family-based identity. However, she also notes that the practice of photography, if anything, augments the sense of temporal dislocation rather than stems its flow: 'To take a photograph is to participate in another person's (or thing's) mortality, vulnerability, mutability. Precisely by slicing out this moment and freezing it, all photographs testify to time's relentless melt' (1978: 15). In its overarching claim to be a representation of the real, the photograph fixes us, so providing us with a sense of continuity. Simultaneously, however, its claim to realism helps remind us of time's passage and the instability of the moment captured by the lens.

This desire for connectedness and the continuity of identity as people age across time is constantly demonstrated. Thus, for example, within Europe and North America, family genealogy is a fast-growing leisure activity. Systems are in place to help adopted people trace natural parents and to address the implications for kinship of new reproductive technologies and, meanwhile, the Internet has made it possible to track down kin long lost to the family. Life-course ritualisation also seems to be proliferating – in the form of evermore costly weddings, celebratory reunions of classmates and mounting floral markers at the sites of tragic death. And an increasing nostalgia for the past is also evident in the burgeoning museum industry and proliferation of heritage trails. However, the sense of rupture, loss of identity and social fragmentation across the life course, for whose repair technologies such as the camera, the video recorder, the computer simulation and the Internet search are used, is one which, ironically, we are now often told we should welcome and embrace! In the name of flexibility, employability and responsiveness to socio-economic change, a process of self reinvention and expression is promoted, with the promise of enhanced personal freedom offered as a goal. Whatever Norman Tebbit meant when he ordered the British unemployed of the 1980s to 'get on their bikes', his words have become a catch phrase for the desirability of 'pushing off' and making a 'fresh start'. Within the sphere of personal relationships, similar imperatives now require the individual to reflect on and be prepared to cast off those aspects of the self and indeed those close personal relationships which are found to be wanting (Giddens 1991: 70–108). Continuity and connectedness thus vie with fragmentation and sequestration in many people's everyday experience of ageing across the contemporary life course and, in the course of this book, we will be examining the grounds of such tensions and contradictions, mapping out their changing territory across time and in social space.

The issues outlined so far therefore centre around three core questions: first, how do individuals make biographical sense of the different social identities which they may take on or relinquish over the life course and what factors pattern and shape this process of self identification? Here, the book concerns itself with the fine-grain of the processes of 'identification', foregrounding the *experience* of ageing to provide a nuanced account of identity-making across time. Second, we ask how important biological ageing is to the adoption or relinquishing of social identities? Here, we question those contemporary theories which seek to replace earlier static models of the life course with a view of ageing that attributes almost sovereign power to the individual to take on whatever identity they wish. To what extent, we ask, are these approaches useful when they take little or no account of the body itself as a material entity which the individual both *has* and *is* (Nettleton, 1998)? Third, we consider what social factors might mediate the experience of growing up and growing old for individuals? How far do gender and sexuality have roles to play? How do ideas of family and kinship impact on the generational alliances and affiliations that individuals make, in and across time? And to what extent do prevailing political and economic factors work to shape and restrict the ways in which ageing across the life course is individually experienced?

Through the course of this book we seek, therefore, to offer a way of theorising the question of ageing which approximates more closely to the lived experiences of people's everyday lives. At different points in the life course, people engage in, or are made subject to, different processes of identification as aged persons. Some of these are welcomed, others rejected; some are open to negotiation while others are heavily constraining of individual choice. This book is not, however, a comprehensive account of theories of social identity; neither is it a handbook of ageing. Rather it offers a perspective from which to see ageing across the life course as a fundamental feature of social identity, a fact which, hitherto, has largely escaped the attention of identity theorists, especially those concerned with identity politics. In charting this path, therefore, this book represents ageing as a fundamentally embodied process and explores how this bodily condition of life is – or is not – managed and negotiated by individuals in different ways, by employing different resources and strategies, at different points in the life course with different consequences and effects.

And in pursuit of such a theoretical perspective, we have ourselves employed a wide-ranging and eclectic series of sources – academic texts of social theory as well as small-scale empirical studies, newspaper articles, advertisements, novels and biographical writings are placed alongside the findings from studies in the separate disciplines of sociology, anthropology, history, social policy, geography, health and gender studies. The breadth of this book, therefore, mirrors the very complexity of the process it seeks to describe: the multiple and interconnected ways in which, across the life course, each and every one of us comes to know that we are ageing.

Identities across the life course

In teasing out the nature of 'social identity', Jenkins argues for the significance of its temporal framing. He says:

> identity can only be understood as process. As 'being' or 'becoming'. One's social identity – indeed one's social identities, for who we are is always singular and plural – is never a final or settled matter (1996: 4).

To purposefully explore questions of identity in relation to time and temporality, as we do in this book through our focus on the life course, is therefore to have identified a critical context within which to theorise and thereby understand not only what is meant by the concept of social identity but how identities come to be formed and are made 'real' in people's everyday biographical experiences. Core to our task in this book is therefore the contemporary work on identity and identity politics which, as Roseneil and Seymour (1999: 3) argue, can be divided into two main strands. The first is a strand within social theory which seeks to explore the development of identity as self-identity and asks about the conditions surrounding an individual's emerging consciousness of the self, whereby we learn to see ourselves by the way others see us (Mead, 1934). The second, linked to poststructuralist cultural theory, is focused more on the politics of identity and cultural difference, highlighting the role of power in the construction of identity through discourses of difference – I know what I am by what I am not. However, though having these rather different agendas, both theoretical strands share a common starting point in rejecting 'the Enlightenment philosophical tradition which conceives of identity as essential, unitary, fixed and unchanging' (Roseneil and Seymour, 1999: 3). Thus, as we will show in the course of this book, in contrast to an earlier concern with social roles and role theory, which sought to show that specific social identities are stamped upon the malleable individual across the life course, this more contemporary work highlights the importance of personal agency for an understanding of how identity comes into being and how the individual, in this sense, authors her or himself in the course of everyday life experiences.

A central task of this book is therefore to engage broadly with the ideas of those who have sought to overcome misleading models which oppose 'society' and the 'individual' and regard social structure as an external force which inevitably shapes human agency. Jenkins (1996), for example, argues that to understand what social identity is, and how the process of acquiring identity takes place, requires us to look at the individual person's engagement with those collective social identities with which he or she may be routinely assigned through, for example, age, or those which arise from their experience of work during the course of their lives. In his view, social identity is both that which is unique to the individual and that which is shared and collective. The one cannot be understood without the other. Thus, a young woman's experience of motherhood and her taking on of the role of, or an identity as, 'mother' both begin with the birth of her baby. Though a unique event for her as an individual, it is also one which reflects and reproduces the symbolic meanings and practical realities through which other births and the making of mothers has taken place within her culture.

Our exploration of these issues is situated against the background of earlier social scientific work on the life course carried out within the social sciences. For example, as Chapter 2 explores, early anthropologists such as Hertz ([1907] 1960) and Van Gennep ([1908] 1960) explained the life course in terms of transition through a series of rites of passage which allowed individuals to enter into clearly differentiated roles and statuses. Working within the shadow of Durkheim, these theorists shared a set of social and political concerns about social stability and coherence, for it was Durkheim's 'discovery' of 'society' as a thing, which existed over and above the sum of its collective parts, that fuelled an interest in how such an entity might sustain itself once it had come into being (1895; 1897). Thus it was that the ageing process was often represented and talked about in terms of the 'life cycle', rather than the life course. Envisaged as a series of fixed stages and roles through which every individual moved as they aged, this cyclical pattern was held to be repeated and to remain unchanged across the generations.

It is precisely in opposition to such a static perspective that the contemporary work on identity discussed in this volume is positioned. Jenkins (1996), for example, opens his account of social identity with a description of the multitude of letters and packages which might land on someone's doormat when they reach sixty-five – birthday cards, pension forms, a concessionary public transport pass, special rates every Tuesday at the hairdresser. He goes on:

> beyond that again, in the promise of free medical prescriptions and the beckoning Day Centre, hover the shades of infirmity, of dependence, of disability. Although it will be the same face you see in the bathroom mirror, you will no longer be quite the person that you were yesterday. Nor can you ever be again (1996: 2).

While this description might seem to reflect the flavour of earlier rites of passage literature, in that the individual is passively on the receiving end of an externally-located transformation of their social identity, he goes on to note that, albeit 'never the same again', different individuals will draw on a diversity of resources to negotiate one among any number of later life social identities. Contemporary theorists such as Jenkins, who concern themselves with change, are therefore more likely to highlight a diversity and fragmentation of paths, rather than a commonality and continuity of experience, as the outcome of life's turning points. We can understand how the identity of the person on the receiving end of the birthday mail might be transformed, whether they like it or not – not just bureaucratically and economically but also phenomenologically. Yet, we must also take account of how they then respond to their altered reflection in the mirror, for this is another matter entirely, It is a matter for the individual. In this way we can develop a model of social identity as a negotiated, processual, inevitably incomplete narrative of identity formation.

In Part 1 of this book (Chapters 2 and 3), we therefore critically examine classical theories of the life course, identifying their limitations but also their strengths. This discussion is taken forward and developed in the following part (Chapters 4, 5 and 6) where we use an historical account of the western life course as a test case for a range of theoretical approaches to human ageing. This critical investigation provides us, then, in Part III, with an empirical basis upon which we can offer a new and innovative approach to ageing which brings together the hitherto disparate areas of identity, the body and the life course (Chapter 7). Through three case studies of gender, the family and work (Chapters 8, 9 and 10), we develop this approach as an alternative to those contemporary accounts which suggest that there is an unproblematic fluidity of personal identity over time and thus the possibility of a postmodern lifestyle, open to all, regardless of their social and material resources is critically challenged.

The process of age identification across the life course

Jenkins suggests that one of the reasons why social scientists have had difficulty recognising that identity is produced within the flow of social processes and social interactions is the tradition of viewing everyday life in terms of a set of conceptual dualisms. Discussions of identity have been limited by working within a set of binary oppositions which can be summarised as follows:

- agency vs. structure
- individual identity vs. social identity
- the individual vs. the collectivity
- group vs. category
- self vs. other
- internal classification vs. external classification
- virtual identity vs. nominal identity
- change vs. continuity

Every one of these theoretical terms is defined by its opposite, so creating a very black and white view of society which cannot easily explain change or ambiguity. To overcome this problem, Jenkins suggests that our task must be to create a synthesis between these dualisms. Instead of thinking of social structure as a rigid framework, we can recognise it as a social process, which incorporates the agency of individuals without whom such a process could not take place. The concept of 'structure' is thus revealed as a kind of snapshot or freeze-frame of something which is in fact in process or motion, the product of individual thought and action, operating on many many levels simultaneously. It follows from this, therefore, that we might also begin to understand social identity not as a thing but as a process, a becoming as well as a being. Indeed, this is the *phenomenological* experience of ageing across the life course (see Craib, 1998).

We began to explore such a perspective in our earlier volume, *Growing Up and Growing Old*, albeit with an emphasis on systems of classification which, to some extent, reproduced a structure/agency binary by focusing on the differences between childhood and old age, as opposed to independent adulthood. Published in 1993, that book not only brought studies of the age-based categories 'childhood' and 'later life' together within a single volume, but also developed a theoretical perspective which addressed the relationship between these periods of life which, in thought and practice, are often separated out. These categories, we argued, although positioned at opposite ends of the life course, could also be seen to share many similarities. Materially and ideologically, for example, children and older adults are often marginalised and made dependent upon members of the more dominant western category of 'independent adult'. Important here were arguments from political economy which revealed the fostering of difference and the construction of identities built around structural dependency and personal vulnerability.

The innocence of 'little' children and the frailty of 'little' old ladies could *both* be seen to have emerged out of the reconfiguration of age-based social divisions during the later stages of the industrial revolution. As disempowered social categories, they share the social milieux of other disadvantaged groups. Compulsory schooling and the provision of state pensions had a common root in the social policies of the late nineteenth century – and similar outcomes in terms of dependency at the beginning of the twenty-first. Thus, although we were arguing that 'childhood' and 'later life' were temporally separate life course categories, their historical and cultural specificity as identity categories could, nonetheless, be made sense of within a single theoretical framework. In identifying the parallel social positioning of children and older adults, and the resulting costs incurred by older people in particular, we were able to expose the structuring of the life course and the relative valuation of its different categorical identities. Positioned at opposing ends of the life course, children and elderly people share, for example, a remarkable range of common experiences in their dual marginal-isation from the mainstream of adult life.

This earlier work was stimulated by our joint recognition of paradoxical similarities between children and older adults. Yet from almost every perspective, children and older adults *are* very different. In a bodily sense they are easy to tell apart. Indeed, their very different forms of embodiment are used to define them in opposition to one another, twin points of orientation for an adult world which looks back nostalgically to the immature, unspoiled bodies of child-hood and reluctantly forward to the physical decrepitude of old age. Entrenched too in different academic disciplines, medical specialisms and welfare provision, the distinctiveness of the body's age-based characteristics is repeatedly reinforced, both in thought and practice. Indeed, it could be argued that our modern preoccupation with systems for classifying and measuring the body has helped rupture any of the connections which bond past, present and future within the individual's memory and imagination. As Foucault (1975) makes us aware, systems of monitoring and surveillance characterise every aspect of contemporary life in western societies and the yard-stick of 'normality' is often drawn up in relation to age-based bodily criteria. Health checks on babies and toddlers pave the way for the later, increasingly regimented age-staged educational SATS (Stand-ard Attainment Targets) tests which, in the UK, go to to make up the national curriculum for school children. Hair, skin and body weight are a focus for self-monitoring throughout middle age, as is memory and mental alertness, adults having an almost moral obligation to make sure their bodies do not conform too soon to the character-istics of 'old age' (Featherstone, 1991). And, in later life itself, competencies are specified on the basis of age, individuals then being measured against standards for senility and dementia.

These examples indicate, therefore, the significance of the body in answering the question: how do we know that we are ageing? However, this is not to say that ageing can therefore simply be regarded as a biological process of cellular growth, maturity and decay. This would suggest that age-based systems of classification are natural and inevitable and such a biological foundationalism would, for example, limit and disempower members of the categories 'very young' and 'very old'. And we know that this is not the case – many old and many young people choose to act outside the supposed constraints of their 'age', often with great success! Rather, as we go on to show in this book, what a focus on the body can achieve is, first, a better understanding and explanation of how bodily-based concepts of age work to mark out different kinds of aged identities across the life course; and second, how, as social actors, different people experience and make sense of the movement from one aged identity to another (Nicholson, 1995). This book explores a wealth of empirical examples and through these we are able to show how particular kinds of subjectivities and identities are produced across the life course, identities which provide us with a personal, as well as a collective, sense of growing up and growing old.

Relations of power across the life course

In arguing that bodily differences are used as the basis for policies and practices which create inequalities between people of different ages, we start with the example of 'childhood' and the space which it occupies within the life course. Arguably, it exists in relation to other categorical and generational spaces and, in contemporary western societies, these might be thought of as 'adolescence', 'youth', 'adulthood' and 'old age'. More emphatically still, Jenks argues that indeed the child 'cannot be imagined except in relation to a conception of the adult' and that it is the 'known difference between these two social locations' which contributes to our under-standing of the identities of 'child' and 'adult' (1996: 3). However, while it may always be possible to acknowledge the binarism of these relationships, the precise ways in which childhood is conceived, understood and ascribed with meaning in everyday social practice alters in relation to the economic and political demands of particular societies at particular historical moments. Thus the experiences and identities of those individuals who occupy the space of 'childhood' – that is children themselves – can be said to be, in part, shaped by the politics and policies through which the conceptual category and social identity of 'child' is given material form in everyday life.

Two important dimensions to understanding identity follow from this: the first is the question of power, the second, that of temporality. Exploring identity across the life course allows both of these features to be critically examined and explored. Jenkins (1996) observes, for example, that, in terms of the individual, the acceptance or recognition of an age-based identity does not always occur. There may be resistance or opposition, confusion and contradiction in the ways in which identities are produced and negotiated in the social realm and, as he goes on to note, it is apparent that some identities are vested with more authority than others. And, indeed, some identities endure longer than others. What is of interest here, then, is the operation of power which, usually within an institutional context, enables the authority of some, rather than other, identities to take hold and which, through the allocation of rules and resources, therefore enables some, rather than other, individuals to assume positions of power.

With respect to the life course, therefore, it can be suggested that identities such as 'adult' and 'child' might be the product of relations of power and authority. Shored up by traditional models of socialisation (Elkin, 1960; Dreitzel, 1973), adults are assumed to be in positions of authority over children, as people whose social identities have been vested with a responsibility for children, a duty to protect and care for them and to work for their best interests. However, the precise ways in which such power and authority are, in practice, enabled and experienced in everyday interactions between adults and children becomes much less clear and, as Christensen and James (2000) note, *negotiations*, rather than uni-directional power relations, are a more common feature of child–adult relations, particularly within the family – as those of us who are parents recognise all too readily.

Once a temporal dimension is introduced, further complications arise. For example, the process of embodiment inevitably means that the 'child' in time becomes an 'adult'. Over the life course, therefore, the individual ostensibly moves from an experience of relative powerlessness as a child to an adulthood vested with age-based authority. But what those identities actually mean to any particular individual and how they are experienced depends, for example, upon how knowledge of what the adult role embraces is acquired and what ideas and concepts of 'adulthood' are brought into play, by and for that individual, at any particular socio-historical moment. As Rapport writes:

Individuals depend upon . . . common attributes of their culture to make meaning, and yet, the vitality of the forms depends on individuals with meanings they endemically want to express through them. Hence, behavioural commonalities are personalised in usage and come to be animated in possibly idiosyncratic fashions. They become instruments of diversity and difference, and yet the conditions of their use remain essentially public, and it is coordination with significant others and in certain routine and limited ways that these meanings come to be made (1993: 170).

More recent work on identity has begun to suggest ways in which such processes actually occur. Giddens (1991), for example, highlights a uniquely self-reflexive or self-aware experience of 'I' which is engaged in a continuous project of self construction across the life course. Through our choice or rejection of everything from jobs and family through to clothing and holidays, we attempt to develop and promote particular versions of who we think we are, or would like to become. If modern identity is characterised as becoming rather than being, as always in process, never tied down, even after death, this means that childhood, adulthood and old age cannot so easily be identified as fixed times and spaces between which the individual makes their transition. In the post-traditional society which Giddens describes, the individual shapes their life course independently, and continuously, according to choice. Indeed, he even argues for such choices among the poor and oppressed:

A black woman heading a single-parent household, however constricted and arduous her life, will nevertheless know about factors altering the position of women in general, and her own activities will almost certainly be modified by that knowledge (1991: 86).

However this is not to say that her identity is simply the outcome of her own choices. Craib, for example, acknowledges that, as a middle-aged man, he can present himself on the World Wide Web as almost anybody he chooses. Yet his physical body will always intervene in any unmediated, face-to-face encounters: 'Once I am *seen*, my ability to revise my identity is limited: I cannot become a blonde teenage girl' (our emphasis, 1998: 7).

Thus, as Jenkins points out, identity has a profoundly political nature: 'social identities exist and are acquired, claimed and allocated within power relations. Identity is something *over* which struggles take place and *with* which stratagems are advanced: it is means and end in politics' (1996: 24). We need to bear in mind, at the start therefore, that not all such struggles terminate in a happy consensus. In many cases – in both private and public spheres – unwanted identities are imposed and desired identities are withheld. And age can be a significant motivating and legitimating factor within such exercises of power. On the basis of age, for example, a job may be lost and an alcoholic drink will not be sold. On the basis of age, a lover may be chosen or rejected. Age therefore mobilises political action – or the exercise of power – and is also an effect of this power. Being banned from a pub, the sixteen-year old experiences themselves as 'young', both in relation to the eighteen-year old glimpsed at the bar and also the publican who asks for proof of age.

It might seem that much of this debate is merely a reflection of a peculiarly contemporary western concern with individualism and personal integrity across time which makes those social and biological factors which change us a threat to the continuity of our personal identity across time. Thus, for example, what we find in Giddens' work is a model of the individual involved in a project of self actualisation, a person who refuses the impositions of 'social structures' and resists the changes brought about by the ageing of flesh. For example, medical technology is increasingly being used to remould faces and breasts; and counselling in its many forms is used to overcome shyness, grief and sexual dysfunction. However, the emphasis on the agency of the individual in theories of the 'social', which such an approach to identity champions, does not refer simply to post-traditional life. In essence, this perspective acts as a brake on the earlier theorising which privileged the social as an overarching superstructure. It allows us to investigate 'structure' as the everyday social processes which society's members everywhere and continuously engage in.

Thus, it can be argued that accounts of how the post-traditional self has become an ongoing, embodied project (Giddens, 1991) share a theoretical stance with the work of some contemporary anthropologists who work in very different social contexts. Seremetakis, for example, rejects the traditional structural model of rites of passage as a way to account for ageing and change across the life course and, instead, argues for the use of the more processual notion of 'ritualisation'. In her ethnography of death in Inner Mani, Greece, Seremetakis suggests that:

> The analysis of ritual in anthropology is informed by the assumption that ritual is an event separated in time and space from other domains of social practice, and thus marked by explicit beginnings and ends (1991: 47).

She goes on:

> I intend to locate death in a more heterogeneous and encompassing context, ritualization. Ritualization here is defined as the processual representation of death in a variety of social contexts and practices that do not have the formal public status of a public rite. The concept of ritualization moves the analysis of death rites away from performances fixed in time and space and resituates it within the flux and contingency of everyday events (1991: 47).

Her re-visioning of ritual, as an ongoing process of change, adjustment and meaning-making, thus parallels Giddens' concept of the ever-present project of the self and undermines the view that the reflexive self is peculiarly post-traditional and western. As Cohen (1994) argues, there has been a common failure to recognise the selves and the self consciousness of people living in other places, and differences in the way selfhood is understood and experienced. Clearly society cannot exist in the absence of people and, in Cohen's view, we need to make the individual our starting point if we wish to understand how commonalities are established between different people (1994: 22). Jenkins (1996: 9) offers a parallel critique, arguing *against* the notion that a sense of identity as something specific to and determined by the individual is peculiarly modern. Instead, he reminds us that Locke's *Essay Concerning Human Understanding*, published in 1694, included a chapter called 'Identity and Diversity', a precursor of literatures on identity which themselves were well-established even before the beginning of the twentieth century.

If we accept these critiques, then, we are left to confront the notion that, on some level, change or ageing is *always* in tension with the possibility of continuous self identity – for the members of all cultures and all historical periods. And the body is central here. Speaking of embodiment, Jenkins argues that for people everywhere it is a core site of resistance to the notion of the self as 'an assembly of different bits' (1996: 45). Embodiment and a consistency of self are therefore closely entwined. Yet, at the same time, as Turner argues, 'we subjectively cling to an image of ourselves as unchangingly young' (1995: 250). While the inside of the body supports this phenomenological sense of coherence and continuity, its external appearance continuously *disrupts* this self consciousness: 'my body is, so to speak, a walking memory' (Turner, 1995: 250). What needs to be untangled here, therefore, are the precise ways in which our bodies are made to operate as both an ongoing location of who we *are* as well as an 'object' which we *have* and need to attend to if we wish to either conform to or avoid particular age-based identities. If, as this book sets out to do, we place ageing, the body and the life course centre-stage in our discussion of identity, we find ourselves re-engaging with notions of the 'I' and the 'me' (Mead, 1934; Cooley, 1964). In their view, the 'I' attends to the ways in which others perceive 'me' and the self is reflexively produced in the process. However, if we acknowledge the biological dimensions of human ageing, we recognise the emergent dilemma of a whole series of mismatches between the 'me' perceived by others and the more consistent 'me' which, via memory, 'I' imagine. It is this kind of discrepancy which allows old people to still feel 'young at heart', and for 'old heads' to be perceived on 'young shoulders'. The question of how the unitary, ageing self attempts to know and reproduce itself across the time of the life course therefore requires us to investigate the interrelationship of socially located *embodied* individuals as they participate in processes of mutual self identification.

Conclusion

This volume examines the ways in which processes of identification unfold for individuals as they age, taking full account of the embodied nature of their experience. Craib, for example, insistent that social and individual identity can never be coterminous, argues that it is the *fact* and *experience* of embodiment which forces this analytical distinction. He says:

> If I suffered a major tragedy in my family life, ceasing to be a husband and becoming a divorced man or widower, my identity would have changed in an excruciatingly painful way but I would still have an identity. Social identities can come and go but my identity goes on as something which unites all the social identities I ever had, have or will have. My identity always overflows, adds to, transforms the social identities that are attached to me (1998: 4).

In this sense, identity is always a state of becoming rather then being. It is something which can be reformulated – even after death. Thus, for example, regardless of our religious affiliations, or lack of them, if our descendants become Mormons then so may we. Traced through genealogical records, we may be baptised after our deaths, so becoming Mormon 'converts' at the hands of future generations who wish to save our souls.

This book drives forward ways of understanding that experience. It problematises the idea that there are social structures which surround the individual who then only exercises agency in response to them. Instead, we start from the indivisibility of both agency and structure, as well as individual and social identity. On this basis, then, we set out to examine critically the contributions and limitations of existing sociological and anthropological theories of the life course. We then go on to show how a processual approach might help us produce more nuanced accounts of the three case study areas of: gender and sexuality; the family; and work. In so doing, we not only draw together studies which are often undertaken within separate disciplines and which map onto discrete categories of the life course, such as childhood and later life, we also merge the currently vibrant literature on identity with established work on the body, so examining the potentiality of a processual approach to ageing for helping make sense of that most extended of human temporal spans, the life course.

2

The Structuring of Age

Introduction

This chapter opens our critical review of the theories which have been developed to explain how individuals make their entries into and exits from society and how, in the process, they come to take on particular identities. We begin with a discussion of the rituals and rites through which human ageing is produced and made meaningful in different societies. To this end, the chapter asks how identification – the negotiation of social identity – relates to the human body and the radical changes which it undergoes between its conception and disposal. Writing as a westerner, J. B. Priestley reveals his experience of a rupture between the personal identity which he has sustained from early adulthood, the ageing of his body, and the social identity which others read off from that body. He describes this experience as follows:

> It is as though, walking down Shaftesbury Avenue as a fairly young man, I was suddenly kidnapped, rushed into a theatre and made to don the grey hair, the wrinkles and the other attributes of age, then wheeled on stage. Behind the appearance of age I am the same person, with the same thoughts, as when I was younger (Puner, cited in Featherstone and Hepworth, 1989: 148).

How, then, have social theorists accounted for this disjuncture between personal and social experience which seems to be part of an ageing identity? Have their accounts addressed the question of whether the ageing process – from birth to death – is similarly experienced, understood and managed at different points in the life course in different societies? In this second chapter we consider the traditional explanations offered by social science.

Social constructionist approaches are our starting point, perspectives which problematise those aspects of human life which other discourses – including popular understandings – often see as 'natural' or biologically given. Its premise, as outlined below, is that there is a social dimension to human life which cannot be reduced to a set of bodily imperatives. Thus, it is argued that 'ageing' is not simply a matter of organic maturation and decay, for the way in which these processes are understood and their import for society's members differ cross-culturally. As Schuller notes, for instance, 'it is said that only the Eskimo seems to view life as an unbroken continuum to be lived out as it comes' (1989: 42). Elsewhere, in societies throughout the world, life is experienced through structured discontinuities, as a series of age-grades, stages, generations and cohorts with the breaks between them marking out forms of age-based differentiation. Social constructionist perspectives have drawn on the concepts of the life cycle and the life course, therefore, to explore these social divisions, to explain how it is that, as they physically age, societies' members seem to pass into and out of a series of age-based social categories and identities.

Using a comparative method, this chapter therefore presents data which show that ages and stages in the life course are indeed 'changeable', depending upon the social context within which they take place. However, while we may recognise the contingency of *social* identities such as 'father', 'intellectual', 'housewife', the *age*-based social categories of 'child', 'adult' and 'elderly person' tend to be read off from and experienced within the body in the same way that 'race' or gender are. The body-centredness of ageing therefore makes it ripe for discourses of biological determinism.

In contemporary western society, these discourses tend to use metaphors which represent ageing as an organic process: thus, the Anglican order for the burial of the dead uses natural imagery to connote the brevity of human life: 'He cometh up, and is cut down, like a flower: he fleeth as it were a shadow'. This discourse even finds its way into the work of sociologists. In Wells and Gubar's typology of the family life cycle, five of its nine stages are represented via imagery from the natural world: 'Full Nest I, II and III and Empty Nest I and II' (cited in Murphy, 1987: 34). It is, however, but a fine line between using the natural world as a source of metaphors through which to classify human experience, and treating embodied experience as if it *were* directly and only driven by biology. The social constructionist approaches, with which we begin our account, thus remind us of the centrality of metaphor to understanding the life course and lead us to question the determinism of the body's biology in making ageing meaningful. Human ageing cannot be experienced as an undifferentiated, embodied process since it unfolds at such an imperceptibly slow and steady pace. Thus it is that the ageing process may only be grasped through metaphor, for it is through this that meaning can be given to bodily experiences which are both intangible and ambiguous (cf Lakoff and Johnson, 1980; Hockey and James, 1993).

Rites of passage

An early example of social-constructionist approaches to the relationship between identity and ageing is the ceremonial schema which Van Gennep identified as rites of passage. Anthropologists such as Van Gennep ([1908] 1960), who were studying society from an outsider position, found themselves beleaguered by the wealth of ceremonial or ritual forms which accompany changes in social identity in different societies. In trying to develop a schema for making sense of this diversity, Van Gennep discovered commonalities across different sets of ritual practices. What he identified were the ways in which individuals move between social locations which are often age-related: for example, between boyhood and manhood or from being single to the married state. However, his overarching concern was with the stability of 'society' itself and thus he saw ritual and ceremonial as ways of ensuring that such transitions and movements were 'regulated and guarded so that society as a whole will suffer no discomfort or injury' ([1908] 1960: 3). These transitions included: 'birth, childhood, social puberty, betrothal, marriage, pregnancy, fatherhood, initiation into religious societies and funerals' ([1908] 1960: 3). By examining their internal patterning, as well as setting each one within the context of the others, Van Gennep identified a common schema: the rite of passage. This comprised three subsidiary rites – of separation, transition and incorporation, each one being developed to a different extent in different kinds of passage. Rites of separation, for example, predominated at funerals while rites of incorporation were central to weddings.

Notwithstanding Van Gennep's concern with the reproduction and stability of social order, it is important to remember that he regarded rites of passage as a flexible, working model or schema, geared towards making sense of diverse, empirical material – and not, as Mauss critically pronounced it, a *law* (cited in Belmont, [1974] 1979: 62). According to the analytic model, passage through each of the three phases of the ritual meant that individuals had been detached from their previous social position, processed through an intermediary state which shared the features of neither the previous nor the successive social position, and then had been incorporated into a new set of rules, roles and obligations. Within this overall schema, each subsidiary rite shared a symbolic *spatiality*, the central, transitional phase being referred to as a 'liminal' period, from the Latin word for threshold, *limen*. What Van Gennep's schema details, therefore, is the *process* of transition, with the notion of passage encompassing a zone which is betwixt and between fixed social positions. The symbolic deaths and resurrections which are often enacted during the liminal phase are analysed as a way of severing connection with a previous social position in readiness for 'rebirth' into the next and therefore of rendering ageing across the life course orderly and predictable. An example here might be Christian baptism where a baby leaves its domestic environment and is brought into the sacred space of the Church. There, it symbolically undergoes a second birth, emerging from holy water rather than amniotic fluid. In the process it acquires its unique 'Christian' name, a prefix to the family name it shares. And through the vows of the godparents it is symbolically re-parented into the social and religious identity it will begin to live out once it returns to domestic space. Van Gennep's own summary of his work is useful to cite here:

> For groups, as well as individuals, life itself means to separate and to be reunited, to change form and condition, to die and to be reborn. It is to act and to cease, to wait and rest, and then to begin acting again, but in a different way ([1908] 1960: 189).

Van Gennep's schema thus provides an account of how individuals enter into and exit from age-based social identities. It is not, however, an experiential account, but one concerned to identify the form and structure of this process, the mechanisms through which society is itself sustained. With a concern for empirical observation rather than 'metaphysical speculation', Van Gennep used a multiplicity of field data to compile graphic accounts of the wide variety of embodied practices which make up rites of passage across a diversity of cultural contexts. But, as his primary goal was to identify a common pattern to the rituals associated with life-course transitions, he shared with other anthropologists of that time a commitment to demonstrating the *social* dimensions of the life course, rather than a concern with individual experience. He therefore insisted that the full complexity of the meanings of these rites could only be gained by adopting an holistic approach in which these rituals could be explored in their *social* context ([1908] 1960: 89). Van Gennep's approach is therefore clearly social constructionist. His was not a model hitched to the determinism of biology represented in the example of bodily ageing.

In a similar fashion, Hertz's account of mourning ritual challenged a cultural bias towards thinking about death as something fixed, essential and biologically grounded ([1907] 1960). His aim was to identify the social aspects of death and he begins his account by defending his apparently 'ridiculous and sacrilegious' project which was to 'apply reason to a subject where only the heart is competent' ([1907] 1960: 27). In his view, 'death has a specific meaning for the social consciousness: it is the object of a collective representation. This representation is neither simple nor unchangeable' ([1907] 1960: 28). As Hertz demonstrated, even death, perhaps of all life course transitions seemingly the least mutable, has to be seen as socially constructed.

The ethnography of life-course transitions further exemplifies this point. Among the Bemba of north-eastern Zambia (Richards, [1956] 1982), for example, the rituals which change girls into women take place only when there are sufficient numbers within a cohort, all of whom will be at different stages of physical maturation. The 'growth' and change which is central to the ritual must therefore be regarded as primarily social. Indeed the Bemba themselves say that 'We do the rite to grow the girl' (Richards, [1956] 1982: 121). It is not, therefore, the growing body of the girl which necessarily determines her transition to the social status of womanhood.

However, it *is* through the medium of the body that this social transition is accomplished. Amongst the Bemba, girls are taken into seclusion for up to a month, are humbled or humiliated, being made to wear short revealing clothes and to crawl backwards, hobble, jump through hoops or be swung over fires. In this and many other examples of age-linked rites of passage, the body is thus made to have life-changing experiences, rather than being regarded as itself a source of change. This is made most explicit in the example of the Maasai of East Africa. Van Gennep describes the changes wrought upon the bodies of their young teenagers, both girls and boys, who undergo the excision or cutting of their genitals ([1908] 1960). In addition to these permanent bodily alterations, which in the case of cliteridectomy in girls has now been recognised as a form of abuse (Shaughnessy, 1998), this rite of passage can also involve more temporary bodily changes, such as shaving the head and painting the face with white clay (Van Gennep, [1908] 1960: 85–6).

All the evidence presented within this early social constructionist framework therefore stresses the cultural and social structuring of human ageing. Things happen to and around the body, rather than biological change being the stimulus for some form of social 'recognition' or 'ordering'. For example, among the Maasai, it is economic rather than hormonal factors that determine the process of 'growing up'. The children of rich parents 'age' faster because their fathers and mothers can afford the ritual more easily, providing as Van Gennep says, 'proof that here, too, social puberty differs from physical puberty' ([1908] 1960: 85). Similarly, when he describes the status of the newborn child among the Rahuna of Morocco as being akin to that of a stranger, Van Gennep details the rites of incorporation into the family and community, which include putting the infant in the care of another woman for a few days, a practice which, he says, 'has no relation to the time required for the appearance of milk' ([1908] 1960: 50). His work and that of anthropologists who later followed his example therefore add up to a powerful challenge to a naturalist approach to ageing across the life course. In such accounts of rituals of transition, cross-cultural comparisons show a clear variation in how the life course is divided up and what different societies expect of human beings at different ages and stages.

Constructing the life course socially

Following on from this early theorising, social constructionist perspectives have continued to predominate in most accounts offered by social science of the ways in which ageing and identity unfold across the life course. Describing the social transition from boyhood to manhood among the Red Xhosa of South Africa, Mayer and Mayer (1990) detail the way these two age-based social categories are constructed through sets of oppositional metaphors – bush: homestead; bull: ox (unrestrained: restrained sexuality); animal: human, each of which symbolically opposes the domain of 'wild nature' to the domain of 'domesticated culture'. These metaphoric binaries are made tangible or literal through ritual practices and rules of etiquette: 'the boy – man opposition has traditionally been dramatised and acted out in the long-drawn-out procedures of Xhosa manhood initiation, but also in numbers of customary etiquettes – almost amounting to avoidances or taboos – designed to separate and distinguish between boys and men in everyday contexts' (1990: 37). In this way, a metaphoric distinction between the concepts of 'nature' and 'culture' allows the social identities of 'boy' and 'man' also to be set in opposition to one another, boys being understood to be incompletely socialised and still partly in the realm of 'nature'.

This abrupt demarcation of identities does not, of course, find any grounding in bodily processes themselves since these unfold only gradually in an unbroken continuum. Yet, as Lakoff and Johnson argue, 'human purposes typically require us to impose artificial boundaries that make physical phenomena discrete' (1980: 25), such that 'boyhood' and 'manhood' are socially constructed outcomes of the Xhosa rituals of initiation and practice. The idea that the life course is a biological continuum which is divided, cognitively, into sets of internal oppositions points towards a view of age identities which are defined in terms of their contrasts with one another, their boundaries and limits, rather than their core features. Indeed, as Barth's (1969) work on ethnic identity makes clear, it is the boundaries between groups which work to confer identity through a process of separating one social category from another.

While these approaches provide an explanation of how individuals move between social categories which are constructed as opposites, they leave aside the wider social effects of individual movements. Thus Turner, who uses Van Gennep's model of rites of passage as a core theoretical resource in his 1967 study among the Ndembu of north-western Zambia, develops it by including an analysis of the internal social dynamics of change. Conceiving of society as a 'structure of positions' (1967: 93), Turner moves his focus away from individual passage through a fixed structure and towards exploring the fluidity of entire networks or matrices of social relationships. As Turner says, 'whatever society we live in we are all related to one another; our own "big moments" are "big moments" for others as well' (1967: 7). Harris (1987: 20) similarly argues that, as individuals who are both embodied and ageing, society's members each occupy a unique space–time location, no two people being able to share the same material space at the same moment in time. Yet each of us follows a life-course trajectory which 'may be plotted not in terms merely of an objective space–time grid, but *relationally* in terms of approximations to, and distantiations from, other members' (Harris, 1987: 20). However, for Harris, as for other theorists of the life course, it is the collective, social *structuring* of such trajectories, rather than any one experience of them or their bodily manifestation, which is the focus of this concern. As our later chapters show, this represents a serious limitation on our under-standing of how social identities are produced in practice across the life course.

As noted, Van Gennep believed rites of passage had a protective function for society as a whole, reducing the 'harmful effects' of passage between groups, roles or statuses ([1908] 1960: 13). However, in a later development of this idea, Turner insists that they 'indicate and *constitute*' transition, implying that ritual also has a creative function (author's italics 1967: 93). In other words, transition rites *produce* the social, rather than just protecting 'society'. In this way, they can be differentiated from ceremony. Thus, for Turner, 'ritual is transformative, ceremony confirmatory' (1967: 95). Bloch and Parry's (1982) later work on symbols of fertility and rebirth in funeral rituals extends this perspective to argue for a model of society which sees it not as an entity acting in its own right which needs protecting from risk, but as an *outcome* of ritual practices. Thus Bloch and Parry share Turner's notion of the creative role of ritual – rather than the stabilising one which Hertz espoused in his work on double burial ([1907] 1960). Bloch and Parry argue that 'if we can speak of a reassertion of the social order at the time of death, this social order is a *product* of rituals of the kind we consider rather than their cause...mortuary rituals themselves being an occasion for *creating* that 'society' as an apparently external force' (1982: 6). However, this is not to say that the notion of ritual as productive was entirely absent from the work of earlier theorists. Van Gennep, for example, describes the different tools used to cut a girl's rather than a boy's umbilical cord in the following terms: 'through their choice of instruments these peoples definitively establish the sex of the child' ([1908] 1960: 51). In this sense they 'create' rather than simply confirm the gender identity of the newborn infant.

However, though Turner's account of initiation rites among the Ndembu focuses on the central liminal zone of a rite of passage and on the question of the production of identity, his account still does not engage with the experience of transition per se. Its overall concern is with the structural outcomes of rites of passage for the ascription or creation of identity. He argues, for example, that if movement is taking place within society's 'structure of positions', those in transition should be regarded as '"interstructural" human beings' (1967: 93). As such, in his model they literally as well as metaphorically become 'invisible' as the people they once were, their previous social identity being submerged within generic terms such as 'initiand' or 'neophyte'. Such terms often have a broad sphere of reference, extending to other people and other transitional circumstances, many of which confuse the gender of neophytes, rendering them asexual. And, in rites of transition, Turner notes that the material possessions which serve as markers of social identity are often removed. This loss of former identity differentiates initiands structurally from other individuals, a difference often further reinforced through forms of spatial seclusion. But none of this tells us much about how initiands actually feel or whether and how they know they are ageing!

Nonetheless Turner's work on the liminal period of a rite of passage marks a significant development in social constructionist perspectives on life-course transitions and the negotiation of social identity. What he adds to our understanding, initially through field material from among the Ndembu, is how material forms work, symbolically, to produce change. For example, separation from a previous status is, as noted, often represented through the metaphors of death and decay, made tangible or literal through practices such as treating the neophytes as if they were corpses, immobilising them in situations which parallel the treatment of the dead. As Turner says, 'the metaphor of dissolution is often applied to neophytes; they are allowed to go filthy and identified with the earth, the generalised matter into which every specific individual is rendered down' (1967: 96). Yet the neophyte 'corpses' remain living people, and are therefore deeply *ambiguous* beings. It is within this state of ambiguity that the creative potential of the liminal period resides, in Turner's view. Thus, while this interstructural or anti-structural period may stand in stark contrast with the structures of the mundane social world, it also contains within it the seeds of that structure: 'liminality may perhaps be regarded . . . as a realm of pure possibility whence novel configurations of ideas and relations may arise' (1967: 97). Turner also shows that many of the symbols of death are themselves ambiguous – huts and tunnels signify wombs as well as tombs, nakedness is associated with both birth and death. It is within this dangerously ambiguous time and space, where the rules and roles of social structure are inverted or put in abeyance that individuals engage with one another more directly, entering into a state known as *communitas*. Individual identities and social hierarchies are here transcended as interpersonal boundaries fade and blur.

By examining empirical data of this kind Turner is able to show, not just the processes whereby social structures are reproduced, but also the ways in which individuals come to take on new social identities, an approach which begins to engage with the agency of individuals. In many societies it is through ritual passage that age-based identities come to be inhabited, regardless of bodily evidence of maturity. Thus, grown Ndembu 'men' would be driven away from rituals because they themselves had not undergone an appropriate rite. As a result they were not men from an Ndembu perspective. But, despite this acknowledgement of individual experience and the need to accommodate it in our explanations, Turner's broader concern still remains the question of how society reproduces the conditions of its own existence. In summary, then, Turner's account provides a far more dynamic model of society, as something generative which contains, in rituals and rites of ageing, the germ of its own transformation. However, it does not engage with ageing as an embodied experience.

Structuring identities across the life course

The model of rites of passage is one example of the ways in which anthropologists and sociologists have sought to understand age-based social status. Using a social constructionist perspective, Van Gennep's approach to the plethora of ritual detail to be found in ethnographic accounts of ceremonial behaviour, reflected the 'scientific' spirit of his time, the belief that 'ethnography is a biological science because it studies living facts in their environment' (Belmont, [1974] 1979: 15). He saw the transience of the individual, a transience which age itself accomplishes, as a form of social disturbance: 'Such changes of condition do not occur without disturbing the life of society and the individual, and it is the function of rites of passage to reduce their harmful effects' (Van Gennep, [1908]

1960: 13). In his view, the fact that individuals age was at best a social inconvenience, at worst a severe disruption.

However, as Baxter and Almagor note 'age-grading whether formally marked by a rite of passage or merely tacitly recognised, is probably universal, and gives the process of ageing a social impress' (1978: 2). As such, then, the concept of rites of passage needs to be set alongside those accounts of other forms of social organisation – age-sets and age grades – through which the relationship between ageing, identity and power come to be articulated in societies. Again, however, such studies have focused not so much on the boundaries of age-based identities and their active negotiation by individuals, as on the structural relationships established between the age categories through which the order of society is reproduced.

Radcliffe-Brown (1929), for example, was one of the first social scientists to identify age and generation as classificatory devices through which social structure is produced and reproduced in some traditional societies by the structuring of 'aged' identities across the life course for individuals. Known as an age-set system and a particular feature of East African societies, the system for which Radcliffe-Brown devised his model is one within which individuals are born into a particular age-set and retain their membership of throughout life. Membership of an age-set determines, for example, when and in what company of cohorts men, collectively, make their transition from youth to manhood. And just as Turner reveals a sense of communitas binding initiands to one another during the liminal period of a rite of passage, so a distinctive comradeship is said to pertain among age-mates, often persisting into old age (1967: 101).

However, significantly, like rites of passage, age-sets are understood and analysed as classificatory devices, and as not necessarily grounded in the biological reality of the ageing process. Indeed as Baxter and Almagor point out, biology and the relentless flow of time frequently disrupt such cognitive ordering systems by throwing up anomalies:

> An age-system implies continuity and replacement of personnel in an orderly and predictable manner through the replacement by birth of new members to replace those who die. Similarly, generation implies begetting, replacement and continuity. When a man's placement within a system is determined by that of his father an underlying assumption is that fathers will beget sons within a limited time space, and that therefore there will be approximate accord between age and generation. In social reality this assumption is false... The biological facts of birth and death must slide out of alignment with the social order with which they should conform (1978: 5).

Thus, although age-sets essentially stratify the society along generational lines, often leading to the establishment of gerontocratic
control, this 'gerontocracy' may be grounded less in the materiality
of age than in its social construction. Thus, as Baxter and Almagor
note, 'age-set rituals provide a platform from which the gerontocrats
(however young in years) can exercise their power and harangue the
youngsters (however old in years) who are encapsulated in a junior
set' (1978: 14).

For Spencer, age-sets are often, in practice, a highly conflictual
form of age-based social organisation. Citing Gulliver's account of
the Arusha, he argues that the age-set system 'extends beyond the
life courses of individuals to the jostling for power between whole
age-sets, notably in the public arena of local dispute' (1990: 7). Privileging structure and social rules, earlier analysts had seen harmony
and stability as the state to which societies continuously return. Yet
this example shows a much more temporary and fragile state of
affairs. In an age-set system, men in early middle age are the holders
of political and juridical power. Yet, their authority is the outcome
of political expedience. Secured at the cost of the older men they
have edged out, they remain vulnerable to challenges from younger
men who strive to wrest their power from them. Here, then, is a hint
that the very embodiment of age may have a crucial role to play in
determining how individuals themselves experience ageing across
the life course. This point we develop later in Chapter 7.

A more experientially-based example is provided in Stamp's
account of the age-grade system among the Kikuyu women of
Kenya which reveals it as 'a collective counterweight to male authority and domination' (1999: 163). Kikuyu women have a dual social
identity, marital role and age being the two organising principles of
its separate halves. Women's identities are made up of their roles as
both the wives of men within the patrilineal lineage system and as
members of an age-grade system. Stamp argues that this latter
dimension of their identity is often ignored, the politics of women's
age-grade systems being rendered invisible in anthropological studies which privilege men's organisations. These 'relegate all social
and economic activity of women to the domestic sphere' (1999: 166).
What her ethnography demonstrates is the way in which the collectivity
of the age-set allows women to enjoy increasing power as they age,
sharing an important political role within Kikuyu society as a whole.

Notwithstanding more recent accounts such as that offered by
Stamp, the examples presented here make it clear that a concern

with social structure and the structuring of identities across the life course has predominated in traditional theorising. The agency and the experience of the individual who is taking on a changed, age-based social identity or indeed the practical outcomes and experiences of different forms of age grading has received comparatively little attention. This may be because, as the next chapter explores, ageing is a process which is imperceptible to the self. It takes place behind our backs, creeps up on us and is not, therefore, easily amenable to self-articulation. Thus, within the social science literature it is usually only in discussions of the transition to non-aged-based identities that the individual's own personal experience of transition and changed identity has been explored. However, we would also argue that this absence of an experiential perspective is a product of the 'scientific', structural-functionalist orientations through which ageing itself has, traditionally, been conceived and framed within sociological disciplines. In other words, the models are as much about the preoccupations of the theorists as they are about the focus of the study.

Disciplinary orientations: rites of passage, the life cycle and the life course

The foregoing discussion shows that theorists such as Van Gennep and Turner were deeply committed to an ethnographic approach (Belmont, [1974] 1979). Nonetheless, they remain wedded to a concern with structure which excluded the agency through which individual identity is formed and then changed. Reflecting both its focus on modern western society and its attempt to achieve scientific relevance by remedying 'social problems' (Giddens, 1989), early sociology construed a relationship between 'the individual' and 'society' which sprang from a concern with the problems caused by the loss of traditional ways of life. Sociologists such as Auguste Comte (1789–1857) and Emile Durkheim (1858–1917) set out to show what kinds of social formation might best be adapted to a developing industrial, urban environment. They adhered to the positivist belief that the social domain of human life could be approached as a set of collective representations. These shared the same status as objective or concrete facts and stood in a causal relationship with the lives of individuals, collectively held structures of thought or systems of ideas being understood to shape and con-strain the actions of individuals.

In addition, early anthropologists looked at societies as they oper-ated in the present, that is synchronically. This was as a reaction to the arm-chair theorising which had underpinned early evolutionary perspectives. This had attempted to explain how society had 'progressed' to its nineteenth-century 'civilized' form. Rather than speculative interpretations of history, the early twentieth-century anthropologists therefore argued that human behaviour needed to be understood holistically within particular, local contexts. Their approach to the relationship between the individual and society thus reflected a more organic and static model of society, within which each part was seen as contributing to its overall functioning. The concept of the life cycle inherent in rites of passage was therefore used to explain the maintenance of society's stability and equilib-rium across time, rather than the adaptive changes to social functioning made by societies undergoing industrialisation and urbanism which was the contemporaneous concern of sociology.

It is within this academic and political context, also, that the concept of the life cycle first emerged within sociology. However, as Chapter 5 shows, this was only in connection with the study of the family as a unit, rather than with the changes occurring for its indi-vidual members. With its longitudinal, diachronic perspective, the concept of the life cycle was embraced as a way of predicting the effects of early events for later transitions on family life in modern societies (Murphy, 1987).

However, the concept of the life cycle was not confined to soci-ology and anthropology. Models of change, development and ageing were to be found in a variety of other disciplines too, psychology and medicine offering a holistic account of systems of growth and change. Central to the study of the natural sciences, the biology of ageing thus seemingly naturalised the concept of the life cycle as a key way to understand human development also. However, as Spencer notes, when applied to the study of *human* 'ageing' it tended to focus on childhood as 'the formative stages of develop-ment almost to the exclusion of adult and later life' (1990: 1). Phys-ical anthropology, linguistics, ethology, developmental psychology and psychoanalytic theory, for example, all concerned themselves with growth, adaptation, character formation and the acquisition of skills in early life. Thus, though Erikson's model of eight stages of psychological development did encompass the entire life course, from birth through to death, the first six stages were argued to occur before the individual reached adulthood. According to Erikson:

> A lasting ego-identity . . . cannot begin to exist without the trust of the first oral stage; it cannot be completed without a promise of fulfilment which from the dominant image of adulthood reaches down into the baby's beginnings and which, by the tangible evidence of social health, creates at every step of childhood and adolescence an accruing sense of ego strength. Thus . . . we must now recognise the place of identity in the human life cycle (1950: 238).

And that place was seen to be very much in the early years as if, after childhood, change, growth and development ceased, that is until the onslaught wrought upon the physical body by entry into extreme old age.

Whilst we might now critically want to argue that change and development continue across the life span, we do need to bear in mind that many of these disciplines first emerged in the late nineteenth century. At that time, only five per cent of the population were over 65 years old, with two-thirds of older men still in paid employment (Arber and Ginn, 1991). Such demographic factors clearly shaped contemporaneous perceptions of ageing, and thus we have to acknowledge the clear relationship between theoretical resources and their social and political context. With this in mind, this second chapter shows how the rigidly defined early models of the life cycle were adapted to meet the research agendas of modernity. The prime concern of earlier social analysts was social structure and the reproduction of the social order. This orientation, we shall argue, has proved inappropriate and constraining for the contemporary study of processes of identification in postmodern culture.

But more than this, the notion of the life cycle as a set of fixed stages was irrevocably wedded to ideas of social structure. As Giddens argues (1984), the concept of the life cycle 'belongs to the succession of generations . . . the "supra-individual" *durée* of the long-term existence of institutions, the *longue durée* of institutional time' (cited in Schuller, 1989: 41). It implies a repeatable pattern, a form of 'reversible' temporality. With such a concept, proper account could not be taken, therefore, of the *irreversibility* of time which is the everyday lived experience of individuals and of families (see Chapter 3).

For anthropologists, focusing on the concept of the life cycle and developing the notion of 'passage' allowed examination of the mechanisms which work to maintain the stasis of social categories – child, adolescent, adult, elder, ancestor. Hence, their focus was on the social processes by which individuals are enabled to move into and out of these categorical identities. This contrasts with Durkheimian sociology and its concern with change, progress and development which is reflected in work on the family life cycle (see Chapter 5). Here, the primary goal was to plot the move from mechanical to organic solidarity, the shift away from traditional, autonomous units geared towards economic survival towards the interdependency necessary in societies with complex economic and administrative systems (Durkheim, [1895] 1964).

However, since the 1970s, both the concept of rites of passage and that of the life cycle have been criticised as over-rigid conceptual devices for making sense of highly diverse data. Anthropologists have suggested, for example, that the model of a rite of passage, identified by the early theorists, does not necessarily harmonise with the way social identity may shift and be shifted across time. This change of heart can also perhaps be seen as a response to new social contexts: the shift from modernity to postmodernity and the reorientation of the anthropological gaze to include complex industrialised societies, as well as holistic and traditional ones.

In addition we need to recognise that these discrepancies between rigid models of the life cycle and how informants actually experience identification may tell us more about social scientists' academic and political concerns than any real differences between past and present societies. The neatly ordered stage models of early anthropologists have to be evaluated within their historical context, an academic era when 'great minds were in the process of exploring the world with a fresh point of view; they were busy organising new acts which were being turned up at every hand into systematic classifications. From these they were constructing conceptual schemes to give expression to the orderliness of the universe' (Kimball, 1960: v). Core to this period were the values of objectivity and rationality, challenges to the supernaturalism which had preceded them. Informed by this scientific spirit, one of the aims of the 'great minds' which Kimball refers to was to uncover the origins and the functions of religious behaviour and in this endeavour 'the creation of classificatory categories was a major concern of scientific thinking' (1960: vi).

Conclusion

The focus of this chapter has been the theoretical resources through which the relationship between ageing and social identity has been made sense of by anthropologists and sociologists. As argued, the concepts of the life cycle and the life course have to be understood against the historical and conceptual backdrop of the development of social science. Note must be taken, therefore, of the *different* ways in which theorists not only achieved accounts of ageing but also delineated how changing social identities accompanied transition across the life course. By locating these sets of ideas within their political and intellectual contexts, we have been able to develop a critical perspective which raises questions about how theorists conceptualised the relationship between the individual and society. As we have seen, models of 'society' have varied throughout the history of the social sciences, a development which has brought us to a contemporary view which stresses the negotiated nature of the social environment and the identities of those who inhabit it, a view to be discussed in more detail in Chapter 7. In the next chapter we take a more detailed look at how the manipulation of time and space takes place across the life course, asking how this serves to generate the experience of temporal change and how it allows for the negotiation of social identity.

3

The Experience of Time's Passage

Introduction

On 8 December 1995, Jean-Dominque Bauby, editor-in-chief of a famous women's magazine, suffered a massive stroke whilst driving through Paris to pick up his son. This completely transformed him from independent adulthood to total dependency. The following year he was helped to provide an account of this rupture of his life course during his forties. In his autobiography, published posthumously in 1998, Bauby looks back to his 'last moments as a perfectly functioning earthling' which feel to him like undertaking a bungee jump. He recalls waking up, routinely, in a city locked in winter weather and the effects of a transport strike, running downstairs and smelling floor-polish: 'It will be the last of the smells of my past' (1998: 128). He describes an ordinary day in the office and then his arrival at the house where his son is waiting: 'From this point onward, everything becomes blurred' (1998: 133), he says, though noting that 'Not for a second does it occur to me that I may be dying' (1998: 134). His account is peppered with highly focused, sensory recollections: the Beatles song on the car radio, the soft click of the door of the expensive car he is driving, his concern to cancel the arrangements he had made for his son, the neon lights in the hospital corridor.

Such changes in social identity which occur in the course of a person's life are experienced as profound, having not only a deep emotional and personal significance but also radically altering the course and direction of their lives. In Bauby's example, we see the dramatic shift in social identity which the sudden onset of serious illness can bring. The rapidity and completeness of Bauby's transition mirrors the more common experience which many of us may have had of the transition to the status of 'patient'.

This is a dimension of contemporary western life which, like traditional societies' rites of passage, has attracted a functionalist explanation. Thus, akin to the three-stage process of a rite of passage, the diagnosis of an acute illness brings individuals a temporary transition to the category 'patient' (Parsons, 1951). The individual benefits by being legitimately released from social participation, although being required to take up the 'sick role' for a limited period. Here, medical diagnosis makes and marks the boundary between illness and disease, the former a bodily experience, the latter a social category. 'Cure', the final stage of a medically legitimated reincorporation back into customary social roles, may or may not coincide with the disappearance of bodily symptoms. Like ritual liminars the sick are betwixt and between categories, in their case, those of 'health' and 'illness' (Turner, 1974).

In contrast to Bauby's description of his changing identity, accounts of the transition between age-based identities have, however, not been so fully-fleshed. Although anthropologists such as Turner have written about the structure of the experience which the initiand or liminar undergoes, as noted in the previous chapter, his account of the transitional phase gives little indication of what that experience feels like. This is a curious omission, perhaps, considering the emphasis which he places upon the sensate body as the material focus for ritual and symbolic action and as the vehicle through which identities are both laid aside and assumed. In this chapter, then, we consider further some of the reasons for such absences in social theorising about identity and explore why it was that more 'agency'-focused perspectives were a long time coming within the social sciences. The chapter concludes by considering other sources which might be drawn on in order to achieve some understanding of the experience of ageing and identity across the life course.

The temporality of the life course

Van Gennep's schema, described in the previous chapter, provides one model of how ageing and the social transition to new aged identities takes place. As such, the model suggests how ritual produces an awareness of ageing by shaping the experience of time and its passage.

This insight is important for, as Leach has stated, 'the oddest thing about time is surely that we have such a concept at all. We experience time, but not with our senses. We don't see it, or touch it, or smell it, or taste it, or hear it' (1966: 132). By contrast, hunger or tiredness are concepts which are closely tied to bodily experiences and sensations. We feel drawn to food or sleep and identify ourselves as 'being hungry' or 'being tired' – '*I* am starving!' '*I* am exhausted!'. Crucially these are experiences which not only have an effect which we know empirically, but which can be contrasted with the very different experiences of being 'full' or 'rested'. When we have eaten a large meal or slept for many hours, the prospect of food or going to bed is unlikely to appeal to us.

Growing older and taking on the identity of an old person, however, occurs too slowly for us to perceive it directly. Moreover, there is no process with which it can be contrasted. We never grow younger. It is only memory, rather than direct bodily *experience*, which can provide some kind of access to time passing, although the surfaces of our bodies, through photographs especially, may serve to remind us that time has passed:

> Despite the fact that nothing in our body, our physical appearance or our knowledge has remained unchanged, we think of ourselves as the same person now as the one that was born many years ago, hated particular teachers, had measles on holiday in Italy, fell in love, married, had children and studied sociology. Furthermore, we relate to each other as selves with an identity whose past has left a record, whether this be an objective biography of significant dates, a record of our own and other people's memory. Some of these traces remain after our death, some fade out of extinction, others are mere flickers known to but a few (Adam, 1995: 18).

Bachelard similarly describes time as something elusive or abstract which cannot easily be recollected in the imagination: 'time ceases to quicken memory...We are unable to relive duration that has been destroyed. We can only think of it, in the line of an abstract time that is deprived of all thickness' ([1958] 1994: 9).

Referring back to Van Gennep's model of rites of passage ([1908] 1960), how might it help to explain the temporal experience of human ageing? First, it suggests that since neither bodily ageing nor time can be apprehended directly, these sensations are only available to us as the outcome of social processes. These, Leach suggests, draw upon the two temporal phenomena which we *can* experience directly: one is repetition such as the cycle of day, night, day, night; the other is irreversibility such as the finite nature of human or animal life. Leach argues, for example, that human beings fear death and are therefore resistant to the idea of the irreversibility or linearity of time upon which ageing is predicated. Thus, in part, what rites of passage do, perhaps, is to recast that experience into something which is both more acceptable and more familiar.

During many rituals of transition, for instance, metaphoric death is followed by metaphoric rebirth, enacted symbolically as in the Ndembu Isoma fertility ritual (Turner, 1969) or the Chisingu ritual among the Bemba which grows girls into women (Richards, 1956). Participants are made to 'die' and to relinquish their previous identity and – rather than coming to an irreversible end – are then 'reborn' anew as fertile or as adult women. And indeed death ritual itself often contains similar representations of rebirth, in either linguistic or symbolic forms. Bloch and Parry describe, for example, how male members of the Bara of southern Madagascar will use a coffin like a battering ram to break through lines of distraught women who block their way to the grave: 'having reached the tomb, the deceased is reborn (head first like a foetus) into the world of the ancestors' (1982: 21).

Another, perhaps more local, example is the Anglican Order for the Burial of the Dead which opens with the words:

> I am the resurrection and the life, saith the Lord: he that believeth in me, though he were dead, yet shall he live . . .

Making metaphorical use of the agricultural cycle of seed-time and harvest, the liturgy itself explains how this 'rebirth' is possible:

> that which thou sowest is not quickened, except it die.

The living harvest follows the death of the seed which was itself produced by the living harvest of the previous year. And, as we have argued elsewhere (Hockey and James, 1993), irreversibility can be side-stepped through the metaphoric use of beginnings, of birth and of growing up, to conceptualise and experience endings, growing old and death. Through active processes of infantilisation – treating elderly people as if they were children – the imminent death of very elderly people may be resisted. Positively perceived images of childlike dependency and wilfulness are foregrounded in the face of the finality of death. Finally, the body-maintenance rituals described by Featherstone (1991) as a feature of the contemporary consumerist attitudes to the body are premised on, if not the reversal of time, certainly an attempt to arrest it via the cult of youthfulness: 'consumer culture imagery has decreed that life can and should be everlastingly happy' (1991: 186).

In all these examples, then, temporal irreversibility is refuted and the unidirectional nature of the life course made cyclical through processes of repetition. However, as Adam (1995) notes, the conventional wisdom that 'traditional' societies employ cyclical concepts of time, in contrast to the linear time concepts of 'modern' and 'western' societies, is based on a set of false suppositions. She argues instead that 'all social processes display aspects of linearity and cyclicality, that we recognise a cyclical structure when we focus on events that repeat themselves and unidirectional linearity when our attention is on the process of the repeating action. Whether we "see" linearity or cyclicality depends fundamentally on the framework of observation and interpretation' (1995: 38).

One way in which we can understand how rites of passage come to construct the ageing process is to see this as a particular patterning of social experience through repetition. Thus, despite the difficulty of grasping time passing, we *can* come to know temporal change via the experience of opposites, such as night and day or heat and cold. The pulse, the heartbeat, the swing of a pendulum are all experiences of change, one state following another in rapid succession. And such 'changes' are more readily perceptible than the slower process of transformation which constitutes human ageing. It is quite possible, therefore, that the acts of repetition which permeate rites of passage give some access to the experience of ageing by symbolically rendering the linearity of ageing as a more cyclical process (Van Gennep [1908] 1960).

Central to this process is Van Gennep's notion of 'the displacement of the sacred'. By this he is referring to the possibility of states or statuses which are not part of the everyday world. They exist but are set apart, taking their shape from their difference from the here-and-now. Note, however, that Van Gennep's theoretical thinking is grounded in spatial metaphors. He writes:

> a society is similar to a house divided into rooms and corridors. The more the society resembles ours in its form of civilisation, the thinner are its internal partitions and the wider and more open are its doors of communication. In a semicivilized society, on the other hand, sections are carefully isolated, and passage from one to another must be made through formalities and ceremonies which show extensive parallels to the rites of territorial passage discussed in the last chapter ([1908] 1960: 26).

The sacred is connoted through reference to a 'place apart': 'as one places oneself successively in this or that spot within the society as a whole, there is a displacement of magic circles' (Van Gennep, [1908] 1960: 16). By thinking in terms of a spatialised binary – the here-and-now of the profane world as opposed to the out-of-bounds world of the sacred – Van Gennep's model allows for the possibility of individuals actually experiencing the repetition of opposites, via the materiality of the body itself moving between different kinds of spaces. Here then we can already detect the importance of embodiment for the experience of agency which, as we show later, is critical to our theorising of age across the life course.

The 'time' of the life course is thus symbolically reproduced and created in rites of passage through the experience of spatialised repetition. 'Ageing' is in this way socially constructed. As they move across the three zones of a rite of passage, participants symbolically step from the profane space of a particular here-and-now, such as adolescence, into the sacred space of transition and then back into the profane space of a new here-and-now, adulthood. And indeed this change is made more meaningful by the literal movement of initiands entering physical spaces imbued with special or sacred meanings. The experience of repetitive change, one thing becoming another thing which then changes back, thus allows the emotionally and conceptually more problematic prospect of one-way transition – irreversibility – to be rendered acceptable and death itself to be apprehended as transition rather than finality.

Nonetheless, despite the spatiality of Van Gennep's work which, as we shall argue, is important for theories of identity, the whole concept of rites of passage as it has passed into anthropological theorising remains problematic in ways which parallel the limitations of Leach's concern with the privileging of temporal repetition rather than irreversibility. As Adam (1990) points out, the separation of repetition from irreversibility is a device rather than a real possibility. Using the example of washing the dishes, she argues that it depends upon your point of view in that while the task is repeated endlessly, the same process does not actually take place every time: 'we therefore need to recognise the separation of linearity and cyclicality as relative to the focus and the framework of observation and not locate it … in logically distinct experiences' (1990: 168). The schema which makes up Van Gennep's model of rites of passage does not, however, take this into account. Spatial metaphors are inextricably intertwined with social structure; 'movement' or 'passage' is visualised as taking place between fixed statuses, endlessly repeated – hence the representation of the life course as life *cycle*.

It is within and through the oxymoron of a static process that social identities are said to be produced. The question emerges then as to whether anthropological accounts of highly structured rituals, such as those discussed so far, can help us make sense of the contemporary experience of changing social identities across the life course. Often, for example, it is literary rather than social science sources which allow us any in-depth insight into such transitions. When Van Gennep ([1908] 1960) and Hertz ([1907] 1960) published their accounts of rituals which had a tripartite structure, as we suggested in Chapter 2, their analyses reflected a Durkheimian concern with 'society' as a reified entity which was more than the sum of its members. Thus, as Bloch and Parry note, practices such as double burial were seen by Hertz and Van Gennep as a way of both disposing of the corpse and recouping society's 'investment' in the dead person. Writing three quarters of a century later, Bloch and Parry do not share a view of society 'as an entity acting for itself'. Instead, they say,

> if we can speak of a reassertion of the social order at the time of death, this social order is a product of rituals of the kind we consider rather than their cause. In other words, it is not so much a question of Hertz's reified 'society' responding to the 'sacrilege' of death, as of the mortuary rituals themselves being an occasion for creating that 'society' as an apparently external force (1982: 6).

Their critique challenges social science's traditional concern with social structure and raises questions, which we shall go on to explore, about the agency of individuals and whether – and if so how – their intersubjective engagement might indeed be the source of the 'social'.

The body, age and agency in the life course

If time is an abstract concept, not easily grasped or made amenable to experience, as we have suggested above, we do nonetheless require an explanation for how it is that we still feel its passage and indeed its pressure on a daily basis. And here, Lakoff and Johnson (1980) usefully highlight the central role of metaphor in making human experience possible. They explain that 'the essence of metaphor is understanding and experiencing one thing in terms of another' (1980: 5). They go on to suggest that the experience of one's body in space, and the materiality of the environment in which it is situated, and with which it engages, provide a basis for metaphorical concepts which allow us to engage with the more abstract or inchoate dimensions of human experience. Thus, it could be suggested that in rites of passage the ritual use of space allows individuals to engage bodily with the temporal distance between two statuses or identities by actively experiencing the process of leaving of one location and entering another.

Aligning his field material from among the Ndembu with other cross-cultural and historical material, Turner, for example, develops his account of the experiences for initiands by suggesting that they are pivoted away from profane time and space and into the ambiguous threshold between what came before and what is to follow. Some anthropologists have therefore stressed the conservative function of liminality as a period during which a play on the status quo serves merely to reinforce it – like a joke, the disorder and misrule of liminality reveals the arbitrary, made-up quality of the powers-that-be without in any way really putting them under threat. Turner, on the other hand, argues that this is a time when social structure is simplified and suggests that this dissolution of profane social structures within the sacred space of liminality allows what he calls 'the central values and axioms of the culture' to be scrutinised (1969: 156). For Turner, then, the experience of liminality is not just about repetition and reinforcement. It contains within it the seeds of change.

This later elaboration of the concept of rites of passage perhaps goes some way to helping us understand a little more about how our identities change across the life course. But, it still tells us rather more about the structuring of experience than about the experience itself. As noted, the classic ethnographies discussed in Chapter 2 make a clear distinction between bodily ageing and social transition. We cannot experience or observe our bodies becoming different across the life course; there is no repetitive oscillation between contrasting states. Yet, by moving out of profane and into ritual space we are pivoted towards re-entry into the profane social space where a new age-based identity can be taken on – we are poised to become someone different. What is central to accounts of ritual processes, then, but hitherto not fully elaborated in social theory, is a view of the body as a site upon which age-related changes can be inscribed and made visible, or a context within which they can be expressed. In such socially constructed accounts, the body is not seen, in and of itself, to initiate or construct the ageing process. Rather, the ageing of the body is regarded as a continuous process which takes place outside such structures, occurring too slowly for us to catch it in motion – no matter how watchful we might be in front of the bathroom mirror. Age has therefore to be stamped upon the body by society, in order for us to 'know' or 'experience' it through the symbolic marking out of differences between 'then' and 'now'.

This process is graphically depicted in one of the very few accounts available in the literature of a personal experience of infibulation (female genital mutilation). Fadumo, a 55-year old Somali woman recalls her own experience as 'a very natural thing' which she always knew would happen because amongst her people this ritual act was the way in which 'girls' were literally made into marriageable women. From her account, we gain a vivid picture of the way in which the body of a nine-year old girl was literally remade to register the 'symbolic' transition to womanhood, a life-course movement metaphorically made in the space of a single day.

> When everything was ready for my operation I was seated on a wooden stool and held by three grown-up women. One of them was my mother. They opened my legs wide apart. Two of the women took one leg each and held them firmly: the other one sat behind me. She held my head between her knees. The circumciser squatted in front of me. As soon as she touched the skin with her knife and began cutting, I shouted and struggled to get loose. But it was impossible ... When the woman was cutting my flesh, I felt as if my intestines were being grabbed and pulled out. After all these years I still feel that particular sensation ...
>
> At last, after what seemed like ages to me, the operation came to an end. I was carried out and put on a mat to rest. My thighs were shaking terribly from the strain that my body had been through ... I had been stitched with five thorns ... my legs were tied from the hips and down to the ankles to make the parts grow together properly ... On the fourth day the thorns were pulled out ... As soon as the thorns were removed, my mother uluated and told me that the place was sewn perfectly and that my opening was as desired (Talle 1993: 89).

Though rites of passage are preeminently social affairs, this account is a powerful reminder that the social inscription of age upon the body *is* itself an embodied experience.

However, as Talle's graphic account affirms, social constructionist theorising which simply privileges structural explanations of change, cannot offer an adequate insight into the experience which such dramatic and powerful rites of passage represent for the individual taking on a changed social identity. Nor can they account for why, in the context of an increasingly urgent call for the ending of such practices, many women themselves continue to offer their support, despite the extreme pain and fear that they themselves have experienced (Flint, 1994). Nor indeed can such approaches shed much light on the more mundane experience which we all share, of our bodies changing as they begin to show the signs of ageing, be it the onset of menstruation and growth of body hair at puberty, or the wrinkles and grey hair of old age. All these are, undoubtedly, signs that ageing is taking place, bodily indications that we might perhaps be about to take on new and rather different social identities.

Within the domain of social constructionist approaches to social identity, we can, however, find some which have attempted to get to grips with more agency-centred perspectives. Our critical review means asking whether these illuminate the materiality and embodied experience of the ageing process itself. As noted in Chapter 2, the concept of the life cycle received little attention outside anthropology, only emerging in sociology in connection with discussions on the family (see Chapter 4). Nonetheless Erving Goffman's (1968) work, which has its roots in the work of G. H. Mead, does begin to offer an early indication as to how such experiences might be incorporated and accounted for, sociologically. However, unlike most of the work we have considered under the rubric of rites of passage, Goffman's work is not concerned with the shift from one age identity to another per se. Rather, it explores other changes in social identity which occur over the life course of some individuals who, through sickness and the onset of physical or mental impairment, law breaking, the ravages of war or the assumption of a religious vocation, may undergo changes in their social identity. This work does however, potentially, illuminate the experience of ageing.

Drawing on numerous autobiographical accounts, Goffman (1963) describes individuals' experiences of stigma and the management of what he calls the spoiled identities which arise with the onset of ill health or impairment. His aim is to discover patterns and regularities in the ways in which the social environment works to shape or construct those experiences and identities *culturally*. Intent upon a micro-sociology rooted in the specificities of individual interaction, the accounts which Goffman draws on repeatedly cite the body as the grounds *of* and *for* the experience of changed and changing identities. As in the rites of passage model, Goffman is concerned with the spatialisation of identity, be it front stage, back stage or behind the walls of a total institution (1968; 1971). The mortifications of the self which occur on entry into total institutions of different kinds – whether religious institutions, residential care homes, prisons, military organisations or mental hospitals – take place through the medium of the body: through changes in diet, through the replacement of personal markers of identity with uniform clothing; through the denial of privacy and other rituals of humiliation designed to level and literally remove the individuality of individuals:

> the new inmate finds himself cleanly stripped of many of his accustomed affirmations, satisfactions and defences, and is subjected to a rather fuller set of mortifying experiences; restriction of free movement, communal living, diffuse authority of a whole echelon of people, and so on. Here one begins to learn about the limited extent to which a conception of oneself can be sustained when the usual setting of supports for it are suddenly removed (Goffman, 1968: 137).

Such a view recalls Turner's perhaps more positive description of the neophyte phase of a rite of passage, the liminal phase of transition and change, where individuals relate to one another not in terms of customary rules and roles but, as undifferentiated human beings, sharing bonds in what he describes as a state of communitas. But, even in the seemingly harsher environments of change depicted by Goffman, a curiously parallel 'togetherness' also pertains. Goffman remarks that

> in thus suppressing externally valid differences, the harshest total institution may be the most democratic; and, in fact, the inmate's assurance of being treated no worse than any other of his fellows can be a source of support as well as deprivation (1968: 112).

In thus seeing total institutions as 'forcing houses for changing persons; each...a natural experiment on what can be done to the self', Goffman's work begins to suggest an approach which might help capture the nature of the embodied experience of changing social identities across the life course (1968: 22). However, as Craib observes in his discussion of another of Goffman's works, *Frame Analysis* (1974), despite his apparent engagement with agency and also with embodiment, Goffman's presentation of the self gets us no nearer to the experiencing self:

> In his production of serial alienation and his reduction of the self he reproduces and, in a sense, lays bare an experience and a way of seeing ourselves and others which is a fundamental feature of life in a social system apparently out of human control (Craib, 1998: 84).

Goffman's overarching concern remains with the identification of a 'similarity of form' within these quite different organisational settings. Thus, for example, he links the common and routine stripping of the individual's markers of self identity on admission to a total institution – hair, name, clothing, personal possessions – with a recasting of a controlling or punitive institution as being beneficial for the unwilling inmate. He does not, however, relate these to the way each individual may learn to make sense of this in terms of their own life experiences. Thus, although as Jenkins (1996) notes, Goffman is clear that identity must be understood processually, his predominant concern remains more with commonalities in the ways in which different institutional structures shape the transitory identities of the individual, rather than how individuals themselves actively experience that changing identity.

Bryan Turner's (1995) later sociological approach to the social construction of ageing, by contrast, rejects the view that people are passively moulded by society in favour of a view which stresses the importance of their embodiment. Describing his body as 'a walking memory', he suggests that though we might not directly experience the bodily process of ageing as it occurs in time, nonetheless, the body *does* provide ample evidence for us that ageing is taking place (1995: 250). Indeed, unlike Leach (1966), who wonders how we know time at all, Turner (1995) sees human beings as continually haunted by their own mortality, living as they do among generational cohorts who act as nostalgic reminders of times past and the people they once were.

It is possible, however, that Turner's suggestion that the body, by its nature, provides us with a sense of the past – and, by implication, the future – tells us more about the technologies of contemporary western society than the body's own capacity to represent time passing, something which Turner himself acknowledges. Photography, for example, which reproduces for us images of our own ageing, operates rather like the scarring which takes place in many rites of initiation. Both juxtapose 'then' and 'now', 'before' and 'after' in the single moment, the western photographed body and lived body being literally set alongside one another, like the imaginative juxtaposing of the unscarred and the scarred body of the Maasai child.

However, the active role of the body in mediating and recording experiences of age hinted at by Turner *does* find support in autobiographical accounts of ageing. Here, changes in the physical body signal to the individual that ageing has occurred, changes brought to our attention by others or through self reflection. This suggests, therefore, that while the social may in part shape the way in which ageing is accomplished as an ascription of identity, any individual's particular embodiment of that identity is neither predictable nor is it shared. In this respect, Denzin's (1989) schema of life-course transitions is particularly insightful. Rejecting the rigidity inherent in models of rite of passage, Denzin explains changes in an individual's life in terms of turning points, which are not necessarily normative or scheduled, but which emerge out of an individual's biographical, and we would wish to say embodied, interaction in the social world: 'biography and history thus join in the interpretive process' (1989: 18).

Denzin describes different kinds of turning points – major ones which irrevocably alter, for good or ill, a person's sense of identity; cumulative turning points, built up gradually over a person's life, which are suddenly recognised as either a barrier or indeed a springboard for change; and minor ones, which, insignificant in themselves, nonetheless turn out to have great symbolic significance in terms of change. Although these may most often be thought about in relation to, for example, the onset of illness, marriage, and the birth of children, there may be scope for thinking about the ways in which the ascription or assumption of a new 'aged' identity may also be regarded as a turning point.

Describing changes in a French rural community, Zonabend, for example, notes the ways in which the life course, and hence the process of growing up and ageing, are constructed around key embodied moments: 'birth, first communion, marriage and death make up the points of reference around which the individual constructs his time' (1984: 197). In this sense, the body is seen as providing both a source of memories and a catalyst for change, a focus for turning points in the life course, Moreover, such embodied experiences also provide the reference points through which external historical events are also recorded: 'When I made my first communion, it was war time' (1984: 198). Recalling an arduous journey to travel to join her husband during the war, one elderly woman vividly depicts the experience of wartime with its rationing and its separations from loved ones through a set of embodied memories:

> the banks of the Ardour were beautiful, but I was sorry there were no potatoes. As for tomatoes, I never stopped eating them, but I would rather have had potatoes. I then asked to be taken back home and I was held up in the station at Tours.

I took three days to arrive at Dijon and I was as thin as a rake! On arrival at the station in Dijon I met Robert Perron's brother, and we fell on each other's necks . . . we had been told not to leave for Minot as there was a curfew and the Boches would pick us up. We left just the same. My husband came along the road to Poincion every evening to see if I had arrived (1984: 197).

In Laurie Lee's autobiographical novel, we have a comparable depiction of an age-based turning point in his life – leaving home at nineteen – as a primarily embodied experience:

The stooping figure of my mother, waist-deep in the grass and caught there like a piece of sheep's wool, was the last I saw of my country home as I left to discover the world. She stood old and bent at the top of the bank, silently watching me go, one gnarled hand raised in farewell and blessing, not questioning why I went. At the bend of the road I looked back again and saw the gold light die behind her: then I turned the corner, passed the village school, and closed that part of my life for ever (Lee, 1969: 11).

Temporal experience spatialised

Both these personal recollections illustrate the importance of turning points in individual lives, examples which, like Van Gennep's account of rites of passage, direct us to the 'spatialisation' of time. As noted, rites of passage, whilst making age and temporality their focus, are persistently couched by Van Gennep in spatial terms. This schema is evident within the Christian marriage ritual, another turning point in the life course. Even though the bride and groom traditionally live separately, they are also kept apart from one another symbolically, prior to the wedding, a spatialised manoeuvre which sets them clearly in opposition to one another. Hen and stag nights take place in different venues, each one potentially involving the ritual practice of tying the bride or groom to a fixed object such as railings or a lamp-post, attempting thereby to prevent, by spatial stasis, the transition of identity which he or she is about to undergo (Westwood, 1984). Traditionally, too, spatial precautions are taken against the engaged couple catching sight of one another immediately prior to the wedding, the final coming together of the bride and groom being ritually orchestrated by the bride's father who passes the bride from his hand to that of her future husband. It is this symbolic use of space which gives social meaning to the house move which the bride and groom will later undertake, and to the carrying of the bride over the threshold of the new house. Simply packing some bags, signing a marriage certificate and moving to a new address is thus not the same as 'getting married'. As this example of a turning point illustrates, rituals of transition, whilst theorised at a symbolic level, are also embodied actions performed by individuals moving from one space to another. Ultimately, it is this which potentiates the bride and groom 'feeling they are properly married'.

It is then through a focus on embodied movement that we propose to explain changes in ageing and social identity across the life course. Early traces of this can be seen in Van Gennep's acknowledgement of the pervasiveness of movement within his metaphoric 'society-as-house' where he notes, for example, that Maasai teenagers cannot 'grow up' into adulthood until their father has performed a ceremony called 'passing over the fence', so making his transition to the age-status of 'old man' (1960: 85). The 'fixed points' between which individuals make such transitions during rites of passage are therefore empty statuses, categories or roles waiting to be inhabited. Embodied experiences of structural transition, carried out actively and in relation to other people whose own identities will change as a result, allow new identities to be taken on. Thus, for example, embracing the social identity of 'parent' involves not just the birth of a child but also, in part, the transition of one's parents to the new identity of 'grandparent' and one's siblings to the new identity of 'uncle' or 'aunt'. One birth, therefore, shifts the life-course positioning of several generations, each one of whom, as a result, feels themselves to be getting older. However, as Pahl testifies, relational shifts of identity are not simply externally driven makeovers. As individuals come to inhabit new statuses or roles, they animate them according to the repertoire of choices available at particular points in time:

> 'You don't look like a grandmother,' they say. As tactfully as I can, I reply that I do look like a grandmother; it is the picture of a grandmother inside their heads which has to be adjusted. The new grandmother of today does not have a bag of knitting and an apron; she has a briefcase and a mobile phone and hurries from her office to help with bath and bedtime. The new grandmother of today does not sit at home waiting to be visited; she finds a holiday bargain on the Internet and flies off around the world to return with exotic presents for her beloved grandchildren. The only thing which has not changed at all is the abiding love which grandmothers have for their grandchildren (2000: 106).

In this sense, as Harris argues, social structure can be seen as 'merely a moment in a process of societal change of which the choices of subjects are constituent' (1987: 24). What Harris highlights, therefore, is the agency of individuals who not only make choices but in so doing produce, reproduce and indeed transform the identities which they take on, and in part the social structures through which those identities are made meaningful.

Conclusion

In this first part of this book, we have explored and critiqued traditional social science explanations of ageing and the life course. We have shown how a social constructionist perspective problematises popular understandings of age as 'natural' and 'biologically given' by demonstrating its cultural variability and its dissociation from bodily ageing per se. Ethnographic material from non-western societies has been our primary source of examples. These provided a focus for early anthropological theorising about the life course, structural theories which take a broad social constructionist perspective to show how *social* divisions order and regulate the ageing process. In this sense, the 'ageing body' *does* ground forms of social organisation of various kinds, although the materiality of the body disappears in accounts which are at pains to demonstrate the contingency of social identities.

Thus, the purely structurally focused accounts offered by social constructionist approaches turn out to be heuristically limited, despite their value in highlighting the social nature of ageing via cross-cultural comparison. Ultimately, they fail to capture adequately the *experience* of the ageing process. Thus, in the next part of the book, we retain this comparative perspective but shift our attention closer to home to examine the changes which the western life course has undergone from the early modern period up to the present day. The following empirically-based chapters engage critically with another set of structural theories about social change which broadly stem from a political economy perspective. Our aim here, as in the first part of the book, is to identify the contributions which such an approach might offer to our understanding of the life course but then to go on to explore their possible integration with more experience-centred approaches. By doing this, we aim to overcome the binarism with which, as Jenkins (1996) has shown, theories of identities are traditionally plagued.

PART II

Understanding the Western Life Course

4

Histories of the Life Course

Introduction

As noted, the literature on rites of passage has provided one of the traditional bases for studies of the life course. Within this, the life course is represented as a series of relatively fixed stages – infancy, childhood, adulthood and old age – through which individuals pass as they grow older. Yet, once we begin to work with historical material within one society we cannot explain differences in conceptualisations and experiences of the life course purely in terms of cultural and geographical distance. Rather, we have to account for change – not just within the individual life course – but also change in the shape of the life course itself. That is to say, it is not only individuals who change, but also the categories they inhabit.

As we shall show in this chapter, new life course categories such as 'youth' and 'deep old age' have emerged in parts of Europe and North America during the twentieth century to accompany the changing demographic profile caused by, for example, a decrease in birth rate and the increase in life expectancy (Bernades, 1997). Such changes, therefore, clearly impact upon individual lives, leading to a changing configuration of the relationship between age and key transitional moments in the life course, such as leaving home, marriage and childbirth, and the significance which these have for age-based identities.

While on the one hand, therefore, we are considering today's very fluid process of classification and transition, as we shall show, the more rigid pattern of the modern western life course which emerged in the mid-nineteenth century continues to occupy a hegemonic position. Highly structured and chronologised, with social roles and

57

stages clearly set out, usually the result of the institutional pressures of employment and the state (Vincent, 1995), its persistent influence is evidenced in the current ideological imperative to 'get a life' by a certain age – and to 'take life easy' when we reach another. Despite the growth of divorce and lone parenting, dominant representations of family structure are still identifiably nuclear, a family-based generational structure remains, and children, adults and older people are clearly differentiable from one another. And still central to this modernist image of the life course is the workplace. This remains a core marker of adult identity, despite some fairly radical changes in the patterning of people's working lives (see Chapter 10).

Thus, although the 'life' we should 'get' is said to have changed and to have become more open, parenthood, for example, is nonetheless *still* perceived as an important temporally located marker or turning point in the biographical movement towards adult identity. Indeed, parenthood remains popularly represented within a life course context via the metaphor of the 'biological clock', an image which exceeds its source in a purely mechanical object. It takes on agency, 'ticking away' the years to remind adult women in particular to hurry up and procreate.

Yet, despite the hegemonic grip which the modernist life course appears to still have on our imagination, there *is* evidence that the contemporary western life course has, in reality, become a much more fluid endeavour, offering scope for individual choice and innovation. Taking marriage as an example of a life-course transition, Elliott's (1991) account of demographic trends in domestic life between 1945 and 1987 shows, for example, that first marriage rates for men and women fell steeply after 1972, halving by 1987. During the 1950s and 1960s there had been a tendency to marry at increasingly young ages, but during the 1970s and 1980s marriage began to occur later, with cohabitation seen as a prelude to marriage. Premarital cohabitation rose from 5 per cent in the mid-1960s to 70 per cent by 1990s (Wasoff and Dey, 2000). Those marrying for the second time were even more likely to cohabit beforehand, marriage being often delayed until one or other of the partners divorced[1]. In sum, then, as an institutionalised life-course transition, it would appear that marriage has undergone rapid changes in terms of its popularity and its necessity as a legitimation of heterosexual relationships and family life (see Chapter 9). In addition, its role as a *permanent* transition to coupledom has also undergone major change during the last half of the twentieth century, the number of divorces in the UK having more than trebled between 1969 and 1994 (Office for National Statistics, 1997).

Rejecting the idea that the western life course is now inescapably standardised or chronologised, White Riley (1986) similarly argues that contemporary American life stages now have relatively blurred boundaries. Nonetheless, the social roles that converge within a life stage may still have entry and exit points which are identified according to a variety of quite *specific*, albeit different, chrono-logical ages. In Britain, for example, adulthood can be differentiated from childhood and youth by the age-specific, *legal* entitlements which adulthood confers: to drink and smoke, to have sex, to marry, to vote, to drive a car or motorbike, to enter the military services. Some of these bring with them social roles: husband, wife, lover, drinking partner, soldier, bus driver. Yet the ages at which *these* roles are assumed can vary quite significantly, by a matter of years. White Riley's distinction between what Kohli terms 'chronologised' social roles (cited in Held, 1986: 157) and these more ragged life course stages is therefore important. What remains open for discussion however is the relative significance – and influence – of *particular* roles as markers of entry into a *particular* stage of life and the experiential consequences for individual identity of the transform-ation of the institutionalised practices which mark entry into an age-based social category.

Developing such an argument, Vincent urges that even closer attention must be paid to the question of how one age cohort succeeds another in our conceptualisations of the life course. His suggestion is that we need to understand how historical events, which produce large structural changes, contribute to the trajectory of the individual life course (1995: 53). In this sense 'structures' such as social class or patriarchy are also life events which, across biographical time, operate as powerful 'external' influences upon the individual's later years. This we term an historio-biographical approach. It is one which, for example, can help illuminate how structural issues of social inequality pattern the embodied moments of individuals' everyday lives over time. At the same time, however, this approach does not suggest that early events have a simplistic or determining effect upon later life experience. On the contrary, the considerable variations in the outcome of childhood poverty or parental divorce highlights the complexity of processes which make up the life course and, in particular, the agency of individuals in authoring their own lives.

Such subtleties need to be accommodated, therefore, in any theorising about the life course and, in the first sections of this chapter, we begin by identifying some of the historical processes which can be seen as integral to the making and remaking of the life course across time. By way of illustration, we take the emergence of pervasive modernist values and images as our focus, tracing their roots in previous conceptions of the life course and considering their role in the experience of ageing today. In this, political economy has been one of the primary explanatory devices used to account for this process of social change, and we therefore examine its contribution to our understanding, as well as its limitations, as an account of how we know that we are ageing. Our focus here, then, is on the shifts in the distribution of power between different social categories which occurred on the basis of age and as the result of processes such as rapid nineteenth-century industrialisation and urbanisation. To illustrate this point, we now move on to discuss the twin study areas of 'childhood' and 'old age'.

Changing conceptions of age in the life course

Bearing in mind White Riley's (1986) reminder that life stages are not necessarily easy to identify, we begin with Vincent's account of the development of the modern western life course as a three-stage historical process which began during the early modern period between 1600 and 1850 (Grillis, cited in Vincent, 1995). At this time, chronological age was of little import, the 'ages of man' being seen to stem from supernatural rather than natural sources. Of the subsequent modern period, Vincent suggests that by contrast:

> in industrial society in the last part of the twentieth century, age is becoming much more important in relation to people's experience. It is becoming a criterion that more people use to interpret and understand their experience of society and to structure their own consciousness and action (1995: 54).

Gillis (1996) shares this view. He argues that from 1870 onwards an acute age consciousness emerged, with the result that 'so as not to appear unnatural everyone did their utmost to act their age from birth to death' (1996: 84). What accounts, then, for the increasing significance of 'age' as a marker of transitions within the life course over this historical period?

We turn first to issues of demography. As already suggested, marriage practices can be a useful indicator of changes in the nature of the life course. During the early modern period, Protestant north-western Europe departed from the practice of multiple-family households which pervaded the rest of the world. Committed to individualism, north Europeans married and made families only after achieving the economic independence necessary to form single-family households. This transition to adulthood was therefore economically determined, though manifested not through entry to employment, but rather in establishing an independent marital household. Whereas people throughout the world married during their teens, in north-western Europe the average age of marriage from the fourteenth century onwards was much later, 26 for men and 23 for women. This age of transition remained in place until the late eighteenth century when earlier marriage again became the norm. However, by the twentieth century, Gillis observes another change: from the 1970s onwards, there was a further shift, away from early to late marriage.

The relationship between age and marriage is therefore subject to considerable variation. This results in rather different outcomes. In the early modern period, though marriages took place later, leaving home often occurred early in life as a consequence of the imperative to set up single-family households. And since the average lifespan for both men and women was only forty years of age – and marriage occurred late – many children were orphaned at an early age and therefore lived elsewhere than their natal homes. Even those with two parents were unlikely to live at home beyond their mid-teens, so that, Gillis reports 'virtually all young people lived and worked in another dwelling for shorter or longer periods of time' (1996: 9). Thus, in the early modern period, neither marriage nor leaving home were determined by the strict age chronology which we take for granted in the modern life course.

Despite Held's (1986) evidence for the existence of certain forms of age-grading in the early modern period in some parts of Central Europe, Hareven (1986) remains persuaded that it was the modern period which saw a marked *increase* in life-course standardization. She shows that, in twentieth-century America, demographic and policy changes increased the segregation of age-groups. This meant that families formerly linked by cross-generational ties became fractured. Family members in one household became isolated from sources of care traditionally found within the extended family. As evidence, she cites data from her study among American families with a parental generation born before 1910 and a child generation born either between 1910 and 1919 or between 1920 and 1929. The parental generation, she found, were more likely to see the life course as a continuous whole, with its major events neither constituting transitions nor discontinuities. Members of the older generation did not talk in terms of 'adolescence' or 'middle age'. By contrast the youngest cohort, born in the 1920s, frequently used terms drawn from popular culture such as 'middle-age crisis' and 'empty nest'.

Hareven goes on to identify the factors which have contributed to this difference. For the parental generation there was often, in reality, no 'empty nest' since one of the younger female children tended to stay at home and care for older adults. In addition, the experiences of migration and economic crisis had often been the most significant turning points of their lives, outweighing any age-bound transition. Thus it was participation in the ups and downs of family life which drove or inhibited life-course changes, rather than chronological age itself. By contrast, by the time the younger generation were growing up, bureaucratic age-based demarcations of the life course were already in place and beginning to govern the boundaries of childhood and retirement.

But why do such changes occur? Is this simply the result of macro-level socioeconomic shifts or do we need somehow to take account of the complex intermeshing of social policy, cultural imperatives and social *action* in the construction of age-based identities? To answer this question we turn once more to the early modern period. Here, we examine the combined forces which gradually worked to shape the ideas of 'old age' which influenced the way elderly people were categorised within the modern life course that emerged subsequently. Roebuck's (1978) account of the development of Poor Law provision for elderly people, for example, charts the gradual chronologising of old age, identifying its base in ideas about older adults' functional role in society. Her evidence shows that chronological age represented far less of a marker of social identity during the Elizabethan period than it did later. She notes, rather, that provision for 'the aged and impotent poor' within the Elizabethan Poor Law was made according to a combination of physical frailty and the *appearance* of being old. She points out that:

administrators seemed to consider old age more a question of function, or lack of it, than a question of precise calendar years. The aged were those who were infirm, frail and suffering incapacities of body and mind to the extent that they could no longer fully support or take care of themselves, and who also gave the appearance of being old . . . it was only when the two conditions came together in one person that that person was considered 'old' by the authorities (1978: 417).

As a result, some individuals became members of the category 'old' in their late forties. Roebuck's historical account therefore documents great diversity in the age at which 'old age' began: 'while local authorities varied in their opinions about the age at which a person became old, most considered people "aged" if they were in their 50s or 60s and unable to support themselves' (Roebuck, 1978: 418). Among those living in the workhouse after 1834, the 'old' were permitted a more luxurious diet which included tea, butter and sugar. Here, a common chronological age was selected and, as Roebuck notes, 'the fact that those over 60 were allowed a better diet quickly created a general impression that the "aged and infirm" were people over 60' (1978: 419). Late nineteenth-century welfare provision via the Friendly Societies produced further digression between chronological age and the social category 'old'. Those who belonged to a society could receive a pension at 50, while those who did not became 'old' only at 60. Another differentiating characteristic was residence and type of work. Charles Booth, social investigator, said that 'In one way or another effective working life is 10 years longer in the country than in the town, or, speaking generally, is as 70 to 60' (Roebuck, 1978: 421).

Roebuck's discussion thus identifies social policy as the mechanism which both contributes to, and draws upon, conceptions of age-based social categories. However, those policies themselves reflect wider forms of social pressure. If we move forward to the twentieth century, for example, we find comparable processes at work in moves to reduce the pensionable age to 60 during the 1920s and 1930s. This reflected the high levels of unemployment during this period and the desire of younger adults to remove the older people who had become impediments to their own working lives: 'the young were dictating the retirement to the old' (Roebuck, 1978: 424). 'Old age' in this sense is the product of intergenerational conflict.

The ragged relationship between chronological age and life course categories – discernible both historically and contemporarily – thus reflects policy-makers' varied and changing welfarist concerns with the properties of particular social roles in relation to particular models of age and ageing. Through these we can see, for example, how the trajectory of the modern life course was initiated. Still ongoing, it is nonetheless often marked by contradiction. Thus, though it is claimed that, in postmodernity, the boundaries of age-based social categories have loosened in terms of what people can do (see Chapter 6), paradoxically this same period has also seen an increased institutionalisation of chronological age. From legal imperatives through to consumer practices, age consciousness has intensified, such that what it means to be a child, for example, has become highly contextualised in relation to the age of criminal responsibility, consensual sex, leaving school, consent to surgery, access to contraception, participation in work and the right to vote. A similar institutionalisation of age is evident in the iconography of birthday cards which, as Bytheway (1995) notes, marks the passage of time qualitatively as well as quantitatively. These can now be purchased not only to mark the early ages of childhood or the key points of transition such as the twenty-first or hundredth birthday, but also every year and every decade in between. Once adulthood has been achieved, reference to ageing in birthday cards often uses humour to make very negative references to bodily decline: wrinkled skin, sexual impotence and incapacity.

Life-course transitions may be more varied and/or less compulsory and yet, at the same time, they are more intensively marked. Consumption practices proliferate around turning points such as: passing examinations, driving tests, changing jobs, acquiring a new home, a new baby, a fiancé, a spouse, the anniversaries of marriages, retirement and death. To unravel this paradox a little further, we now turn, therefore, to the complex of factors which are said to have been fundamental to the emergence and persistence of the concepts which make up the modern life course. We do this by looking in more detail at an historical case study of the relationship between work and age-based identities to show how these developed in parallel to exclude certain categories of people from social participation.

A Working Life?

As Chapter 10 will detail, children, older people and those who were sick came to be excluded from *selling* their labour during the nineteenth-century processes of industrialisation and urbanisation.

This trend enabled the mapping of particular evaluations on to stages of the life course, with dependency rapidly becoming regarded as a marker of the very young, the very old and the sick, and independence becoming increasingly valued as the mark of full adulthood status. However, as discussed elsewhere (Hockey and James, 1993), this had rather different consequences for those at either end of the life course. While children came to be seen, increasingly, as in need of the care and protection of state systems of education and welfare, a parallel pattern of progressive margin-alisation had more negative implications for the position of older people. As noted earlier, Poor Law provision produced a staggered chronological boundary to the category 'old'. In addition, however, it played a key role in shaping older people's social participation and therefore, subsequently, their citizenship rights. Thus, the Poor Law Amendment Bill, introduced in 1834, was a bill which not only reduced the traditional sources of poor relief but, via the new 'bastille' workhouses, aimed to keep older people in work by making the living conditions within these institutions harsh enough to deter malingerers. However, that there was a steady *rise*, rather than fall in paupers placed in workhouses between 1838 and 1843 suggests that the factory system was serving to *exclude*, rather than include, particular categories of people. As Thompson (1968) wryly notes, no one, if they could have helped it, would have surely voluntarily offered themselves up as workhouse fodder. According to Thompson, in 1838 there were 78,536 workhouse inmates regis-tered, a figure which had more than doubled by 1843 when 197,179 inmates were recorded. It must be surmised, therefore, that many of these destitutes were in fact older people who, because of their physical condition, could simply no longer keep pace with the demands made by machines, the cornerstone of the factory system. Thompson records the words of a Bolton muslin-weaver in 1834:

> I am in a certain situation; I am now at this moment within a twelve month of 60 years of age and I calculate that within the space of eight years I shall myself become a pauper. I am not capable, by my most strenuous exertions to gain ground to the amount of a shilling; and when I am in health it requires all my exertions to keep soul and body together (cited in Thompson, 1968: 334).

Older people were thus gradually being excluded from continuing a working life within mainstream economic settings, any opportunity for them to sell their labour being confined, like that of children and disabled people, to marginal piece-work outside of the factory system. Oliver sums up this process:

> the new mechanism for controlling economically unproductive people was the workhouse or the asylum, and over the years a whole range of specialised institutions grew up to contain this group. These establishments were undoubtedly successful in controlling individuals who would not or could not work. They also performed a particular ideological function, standing as visible monuments to the fate of others who might no longer choose to subjugate themselves to the disciplinary requirement of the new work system (1989: 10).

For elderly people, the once cherished independence of adulthood was lost through ageing or sickness. Older people became seen as part of the 'burden of pauperism' during the early twentieth century, a view which undoubtedly laid the grounds for the growing stigmatisation and infantilisation of elderly people in the second half of the twentieth century (Hockey and James, 1993). During the early nineteenth century, even those who *died* in the workhouse were penalised, experiencing a social death which was felt to lead to their spiritual annihilation. Thus their bodies were made available for dissection within the terms of the 1832 Anatomy Act. This failure to be buried whole robbed paupers of their hope of resurrection in Paradise (Richardson, 1987).

For children, by contrast, enforced exclusion from the factory system by the end of the nineteenth century, via the Factory Acts, went hand-in-hand with the rise of compulsory universal education, heralded in by the Education Act of 1870. The child's workplace became the school room, with children's dependency being recast more positively as a childish need and, unlike the position of elderly people, as something which was very much in their best interests.

Ideologies of the life course

While it is clear from this case study that the shape of the modern western life course has indeed developed as a byproduct of the changes in social relations which were set in motion by the process of industrialisation, such a determinedly materialist account brushes over the complexity of the processes through which this was actually accomplished and experienced in the lives of individuals. As Rose (1989) has argued, chance needs to be reinstated as an explanation of change to capture its essentially messy, often incidental, character with spin-offs in unforeseen directions:

> innovations made have sometimes arisen from radically new inventions, but at other times, they have involved the ad hoc utilisation, combination, and extension of existing explanatory frameworks and techniques. Sporadic innovations like these have often come to nothing, failed or been abandoned or out flanked. Others have flourished, spread to other locales and problems, and established themselves as lasting and stable networks of thought and action. And out of these small histories, a larger pattern has taken shape in whose web we all, modern men and women, have become entangled (1989: 9).

Such a view of history opens up the possibility of a more rounded account of the forces which have been integral to the modern life course. Although writing primarily about the twentieth century, Rose's observations about how regimes of truth come to establish particular kinds of subjectivities through particular forms of governance are especially instructive for us here. They suggest that we need to pay attention to the ways in which ideas about the child's nature, adulthood and old age came to prominence and how they subsequently became established as 'truths'. These can tell us a great deal about the cultural construction of the life course, as one representation of the transition from birth to death. For example, as Rose points out, in the twentieth century it was 'the new vocabularies provided by the sciences of the psyche [which enabled] the aspirations of government to be articulated in terms of the knowledgeable management of the depths of the human soul' (1989: 7). In the eighteenth and nineteenth centuries, parallel concerns had been expressed about the nature of 'the child' and the child's nature. These were instrumental in ensuring childhood's governance through framing the social exclusion of children, increasingly, as being in their best interests. As Steedman observes, 'children were *both* the repositories of adults' desires *and* social beings who lived in social worlds and networks of social and economic relationships, as well as in the adult imagination' (1995: 97).

To explore this idea in more depth, we offer a second case study and consider Hendrick's account of the ways in which, in the context of the UK, the category of 'child' became firmly entrenched in its particular niche in the life course. Thus, Hendrick writes:

> in 1800 the meaning of childhood was ambiguous and not universally in demand. By 1914 the uncertainty had been virtually resolved and the identity largely determined, to the satisfaction of the middle class and respectable working class' (1997: 35).

And it was in part through the chance actions of individual reformers, engaging with particular philosophical traditions and having recourse to certain political resources, that the idea of the child became reinscribed in the life course in new and rather different ways during the nineteenth century. No longer fragmented by class, a more universal notion of the 'child' emerged to occupy a place at the start of the life course. Thus, for example, as Hendrick notes:

> the reconstruction of the 'factory child' through the prism of dependency and ignorance was a necessary precursor to mass education in that it helped prepare public opinion for shifts in the child's identity: from wage earner to school pupil; for a reduction in income of working-class families, as result of loss of children's earnings; and for the introduction of the State into the parent–child relationship (1997: 46).

Central to the reforming zeal of the mid-nineteenth century were the twin themes of innocence and experience – the legacy of the earlier Rousseaunian romanticism – which became focused upon the idea of the delinquent child. This child, the child of the poor, was by the mid-1850s, not seen as conforming to the 'middle-class notion of a properly constituted childhood, characterized by a state of dependency' (Hendrick, 1997: 43). A series of legislative Acts between 1854 and 1866 sought therefore to define the juvenile delinquent as the child in need of care and protection, its delinquency seen as the product of poor parenting and the lack of adequate discipline and control. Hendrick cites Mary Carpenter, a keen social reformer of the 1850s, who regarded delinquent children as the precise opposite of what children should be: 'independent, self-reliant advanced in knowledge of evil but not of good, devoid of reverence for God or man, utterly destitute of any sound guiding principle of action' (1997: 44). In short, such children, it was thought, needed to be restored to 'the true position of childhood' by instilling in them 'a sense of utter helplessness from a confidence in the superior power and wisdom of those around' (1997: 44).

In such statements, the child's difference from the adult and its necessary separation from the adult world is being decisively claimed through recourse to a set of assumptions about the distinctiveness of the child's nature. And it was these same assumptions about the universality of childhood that laid the foundations for universal education for all 'children': 'wage-earning children were not proper children and, therefore had to be made innocent of such adult behaviour, and the school was the institutional means for achieving this' (Hendrick, 1997: 46).

However, as Williamson notes in his biographical study of change in a mining community, school as a marker of the 'universality' of childhood in the life course came first for the urban middle and upper classes. For many rural working-class children, school attendance was often erratic. School was in many ways irrelevant for 'the work children would do on the farms, in the pit and in the home [and] ... that they did rather badly at it anyway, persuaded them that school offered very little indeed' (1982: 28). In addition, they were inspected by middle-class educators who all too often 'equated dialect and forms of speech with intelligence and potential so that deviations from educated styles of expressions were taken as evidence of failure' (1982: 28). And schooling was also at first regarded as more of a male than female preserve, an attitude persisting well into the 1950s as Dennis *et al.*, observed in their study of a Yorkshire mining community:

> parents are much more interested in the educational progress of their sons than of their daughters, many of them regarding education for women as a waste of time, since they are destined to spend their time as mothers and housewives. For the boy who does not gain entrance to the grammar school at the age of 11, this interest ceases but there will usually be some concern about what sort of a job he is going to take, some concern for his future. For the girls this is not true at all (1956: 239).

As Steedman remarks, the making of 'childhood' as a particular kind of life course space during the nineteenth century was also achieved through the 'building up of scientific evidence about physical growth in childhood, the marking out of stages of development and the processes of language acquisition' (1990: 79). Through their writings, particular educational theorists disseminated ideas about the nature of children and of childhood, ideas which, in turn, came to buttress the political and economic processes outlined above which were removing children increasingly from public adult work, confining them further into domestic and school environments. Steedman describes how Freidrich Froebel (1782–1852), for example:

> working within a Romantic appropriation of Kantian philosophy, evolved an educational system for young children based on a notion of the human being as an organic unity, with the human mind as a spontaneous formative agency (Steedman, 1990: 82).

Writing in childcare manuals and magazines destined for the middle classes of the 1860s and 1870s, Froebel promulgated the importance of 'child-gardens' which would 'allow the developing child to be active in a fitting way, and activity would permit the flowering of inborn capacities' (Steedman, 1990: 82). Though such ideas were in part metaphorical in intent, they were also translated into practice by, for example, the establishment of kindergartens in the poorer districts of many industrial cities, with kindergarten education being adopted as official policy by the Board of Education from the 1890s onwards. The reformer Margaret McMillan established a camp school in Deptford, London in 1911 as part of a treatment programme to improve the health of young girls. Her journals indicate the ways in which such practical activity was sustained by a particular ideological vision of children's needs and nature:

> here the little girls gathered each evening, as the sweltering day turned to twilight; pale faces brightened at the sight of the sweet-williams and white fox gloves which 'I can look at after I'm in bed'. Here, sleepy eyes looked from their pillows at points of starry fire in the indigo blue depth; the night wind cooled their little heated bodies, and a primrose dawn called them awake. Will these children ever forget the healing joy of such nearness to the earth spirit as is possible in Deptford (cited in Steedman, 1990: 85).

Turning now to consider the later years of life, we find an imagery of ageing which is much more variable in content and tone. These representations begin with medical formulations during the nineteenth century, followed by a blend of consumerism and health promotion during the twentieth. However, as Zeilig notes in a discussion of the relevance of literature for gerontology, 'when one is contemplating old age, older people and what it means to grow old, no single answer is possible, and the variety of perspectives afforded by different authors at different epochs who have tackled the subject demonstrate this' (1997: 43). For example, Featherstone and Hepworth (1985) note the contradictions inherent within nineteenth-century constructions of the menopause. The bodily changes which occur within women's reproductive lives, associated with the ending of menstruation, were projected in the medical literature onto the more diffuse experiences of men – a loss of interest in sex and flagging capacity for sexual penetration (see also Chapter 8). However, these phenomena were interpreted in two different ways, both of them in keeping with a Victorian scientific and moral conception of the life course as 'a road from physical to spiritual perfection'

(1985: 251). Dr William Acton's book *The Functions and Disorders of the Reproductive Organs*, published in 1857, assumed a natural complementarity between the sexes which paved the way from physiological to spiritual maturity, women losing the capacity for reproductive sex, men losing the urgency of their sexual desires. Later, a contrasting conception of mid-life was proffered: the notion of a transient period of change, occurring among both women and men, which prefaced a period of stabler health, fortified by a continuing pursuit of sexual pleasure. During the 1920s and the 1930s, Marie Stopes, for example, worked hard to promote the idea of lifelong sexual pleasure for both women and men. By the twentieth century, this possibility of a positive outcome to the menopause, whether male or female, was complemented by literatures which advocated a much more active approach to mid-and later life (Hepworth and Featherstone, 1982). Here, the emphasis is less on the potential long-term benefits of naturally occurring changes and more on the moral duty of the individual to adopt regimes of diet and exercise which will bring older people's appearance and lifestyles closer into line with younger ones, so differentiating themselves from 'the elderly' who are past saving.

The ambiguities and contradictions inherent in this literature on middle age are also evident in the gerontological literature. Immediately after the Second World War, and in fairly rapid succession, we find, for example, activity theory (Cavan *et al.*, 1949) which stressed the likelihood of older adults continuing to adhere to their more youthful identities and, if unable to do so, then discovering ways of adapting which reflect their existing cultural frameworks; disengagement theory (Havighurst *et al.*, 1964; Cumming and Henry, 1961) which took a functionalist approach to argue that it was natural and socially appropriate for older people to withdraw from active involvement in their earlier social roles and networks; and dependency theory which argued that the profile of later life as a time of waning personal resources was a product of social and economic structures which excluded older people from participation in the mainstream economy (Townsend, 1981).

These varying and often contradictory representations of the later years of the life course, when compared with those associated with childhood, can perhaps be seen as the necessary ideological backdrop for the changes in policy-focused rhetoric which have persistently re-represented later life as, variously: a time of welcome rest, an opportunity for self-fulfilling leisure or a period during which there are still contributions to be made to mainstream life. Blaikie, for example, notes that 'history reminds us that retirement is a decidedly malleable concept, its ideology varying according to manpower (sic) requirements' (1997: 11). He exemplifies this point with citations from the social investigator, Seebohm Rowntree, the first being written in 1931 at the time of the Depression:

> it is one of the sources of our industrial weakness to-day that men whose powers are thus waning are often excessively unwilling to resign one shred of their authority (cited in Blaikie, 1997: 11).

As labour shortages emerged after the Second World War, however, Rowntree came up with a different take on this period of the life course:

> the [Nuffield] enquiry pointed clearly to the fact that many old people can render valuable service in industry – service which should be made full use of . . . (cited in Blaikie, 1997: 11).

In contrast with these persistently contradictory trends with respect to older people, the policy-focused rhetoric surrounding childhood was far more consistent, constantly reinforcing notions of children's dependency, vulnerability and innocence (Stainton Rogers and Stainton Rogers, 1992). Thus by the 1990s, when two ten-year old boys were arrested for the murder of a toddler, they could not be incorporated within the category of child. Through their actions, they had forfeited any claim to childhood innocence or vulnerability (James and Jenks, 1996).

Age and citizenship across the life course

In our discussion of the historical case study material above, we have drawn heavily upon a political economy perspective to reveal the importance of processes of social inclusion and exclusion in the establishment of the categories of 'childhood' and 'old age' within the modern life course. However, in order to understand how power is actually withheld at different points in the life course, a third element needs to be incorporated into our discussion. This is an account of the nature of citizenship – since citizenship varies in relation to age across the life course.

Marshall's (1950) analysis of the development of citizenship, based on the British experience, details the progress of citizenship rights through three phases: the seventeenth century saw the development of legal rights, followed by the emergence of political rights during the eighteenth and nineteenth centuries and culminating in the twentieth century with the implementation of a raft of social rights, epitomised in the emergence of the welfare state. However, as Turner argues, while in general this model is useful in outlining the three-pronged aspect of citizenship, its essentially evolutionary thrust fails to acknowledge that 'different social groups may experience the rate of social change in very different ways and within a different sequential order' (1993: 8). Thus women, Turner argues, may be said to have achieved a certain number of social rights before many of their civil and political rights were secured.

Similarly, although children have had their rights to welfare increasingly being affirmed and secured since the late nineteenth century, the question of whether children should be permitted political rights still remains highly contentious. Thus, it is still questionable as to the extent to which children can yet be regarded as citizens, despite Britain signing up to the UN Convention on the Rights of the Child in 1990. For example, though the Children Act, 1989 was hailed as 'a children's charter' and ostensibly is an Act which incorporates the principles and rights of the Convention, there is strong evidence to suggest that the practical implementation of those rights is proving more difficult. In brief, the Act provides that in matters concerning their own welfare children should have a proper say and that any decisions taken by adults on children's behalf must take account of their wishes and feelings and be in their best interests. However, work carried out within the family justice system, for example, reveals that courts still do not always take account of children's wishes and feelings (Lyon, 1995; Murch, 1995; Parry, 1994). In other settings – such as hospitals or schools – routine consultation with children is even less well established as a practice (Alderson, 1993; 1995). Thus, as James and James observe, New Labour 's initiatives with regard to the position of children and young people in the UK reveal,

> areas of concern in relation to the status of children as citizens, as members of the community, and of the community's attitudes towards them. In spite of the UN Convention . . . and all of the political rhetoric about the emphasis in recent legislation on children and their rights to be heard, it can be argued that these may, in effect, amount to little more than an artifice which conceals the real nature of the way in which mechanisms for retaining and increasing the control over children

are being sustained and extended, creating a wider net of social control, with an increasingly finer mesh, which is permeating more areas of more children's lives than ever before (2001: 225–6).

Thus, despite there being a continual exhortation to children to fulfil certain responsibilities and obligations to society, their rights remain, on the whole, poorly articulated (James and James, 2001).

The pertinence of the question of citizenship arises therefore out of the intimate links between citizenship and access to rights and resources. As Rose (1989) has suggested, it is indeed quite possible to argue the case that the growth of citizenship, envisaged through the expansion of the welfare state and the extension of its reach across the life course, may have worked *against*, rather than for, the rights of particular social groups. It may have increased rather than decreased processes of social exclusion. Thus, it may be the case that for people with disabilities, young children and older people:

> the policies and practices of welfare, far from extending citizenship in any benign sense, have in fact functioned to maintain inequality, to legitimate existing relations of power and to extend social control over potentially troublesome sectors of society (1989: 123).

Higgs (1995) shares Rose's critical stance. He critiques the political economy perspective on later life which argues that the dependency of older people is created socially and which envisages the extension of citizenship rights to older adults as an a priori requirement for overcoming their marginalisation. Challenging this perspective, Higgs argues that citizenship now operates within a social and political reality where personal responsibility has been made core to programmes of welfare. The citizen has become a kind of informed social consumer who is offered equality of opportunity rather than guaranteed an egalitarian social environment. The citizen is therefore active in the public sphere, their rights being met as part of a contract which involves obligations on the part of both the state and the individual. But, if individuals *cannot* fulfil their part of the contract they are likely to become a focus for surveillance, oriented towards either returning them to conformity with social norms or giving them special attention if this is not possible. Welfare for older adults is therefore no longer a matter of right. Rather it is the outcome of forms of surveillance which discriminate between those in need and those who have been able to provide for themselves. As a result, the life course bifurcates in old age and in health care; for example, 'older people are presented with two images; one is physically frail and dependent while the other is active and healthy – a third ager' (Higgs, 1995: 547). Rather than consumers, therefore, very elderly people become objects of consumption, the focus of the medical gaze. As a result, those older adults who are able to evade surveillance distance themselves all the more determinedly from their more needy peers. The likelihood of any collective politics of age retreats as a consequence.

Two questions arise from these responses to individuals at different points in the life course. First, to what extent has the rise of the welfare state simply provided 'antidotes to social unrest and... [warded] off demands for truly progressive measures of equalisation of wealth and status' through the provision of just the minimum necessary social support for those sections of society who cannot, through age and or ill health, contribute their labour power to the collective good (Rose, 1989: 123)? Second, given the attenuation of the modern life course, has consumption, rather than production, become a key marker of citizenship status and, if so, is this now offering a challenge to the ways in which social identity is being ascribed across the life course?

Conclusion

In Part I of this book we presented a critical account of early theories of the life course, assessing the extent to which they explained how it is we come to know that we are ageing. These theories concerned themselves with the nature of society, whether as a static entity or as an evolutionary, developmental process. Following on from this, the present chapter has outlined the legacies of this macro-level orientation through looking at the ways in which conceptualisations of age and the life course can be explored from the twin perspectives of the sociology of the family and the political economy of ageing.

However, as we shall go on to elaborate in the next chapter, the adoption of the more flexible concept of the life course by family life cycle sociology allows scope for examining individual 'careers' as well as change within family units. For example, in his discussion of the social reconstruction of retirement, Blaikie argues that, 'the post modern culture of today suggests that rather than focus on the social construction of the life cycle, as a fixed set of stages occupied by people of particular age-bands, we analyse the ways in which it is being reconstructed by individual elders, or groups of older people, negotiating their own life courses' (1997: 10). Thus, as we suggested at the start of this chapter, an historio-biographical approach is needed which can take full account of the historical and generational factors that come into place, and yet also explore the broader processes of development and social change, such as the industrial revolution. Through this, the intermeshing of private life and public events can be mapped out. In contrast to the structural focus adopted in this chapter, therefore, the following chapter goes on to examine theories which highlight the agency of individuals. These show how ageing and the life course constitute important dimensions of the processes of social identification with which society's members engage.

Note

1. These statistics appear therefore to document choice and agency. However, it is also clear that structural factors such as unemployment and poor housing have a part to play, potentially curtailing the life projects of individuals who might otherwise adhere to more traditional patterns.

5

The Making of Life-course Histories

Introduction

Institutions such as 'the family', 'work' or 'social policy' have been adopted as broad schema within which we might make sense of social change and the ways in which social identities are produced and reproduced over time. Such structural representations of the life course tell us little, however, about people's experience of the identities through which the life course is constructed. As noted in previous chapters, awareness of this omission within many accounts of ageing has led social scientists to take a quite different theoretical direction. They have adopted either micro-level, 'actor-oriented' sociological perspectives such as symbolic interactionism or ethnomethodology; or have had recourse to more literary or auto-biographical sources.

Giddens (1979) does endeavour to reconcile these two avenues in his concept of structuration, an attempt to overcome the inadequacy of 'social structure' as a concept which might help us understand how social identities come into being. However, as Cohen argues, this concept of structuration still retains the notion of society as separate from its individual members: 'Giddens' "structuration theory" treats society (rather than self) as an ontology which somehow becomes independent of its own members, and assumes that the self is required continuously to adjust to it' (1994: 21). As a result, selves are not regarded as creative and any notion of agency falls short of actual motivation, remaining merely a form of reflexivity. Cohen concludes that Giddens' individuals 'seem doomed to be perpetrators rather than architects of action' (1994: 21). This point is echoed by Craib who argues that 'a social theory which moulds its conception of the actor around the demands of more abstract levels of theory will always be inadequate' (1998: 74).

In this chapter, therefore, we not only begin the task of showing how age-based social identities are *experienced* across the life course, but also develop the debates introduced in Chapter 1 about how the nature of identity and selfhood might best be theorised. To do this, we move from a political economy perspective to consider different ways in which we might access and theorise experiences of the life course. Autobiographical data clearly represent a very valuable resource here, albeit one we may have qualms about using, since its relationship with the actual experience of its author is often hidden within the text itself. The status of autobiography as a source of research data is therefore difficult to define and thus, as social scientists, it is more likely that we will privilege qualitative data, gathered firsthand via in-depth face-to-face interviewing. What needs to be recognised, however, is that, like the autobiography, the life history interview is also a remembered account of embodied experience, of necessity a representation.

This chapter provides, therefore, a critical account of those theories of identity which give prominence to discourse and representation. Contemporary readings of historical and cross-cultural materials are, for example, often put to rhetorical use within political and policy agendas, representing the past as a 'golden age' of 'childhood innocence' or 'family care for elders'. Similarly, contemporary representations of 'mid-life' as a time of crisis or as the product of significant changes brought on by the escalating demands of work or domestic spheres contrast with the image of stability which was previously attributed to 'middle-age' through the icons of slippers by the fireside and middle-aged spread. In this way, historically located discourses inflect policy documents as much as they do autobiographies and life history data.

A critical lack of fit

In considering questions of cultural identity, Hall's (1996) work parallels Jenkins' (1996) understanding of identity as processually produced. Hall says, 'precisely because identities are constructed within, and not outside, discourse we need to understand them as produced in specific historical and institutional sites within specific discursive formations and practices, by specific enunciative strategies'

(1996: 4). By this, he means that identity cannot be seen as a fixed or enduring aspect of the self. Rather it is something which emerges, for a period only, out of what it is not, or that which it lacks. The Other therefore crucially constitutes the self. Using the term 'identification', Hall describes this as a process of becoming and as a process which is subject to fragmentation and change across time. He therefore favours the notion of identification precisely because it forces consideration of the active processes through which collectivities come to be identified or through which individuals find some points of connection, or suture, between themselves and others.

Thus, according to Hall, exploring how identities come into being means seeking out:

> on the one hand, the discourses and practices which attempt to 'interpellate', speak to us or hail us into place as the social subjects of particular discourses, and on the other hand the processes which produce subjectivities (1996: 5).

And most importantly it involves locating these practices and processes 'within the play of specific modalities of power' for, as already demonstrated in Chapter 4, identities can be invested with varying degrees of moral worth and degrees of stigmatisation (1996: 4). When it comes to understanding age-based identities, Hall's approach is highly suggestive on at least two counts. First, he argues that the identities we produce are never complete. In some sense, we always experience a lack of fit with what we think we are or should be – or with what others project upon us, or the self we remember ourselves to have been. This is particularly evident for those hidden by the 'mask of ageing' (Featherstone and Hepworth, 1991) Explored more fully in Chapter 6, the 'mask of ageing' describes the experience of a mismatch between the self we think we are 'inside' and the much older self which others read off from the exterior of our visibly ageing bodies. In that our identities are always conditional, or as Hall says 'lodged in contingency', they contain within them scope for fluidity, for combining or moving between identities (2000: 17). Thus, for example, a seven-year old boy can perform the identities of schoolboy, big brother, doctor, runaway horse, aeroplane and babytalking toddler. However, he is unlikely to 'fit' any one identity entirely, the horse and the aeroplane being particularly challenging. But even the 'schoolboy' may feel at odds with his playground peers and the 'big brother' may choose not to stick up for his little sister. As the seven-year old boy grows up he may still move between partial fulfilment of the identities of husband, student, father, son, football player and butcher. More covertly, he may engage in other processes of identification, imaginatively taking on the identities of hero-who-rescues-the-world-from-destruction, goalkeeper for England, lead singer, fighter pilot and so on. Here, film theory points us towards the 'unconscious dynamics [which] motivate the individual's "stitching into" or "articulation" with the subject positions made available in language and wider cultural codes' (du Gay *et al.*, 2000).

Thus, although this book makes age-based identities its primary focus, we recognise that categories such as 'elderly' are umbrella terms which can include 'chronically sick patient', 'gardener', 'great granny', 'charity worker', 'community carer' and 'little old lady'. Any one eighty-year old woman may move between all these identities, many of them defined by what they are not – 'chronically ill' and 'worker', for example, being seen as mutually exclusive categories As Hall reminds us, the fit with any one identity is likely, therefore, to be approximate.

This links with his second important point: that identity emerges more out of difference than sameness: 'throughout their careers, identities can function as points of identification and attachment only *because* of their capacity to exclude, to leave out, to render "outside", abjected' (2000: 18). Though Hall makes questions of ethnic and gendered identity his primary focus, his work can illuminate age-based identities in a particularly helpful way. While 'race' and gender-based differences rarely collapse into one another, age-based categories, by their very nature, do. They are temporary and contin-gent, their separation from one another unravelling day by day. Thus, to order this progression we therefore work hard to shore up age-based differences. Children, for example, are often defined by their *lack* of adult competencies, a western conception which, as Chapter 9 will argue, grew in response to ideas about the nature of factory work and the suitability of particular kinds of people to undertake it. If children are small it is because they lack height. If they are innocent, it is because they lack worldliness. If they are unruly it is because they lack discipline. These lacks and limitations are, however, only temporary, particularly in a society where children are frequently urged to be 'grown up' about things. The lack or the possession of competence therefore represents an insubstantial, time-linked boundary which tends to submerge within the flow of young people's everyday experiences. Hall, for example, describes identity and exclusions in terms of identity being 'constantly destabilized by what it leaves out' (2000: 18). And, as we know, children 'grow' taller, more worldly and more orderly as the years pass. Thus, acquiring what they lack makes them no longer able to perform their identities as 'child'. Tall children, for example, may have difficulty getting a half fare on the bus.

However, as we have shown, the category 'childhood', whilst intended to be transitory, is nonetheless required to persist as distinguishable from adulthood for a culturally specific period of time. Reports of categorical trespassing therefore often use language which reflects Hall's notions of 'threat' or 'destabilisation'. Describing a victim of rape, for example, a National Children's Home advertisement said 'Kevin's 8, but for him childhood's over' (Kitzinger, 1997). But once adulthood has been legitimately attained, children enter into the dominant half of what Laclau calls 'a violent hierarchy': adult/child (cited in Hall, 2000: 18). Here adulthood is essentialised and 'adult' is left to stand as an untheorised status. In the parallel example of 'race', as Laclau argues, 'white', as the dominant half of the 'violent hierarchy' of white/black is unremarked and taken as the equivalent of 'human being' (Dyer, 1997).

Compared with the essentiality of adulthood, childhood studies has provided ample evidence of the problematic, unresolved status 'child' when compared with the 'essentiality' of its 'unremarked' oppositional half – adult. In adulthood one's age no longer constitutes an aspect of social identity in the same way as it did whilst 'growing up', nor as it will once 'grown old' (Hockey and James, 1993). Curiously, age does not come into it. Thus, childhood and old age are constituted either through their lack of 'age' or through their excess. Neither fit. Both are the marked halves of the twin hierarchies of child/adult and adult/elderly. In the privacy of family birthdays and on tax forms, adults may disclose their age, albeit reluctantly, but within many other social interactions it is not something readily enquired about, referred to or declared. Yet, as Laclau argues, the apparent objectivity of dominant categories or identities is affirmed 'only by repressing that which threatens it' (cited in Hall, 2000: 18). Once achieved, however, adulthood is constantly under threat from *old* age, a threat which is intensified in relation to the extent to which it is feared or made abject.

Thus Sontag (1978), for example, highlights the particular losses which women suffer as they age, their sexual and reproductive roles being both core to their social identity and, at the same time, seen as transitory. Men by contrast draw more on their work-based identities and, once retired, are less harshly judged in terms of their looks. Reproductively they suffer no evident cut-off point to their capacities. Women, however, are likely to monitor their 'adult' bodies for signs of 'old age' almost as soon as they have made the transition from 'youth', in Sontag's view. The repression of old age, that which threatens women's adulthood – or, as Hall would argue, the aged Other through which their adulthood is constituted – requires sustained surveillance and intervention in the form of cosmetics, dress, exercise, diet and possibly plastic surgery (see also Chapter 8).

'Age' as discourse

Hall argues that representations constitute the 'discourses and practices which attempt to "interpellate", speak to us or hail us into place as the social subjects of particular discourses' (2000: 19). And indeed, in popular representations of the life course, the passing of time is rendered orderly through a series of age-based identities which, it is implied, each individual will naturally take on. From the mediaeval great wheel of fortune, through Shakespeare's seven ages of man, to Wordsworth's 'Intimations of Immortality' such controlled sequencing of age-based identities seems, ironically, both timeless and enduring: childhood leads to adolescence, and is followed by middle age, old age and death. And associated with each 'age' are particular aged identities, albeit inscribed with culturally specific social roles and experiences. These influence the ways in which the individual is conceived to move from, for example, his or her family of birth to a later family of marriage or to shape the life course of the younger person who leaves school to enter the more adult world of work. At the same time, however, we are aware that these images which so permeate popular mythology are often contravened by examples of people who assume identities which their age belies or which are somehow out of step with such a 'naturalised' sequence. But the prominence given to such figures in media and press reports, however, underscores the hegemonic hold which very particular images of the modern life course still have over our imagination about where people are presently positioned and the direction in which they are heading (see Chapter 4). Thus, a recent article about the novelist Saul Bellow, was headlined by reference to a set of life course events thought especially note-worthy:

The worldly mystic's late bloom. He is one of our greatest novelists and has a Nobel prize to prove it. Married five times, he describes himself as a serial husband. Now at 84, after a near-fatal illness, he has produced a vibrant novel and a baby daughter (*Guardian*, April 15 2000).

In a few short lines Bellow's life is summarised, its key features highlighted and made to appear unusual or transgressive. It is an instructive example. Bellow is multiply identified through contrasting and competing identity locations: by his work, by his international acclaim; by his repetitive marital status; by his age; by his health; and by his familial role – and in that order. Here is a man, famous not only for his great literary skills, but made infamous it would seem through his apparent defiance of the natural order of things. At 84, he has not stopped work, but instead produced a new novel; he has cheated death at an age when death is not uncommon; and, in this very moment of defiance, Saul has demonstrated a virility normally associated with younger men by fathering a child, a feat which is enhanced by its context, the 'social problem' of men's diminished sperm counts. Marriage, for Bellow, has not been a one-off and enduring state, but a serial affair – and not just once, but five times. Thus the 'normal' social sequencing of life events – work, marriage, child birth, retirement and death – has been massively disrupted. Bellow's life course is not an orderly sequence of moving between age categories and status positions. Instead, it is a recursive spiralling between different identities and social roles, identities to which he has returned, time and again, at different historical moments over a period of 84 years.

Others, who likewise contravene either the expectations of age or the expectations of the sequence of life course roles, also make the headlines: older people who get degrees; grandmothers who give birth; mothers who give birth alongside their daughters; children who run successful businesses. The intersection of ageing with these events potentially disrupts chronologised representations or discourses of the life course which normally interpellate us to regard reproduction and creativity as the prerogative of the category adult. Mismatches, or poor sutures, may attract wonder, as in Saul Bellow's case. Or they may attract condemnation, as in the case of women who reproduce either 'too early' or, with the aid of medical science, 'too late', as, for example in the case of Lynne Bezant who became pregnant with twins in her mid-fifties following *in vitro* fertilization (IVF) (*Guardian*, 23 January 2001). Here, however, age, gender and celebrity status intersect differentially to produce applause for older fathers and castigation for older mothers. Within the dialectical relationship between media, popular discourse and everyday life, therefore, 'ageing' can be seen to take place as a self-reflexive practice. As a contributor to the *Guardian* letters page pointed out:

> I don't recall anyone making such a fuss when Michael Douglas became a dad last year, age 56. Nor when an elderly Les Dawson sired a child, only to die soon after, thus cruelly denying 'the fruit of his worn-out loins' child the opportunity to know her father . . . (Laura Marcus, *Guardian*, 23 March, 2001).

Similarly, as Bytheway and Johnson (1996) note, in obituaries, alongside the detailing of a person's career and achievements, it is any transgression of age expectations in relation to social roles which is picked out as a key signifier of a person's identity. They cite an extract from the *Guardian*'s obituary of Dilys Powell, the film critic, as an example:

> Perhaps the Sunday Times became nervous that films increasingly styled for the under twenties were being reviewed by a critic now in her seventies. Rumour had it that the then editor, Harold Evans, had taken her out to lunch to broach the question of retirement, but was so charmingly sidestepped that the subject was never raised' (*Guardian*, 5 June, 1995, cited in Bytheway and Johnson, 1996: 226).

But, as noted, the transgression of such hegemonic models of 'how life should be lived' are not always approved or heralded as inspirational. Individuals may become outcast or stigmatised as a result of transgression. Thus, up until the 1950s in the UK, for example, the stigma of being an unmarried mother was paramount, haunting both the mother and her illegitimate 'bastard' for much of their subsequent lives. In the 1950s, motherhood had to follow rather than precede marriage, and a child's status and membership of a family of birth only received social legitimation through the prior ritual of marriage. The hasty 'shotgun' weddings of pregnant teenagers during this period can be seen as attempts to repair the rift between the life course as imagined and as lived, age and stage here being out of kilter with the required rigid chronology of the 'life cycle'.

The idea that the life course has an inscribed and natural 'order of things' is further and more starkly underscored by the notion of a 'bad death', a description often attributed to the death of a child. At the turn of the twentieth century, it is regarded as untimely for a child to die before its parents, with even the death of children not yet born, through miscarriage, now being socially acknowledged and mourned. Such events transgress what is regarded as the natural order of things, increased longevity making it even more common for 'parents' in their nineties to suffer as their 70-year old 'children' 'unnaturally' pre-decease them (Komaromy and Hockey, 2001).

The historio-biographical approach which this book develops permits us, however, to engage with such examples of a critical lack of fit by showing how the passage of time in an individual's life may not conform to popular representations but instead reflect the contingencies of an individual's historically and generationally specific biography. Indeed, it is as a result of this that the process of identification comes into play, as individuals seek to conform to the subject positions made available through the life course. It is also through this that new life course identities emerge when critical lack of fit is eventually anulled – for example, the stigma of young people 'living in sin' up until the 1960s giving way to the accepted practice of 'cohabiting with a partner' in the 1990s. Thus, in the sections which follow here, we explore how ideas about the life course have changed historically and how discourses of the life course work to culturally construct ageing – time passing – in particular social and cultural ways.

Life histories, history and the life course

The use of the life history approach as a method for the study of social life, though not very common, has nonetheless a long and respectable history within the social sciences, from Thomas and Znaniecki's (1918–20) five-volume collection of autobiographies of Polish peasants, through to the more recent experimental work of anthropologists such as Shostak (1981) and Crapanzano (1984). Such work, varied though it is, can nonetheless be said to have been undertaken with a common, albeit not uncontroversial intent: to reveal or uncover aspects of a particular culture or epoch through recording and writing down the biography of an individual life. However, as Crapanzano (1984) notes, such an undertaking is not unproblematic, raising questions about the extent to which a single testimony of a life recalled can, indeed, stand for or be typical of a whole culture? Further, we might ask to what extent can life histories, enlisted by a researcher for a particular purpose, be regarded as unmediated and unambiguous accounts of the complexities through which social life has taken place in another geographical setting or epoch? How far does the translation from verbal account to written record transform the meaning of a life recalled and what roles do memory and forgetfulness play? Indeed, so vexing are these issues, that Crapanzano is led to suggest that 'when we analyse a life history, we are analysing a text, not social reality, and this text is itself the product of a complex collaboration' (1984: 959) (see Chapter 11).

Notwithstanding these critiques, we would argue that the presentation of the life course, via the recording of life histories, does, nonetheless, have some analytical and methodological utility for engaging with the ongoing processes through which social and personal identity is produced. And, once again, it is within the historical study of the family that the value to be gained from such a perspective is most clearly revealed (Hareven, 1982). Indeed, the very concept of the family life cycle has its roots in the nineteenth-century practical, welfarist approach of Rowntree who demonstrated the great potential of the life cycle schema when he identified alternating stages of need in the life cycle of labourers (Rowntree, 1902, cited in Murphy, 1987: 31). Later, during the 1950s and 1960s, an American sociology of the family similarly outlined the stages through which 'the family' could be expected to pass[1].

This systematising dimension of a family life cycle approach within sociology began to be experienced, however, as a limitation by researchers. Not only did they take issue with the normative, value judgments which it represented; they also found it a constraining model which failed to make sense of the diversity of family lives which included, for example, divorce or pre-marital child-rearing. In addition, the concept of the life cycle was deemed to be ethnocentric, making no sense of family life outside the West. For example, in Benares, India, early marriage, prolonged childbearing and early death combined to produce an entirely different form of family and produced very different life experiences (Murphy, 1987: 39). Thus, by the end of the 1970s, family life cycle sociology (or FLC) had begun to be influenced by a life-*course* approach which was being developed by the family historians such as Hareven. This work demonstrates that 'life trajectories cannot be understood without taking into account the inner economies of families' whose collective needs often dominate those of the individual (Bertaux and Kohli, 1984: 220). Such a perspective, therefore, immediately draws attention to our own expectations of personal autonomy, as well as to the difficulties incurred by thinking about personal and social identities as separable (see Chapter 1) and reinforces the need to examine their intricate interplay. And indeed, in the historical study of the family, the complex patterning of social identities across the life course has been revealed precisely through a commitment to viewing families as composed of individual people, embedded in and responding to broad processes of social and economic change, rather than as disembodied collectivities.

However, despite recognition of the variations in experiences which these processes bring, the essentialist ordering of the modern life course remains intact in our thinking and its robustness prompts enquiry. This is especially intriguing, given that, as Hareven has argued, the attachment to uniformity and regularity in the patterning of life transitions, which is so characteristic of the twentieth century and largely regulated by norms and expectations of age, is a relatively recent perception of the 'natural order of things'. In the nineteenth century, the pattern of the life course was far more varied. The death of children before their parents was, for example, a common, rather than a rare event. Moreover, that the needs of the individual were overshadowed by the needs of the family unit or community meant that individual life courses were necessarily very varied in terms of the sequencing of roles and responsibilities. Thus, as Gillis (1997) shows, for example, in the early nineteenth century a working life did not always or necessarily follow schooling; young men (for few girls were educated at this time) might go in and out of education over a protracted period of time until they were quite old, with work interspersing education as and when more communal needs demanded it. Hareven, for example, in her historical analysis of the family, argues therefore that the family has to be seen as a 'process', rather than as a static unit, and suggests that in order to understand the changes that have occurred in the family historically it is neces-sary to grasp 'the interrelationship between "family time", "individual time" and "historical time"' (2000: 4). Central to this is what she terms a life-course approach to family history. This focuses on 'age and cohort comparisons in ways that link individual and family development to historical events' (2000: 4). Such a perspective enables the family to be seen as a 'lived' experience, enacted by individuals, rather than simply as an institutional structure comprising sets of fixed social roles. This entails seeing different family members as therefore engaged with, rather than simply positioned by, those familial and social roles. Citing research by Berkner on eighteenth-century household composition in Northern Austria, Hareven underlines, for example, the important distinction to be made between 'family' and 'household' and shows how, during this period, for one man the form and composition of his family of residence would change throughout his life course. Thus the social identities he could assume also changed in terms of their associated roles and responsibilities, rather than in line with the chronology of ageing:

> after a man's marriage and his father's retirement, the man lived in a stem family; after his father's death he lived in a nuclear family; but later in life, he found himself again in a stem family, when he co-resided with his married son following his own retirement (2000: 11).

And this is not simply an eighteenth-century phenomenon. In many parts of the world, such ebbs and flows in family and household patterns may be occurring even more frequently, as Goody (1972) notes, in relation to yearly migratory movements and the demands of agricultural production and the labour market. Divorce, remarriage and the shift to later life single-hood, post-45, have also, by the dawn of the twenty-first century, ensured that 'the family' cannot be regarded as a static, unchanging and enduring structure in the life course of its individual members.

Given the possibility of such flux in family form within a single lifetime, for any individual, therefore, familial social identities – those of son or daughter, sibling, mother or father – and the expectations, responsibilities and attitudes tied to these social roles, will shift and change throughout his or her life course (see Chapter 9). This is not only in relation to the individual's position within the family at any point in time and thus his or her responses to the demands of family members, but also a result of the wider social, political and economic frameworks within which their family is embedded. A life-course approach to family history, as advocated by Hareven (2000) and others, therefore underscores the importance of adopting such a perspective for gaining insight into not just how the family was structured, historically, but what the experience of family life was like.

By way of illustration, the critical importance of simple demographic factors in shaping family forms, household structure and, most importantly, in ascribing experiential meaning to the social identities of mother, father and sibling can be pointed to. Hareven notes, for example, that during the nineteenth century the experience of childhood for any one child within a family was likely to be quite distinctive, as a result of demographic factors such as the decline in mortality, birth order and family size. Prior to the 1870s, which marked a sharp decline in infant mortality, in any family children would be likely to grow up with a large number of siblings of a great age diversity. Breast feeding of infants usually ensured the spacing of births between two and three years apart, so that in a family of five children, the oldest child might be ready to leave home just as the youngest was being born. As Hareven notes, in many families this meant therefore that young children quite often had more contact with older siblings who acted as their caretakers, than with their parents. The experience of being a 'mother', 'father', 'son' and 'daughter' was, as a consequence, likely to be rather different for different family members, even within one family:

> Before the turn of the twentieth century, in the demographic regime of late marriage, high fertility and lower life expectancy, the overlap in age between children and their parents also differed significantly. The oldest child in a family was the one most likely to overlap with his or her father in adulthood; the youngest child was the least likely to do so. The oldest child in a family was the one most likely to embark on an independent career before the parents reached old-age dependency; the youngest was most likely to be left with the responsibilities for parental support and to overlap in adulthood with a widowed mother (Hareven, 2000: 109).

In comparison to children in the twentieth century, who are likely to know their parents as young people, only the oldest children in families of the nineteenth century would do so. The youngest children in a nineteenth-century family were likely to know their parents only in their middle to later years of life.

The critical importance which such demographic factors play in contextualising the history of the life course and individual life trajectories and experiences of ageing sharpens up our theoretical perspective; it provides additional evidence of the life course as a fluid and ever-changing experience, not susceptible to fixed or even sequential stages. Thus, if we turn now to the example of contemporary UK patterns of divorce and remarriage, we can similarly see individuals moving between, and perhaps returning to, different kinds of social and familial identities throughout their life course in a way which is reminiscent of a much earlier period (see Chapter 9).

Representing the life course in time and space

In discussing recent theoretical approaches to the life course, Cohen argues that the intention is to relate biographical and subjective processes to broader social changes and that this means, in part, focusing on the dynamic relations between individuals and the changing political economy (1997: 220–1). These relationships are, however, multifaceted and varied. They range, for example, from the more overt impact that unemployment might have on the different life trajectories people follow, to the more subtle and less obvious effects which the broader sweep of social policies may have on the shaping of available life course positions, status roles and categorical identities within particular cultures.

As noted in Chapter 1, for example, the space occupied by 'childhood' within the life course exists in relation to other categorical and generational spaces such as 'adolescence', 'youth', 'adulthood' and 'old age' (Jenks, 1996: 3). However, while it may always be possible to acknowledge the oppositional nature of this relationship, the precise ways in which it is conceived, understood and ascribed with meaning in everyday social practice alters in relation to the economic and political demands of particular societies at particular historical moments. Thus, the experiences of those who occupy the space of 'childhood' – that is children themselves – can be said to be in part shaped by the politics and policies through which that conceptual category and social identity is given material form in everyday life.

The need for such contextualisation of the family and its members within the broader political and economic context has also been pointed out by Hareven. She suggests, for example, that when studying the history of the family at the time of industrialisation it is not enough to ask, as has been traditional, about the impact which industrialisation had on the family. An equally important question is: what impact did the family have on industrialisation? Her studies of family and work in Manchester, New Hampshire, between 1880 and 1930, for example, shows the family taking an active stance and developing particular strategies in response to the demands of the factory system.

> Family strategies involved not only the decisions of individuals or families made but also the actual timing of such decisions in response to opportunities or need: when to send a son or daughter to another community, for example; when to join other kin; and when to change residence. Strategies involved, at the time, calculated tradeoffs in order to find employment, achieve solvency, buy a house, facilitate children's education or their occupational advancement, control or facilitate a child's marriage, save for the future, and provide for times of illness, old age and death. Strategies were part of a larger life plan (Hareven, 2000: 23).

Hareven's life-course approach to family history underlines, therefore, Cohen's (1994) insistence on locating social and age-based identities not only within the life course but to see the life course itself as temporally and indeed spatially framed. It highlights, too, the importance of the historical moment as an age cohort experience and postulates this as a key variable for gaining insight into the experiential aspects of the life course. Thus, while in some senses the life course *does* follow the biological processes of birth, maturation and decay – the precise experience and nature of that passage, and how the transitions between its various phases are encountered and experienced by individuals are very much dependent on the passage of time itself and, significantly, on the spaces within which such transitions occur. Thus, as noted in Chapter 3, it is the spatialisation of identity which perhaps allows us to apprehend its temporality.

Hareven, for example, argues that throughout the life course the pace and timing of life-course transitions and thus transitions between different social identities – say from school to work or from work to retirement, from school child to worker to old-age pensioner – hinges upon 'the social, economic and cultural contexts in which transitions [occur] and the cultural constructions of the life course in different time periods and in different societies' (2000: 129). She identifies three key dimensions which need to be explored in adopting a life-course perspective.

The first dimension to be considered is the timing of life transitions over an individual's life path. When and how do people enter and exit different social roles over the course of their lives and what sequence do these take? The second dimension involves exploring how individual life transitions synchronise with more collective transitions such as those occurring within the family. Additionally, when exploring the life course at the start of the twenty-first century and cross-culturally, it may be pertinent to ask about the significance of synchronisation with other collective transitions, such as those made by one's peer group. For example, today in the UK, we might want to ask how and why are decisions to marry made by individuals in a social climate when living together commonly precedes, or indeed is replacing or delaying, decisions to marry and when it has become more acceptable to speak of one's partner than of one's spouse.

The third, and most critical dimension, is to explore the cumulative effect of earlier life events on later ones and to investigate how the timing of one event – child birth, for example – might shape the subsequent life trajectory of any one individual. And here, acknowledgement of the importance of historical time is considerable for, as

Hareven remarks, 'historical experiences have a direct impact on the life course of individuals and families at the time when they encounter them and continue to have an indirect impact over the entire life course' (2000: 131). The impact of the two world wars on an individual's life course are obvious examples, affecting not only the first generation but subsequent ones. Other effects, more closely linked with policy-making at particular points in time, include the influence of women's uneven patterns of paid employment, particularly during early, child-bearing years, on the income they derive from their pensions in later life (Arber and Ginn, 1995); another example might be the long-term financial benefits which men accrue from divorce. Thus Jenkins and Jarvis (1999) showed that ten years after divorcing, men's disposable incomes had increased by an average of 15 per cent while women's had decreased by approximately 28 per cent. This was explained in terms of the rising costs of bringing up children which soon exceed the amount agreed during the divorce settlement, something which women are often reluctant to bring back to court. In addition, men's anxiety about supporting the family they have left behind often stimulates them to advance their careers, particularly since they no longer have the impediment of a young family to care for at the end of the day. Finally, when we examine the individual life course within the context of the extended, cross-generational life course of the family, we need to take account of the process of will-making. This may take shape as a result of life events which have occurred during the will-maker's young adulthood; yet it can have a beneficial effect on subsequent generations' livelihoods and education, as well as a longstanding deleterious effect on existing family rivalries.

Less dramatic perhaps, but as significant in terms of how historical time patterns the life course, are the ways in which particular cultural contexts, such as legislative and policy arenas, come to shape the generational experiences of particular age cohorts. With regard to healthcare, for example, one could suppose that rather different life trajectories were experienced by those individuals in Britain born before the creation of the National Health Service and improvements in public health and those who came after; similarly, the timing of scientific advances in healthcare have a significant impact, witness the greying of the population due to the increase in life expectancy. And cross-culturally, even within an age cohort there are wide diversities between those, in the United States, for example, who have to rely on medicare and those individuals who have private health insurance. Such diversities in life-course trajectories are greatly magnified when comparisons are made between developed and developing countries.

It has been well documented, for example, that parental unemployment and/or low income has a direct and unequivocal relationship with childhood poverty. The contemporary position of children in the UK illustrates this well. In 1992, 4.1 million children (32 per cent) were living below 50 per cent of the average income in comparison with 25 per cent in the population as a whole. This means, therefore, that, at that time, children comprised 30 per cent of the poorest tenth of the population whereas they constituted only 20 per cent of the total population (Daniel and Ivatts, 1998: 57). By contrast, in 1979 only 10 per cent of children were living below half the average income. Children, it would seem, are some of the poorest members of society and, in the UK, getting poorer. Cross-culturally, the position is worse both in terms of absolute and relative poverty (Huston, 1991) and, as Duncan (1994: 23) observes, there is strong evidence for the intergenerational transmission of social status. This suggests that the income and assets of the family have considerable impact on children's life chances and on the course their lives take to adulthood.

However, Duncan also makes clear that children's individual experiences of poverty in terms of a biographical life course are, nonetheless, shaped by factors other than their *structural* experience of persistent poverty. While there are, as he says, 'highly suggestive links between the persistence of poverty during childhood and adult attainments' very little is known about the precise mechanisms at work and why some children, rather than others, seem to elude such determinism in their life course (Duncan, 1991: 42). Explanation might be sought, for example, in the fact that very few children *always* live in poverty. Family income can be highly volatile, due to the effects of divorce and remarriage as well as unemployment, across the years of childhood. Without documented longitudinal studies linking childhood experiences of poverty with educational attainment and adult outcomes, snapshots taken at one point in the life course can be misleading. In addition, is it income *per se* or 'other factors correlated with families with persistently low income' which affects a child's life course trajectory towards adulthood? (Duncan, 1991: 44).

Following Townsend's study in the 1960s, which used poverty as an index of social participation, other studies have endeavoured to tease out the significance of some of the broader cultural contexts within which poverty may be experienced by children and which might account for differences in outcome for children who are ostensibly occupying similar economic positions. Coffield's (1987) study of youth unemployment, for example, highlights the importance of regional variations and thus the importance of space in shaping the actual experience of poverty for individuals with regard to their own life course:

> to grow up in a region like the north of England with its long tradition of high unemployment and . . . to live on an estate where seven out of ten males are unemployed is obviously to be in a social setting of a different order, irrespective of one's class or sex, from leaving school in a town with 4 per cent unemployment and factories specialising in the latest technologies. . . . the combined effects of the historical experience of joblessness and the resulting system of local support are likely to lessen the psychological impact of unemployment (Coffield, 1987: 98).

Such observations call into question, then, making any simple causal relationship between family income and childhood poverty and force us to begin to differentiate between children in terms of how 'childhood poverty' is actually experienced and how agency is exercised in relation to identity. As Daniel and Ivatts (1998) point out, statistics on childhood poverty, while providing a macro picture of the dreadful conditions that many children endure, nonetheless disguise the variations and trends contained within the big picture and tell us little about the nature of that experience. Parental divorce may impact adversely on some but not others and it may be the interplay between different cultural factors and patterns of social relations, rather than economics alone, which can account for these differences. In underscoring the importance of the cultural context in relation to how individuals' experiences of poverty impact on, or are made sense of, in relation to their own life projects, Coffield (1987) indicates, therefore, the ways in which agency is and can be exercised in the face of seemingly oppressive economic and political structures. Indeed, such examples provide a counterweight to explorations of the life course which, from a purely macro perspective, would seem to suggest that the experience of economic deprivation is inevitably circular and unremittingly transmitted across and through the life course from one generation to another.

The importance of attending to variation in terms of the biographical life course is illustrated most obviously in those autobiographical accounts of children who outwit the strictures of cycles of deprivation. The stuff of much popular fiction, these accounts give us evidence that children born in grinding poverty can and do manage to alter the seemingly set path of their lives. They can and do grow up to lead rather different kinds of lives than those for which they seemed destined. But that these individuals, as adults, choose to author their own childhoods in this way suggests that it is precisely because they *have* managed to go against the grain, to wrench a new and different life out of unpromising circumstances that their life stories are deemed worthy of note. Bromley writes:

> it becomes possible to extrapolate from certain autobiographies carefully quantified images of hopelessness (seven in one room, no shoes, two pence to last the week) and yet from within the same text or range of texts to mobilise a different set of abstracted qualitative images representing 'the human spirit' – tireless mums, resourceful kids, community feeling. The dominant image is of the *survivor* – figures who have 'made it' despite demoralising conditions (1988: 29).

For Bromley, such an image is double-edged, particularly in terms of the role it plays in the popular imagination and memory. In the hey-day of Thatcherism in the UK, the idea of 'people building their own lives in their own way' had immense political appeal which, he suggests, accounts for the flood of books and TV programmes which colonised people's memories by repackaging the past in this way (1988: 189).

Conclusion

Undoubtedly, not all children remain locked in poverty. Nor, unlike the Jesuits' claim, are all adults' lives set in stone by the age of seven. Class position, family income, gender patterns, ethnicity, regionality, family form and style intersect to differentially fashion the shape and outcome of children's passage to adulthood. Theories of the life course must, therefore, pay attention to such variations and unlock the complexity of that passage. On the other hand, recognition of that complexity and diversity makes generalisations and comparisons the more difficult. This book treads a fine line between these traditions and Qvortrup illustrates our dilemma well:

> Who can possibly claim there to be only one childhood when it is so obvious that children lead their life under a variety of conditions, depending not least on the socio-economic background of their parental home? On the other hand this view would if followed to the end constitute an insurmountable obstacle to any generalised

insight, because it indicates the preponderance of what is unique over what is common (1994: 5).

As this chapter has argued, any study of the life course must engage critically with both structure and agency perspectives, and, in particular, with the dialectical interplay prescribed between them. Reflecting the approach taken by Harris, we have presented evidence which reveals the life course as a 'process which is both unintended and the results of intentionality and in which earlier events condition later events' (1987: 22). Harris highlights three points which he believes crucial to such an approach and these, as we have seen, also inform the work of Hareven. First, a recognition that societal events will *constitute* biographical events in the lives of some people – the Second World War, for example, had a profound impact on people's individual lives and career trajectories; second, that the events in some people's lives will become *constituents* of events in society – for example, widespread, but nonetheless individual, decisions to limit family size will eventually lead to a changing demand for education; and third, that social events will *condition* biographical events in people's everyday lives – high unemployment and limited job opportunities for women often accelerate the pattern of early childbirth. Formulated in this way, and working within this kind of framework, it becomes clear, then, that any account of the life course has, of necessity, to engage critically with the 'duality of structure' (Giddens, 1979), taking on board the insights made possible by engaging with the *dialectics* of identity (Jenkins, 1996).

Through its presentation of a wide variety of historical and contemporary material, this chapter has thus demonstrated the value of the theoretical issues raised by authors such as Hall (2000) with regard to processes of identification. The processes whereby individuals come to live out different social identities as they age, as we have seen, involve not only the processes of interpellation which, in Hall's terms, hail us as individuals, but also, and importantly, 'the processes which produce subjectivities, which construct us as subjects which can be "spoken"'(2000: 19). Hareven's work, in particular, brings out the mismatch, the lack of fit, between 'structure' and 'experience'. And, having recognised this disjunction, she goes on to argue that it is precisely this insight which allows us to grasp the creative agency of individuals in producing those 'structures'. This produces a more fully fleshed account of the self than that vouchsafed by structuration theories where identity amounts to little more than a process of reflexive adaptation to externally derived values, beliefs and institutions. But the extent to which the creative energy of individuals permits an endless and open-ended remaking of the self, as postmodern theories would suggest, is questionable. This is our central concern in the next chapter.

Note

1. It did so, however, by extrapolating from the normative expectations of white American middle-class families, a typology which thus reflected the interests of particular groups and worked as a form of surveillance, allowing 'atypical' or 'deviant' families and individuals to be identified and potentially brought under control.

6

Postmodern Lives?

Introduction

The question mark which punctuates the title of this chapter reflects a pervasive critique of postmodern approaches to social life. The notion that we can exercise choice and agency in our lives is often met with hollow laughter, the product of day-on-day frustration with unbending institutions or bureaucracies and wilfully non-compliant bodies. Laurie Taylor (1982), for example, introduces an account of the social construction of middle age with a description of his failure to exercise control over his ageing body at the health club:

> For the first six months I was along there three times a week, riding bicycles into the ground, running no further than the spot on which I stood . . . this was the way to give new meaning to life, the key to a vigorous and productive middle age . . . it took me time to realise that the damn weights were interfering with almost every other aspect of my life . . . I was also permanently tired – something which wasn't helped when a colleague pointed out that my second-floor health club was located directly above a business which described itself as *The Tyre and Exhaust Centre* (Taylor, 1982: preface).

Taylor then finally abandons his attempts to 'look ten years younger', choosing to settle for 'the old comfortable version' of middle age (1982: preface). Whilst acknowledging such criticisms of postmodern perspectives, this chapter makes their contribution to social theory its core focus. It does so by asking whether, and if so how, some of the inadequacies of structuralist and political economy accounts of human ageing discussed in previous chapters might be remedied by the postmodern focus on agency and choice.

Standard life?

Featherstone and Hepworth's account of the postmodern life course opens with a critique of psychological models of the stages of human development, arguing that its social dimensions get written off as 'variables'. In their place, these authors call for models which recognise the life course as a 'social institution in its own right' (1991: 371). Approached in this way, the life course becomes one of the structures which has undergone change within the processes of western modernisation. And, as we saw in Chapters 4 and 5, it can be placed alongside other social institutions such as the family or the organisation of work or leisure. Indeed, in some senses it can be seen to be inextricably intertwined with them, changing patterns of family life and work responding to and reflecting both demographic shifts and change in social expectations and attitudes.

Such a critique already moves us away from essentialist, biologically grounded psychological categories, a point underlined further by Gillis, who argues that the assumptions one might make about chronology and ageing are more socially, than biologically, based. He proposes, for example, that before the nineteenth century, the highly unpredictable length of any individual life meant that the future, like the past, was without depth. Numerical age had little meaning; the life course had yet to be 'chronologised' (see Chapter 4):

> Time, measured out in quantitative units of years, months and weeks, and days mattered less to both the individual and the community. Time and age had not yet separated themselves from place, so that, while most rural people could not tell their numerical age with any great precision, they could make rough calculations of how young or old a person was by his or her relationship to certain remembered events – a saint's day, a flood, a harvest. In rural England time was still counted in the same way as late as the First World War (Gillis, 1999: 113)

And indeed, formal registration of births in England and Wales was introduced only at the end of the nineteenth century as an aspect of a growing, age-based institutional control of the individual (Bytheway, 1995: 18). Of the period up till the nineteenth century, Gillis therefore says:

> all generations occupied the same capacious present. The young were not necessarily identified with the future, nor the old with the past. In the pre-modern economy of time, all ages were conceived of as equidistant from death... (1997: 17).

As noted in Chapter 4, chronological age, now a seemingly incontro-vertible material reality, is only a relatively recent social indicator of life course passage within western societies. Previously, a person's location within sets of cross-generational family relationships acted as the more important indicator of life course stage. People there-fore 'aged' when they became parents or grandparents or took over as heads of households. As historical demographers have shown, only when more people lived predictably longer could a standardised passage across the life course be conceived. The taken-for-granted shift from childhood dependency to adult independence, with the prospect of an eventual slide into 'old age' dependency, thus only gradually materialised from the 1870s onwards. Only during the last century, therefore, has 'age' supplanted the family as a site within which 'questions of maturity, independence of action and power' are determined (Featherstone and Hepworth, 1991: 372).

However, this predetermined vision of the life course has not remained a norm for long. As Chapter 4 detailed, since the 1960s, new patterns of divorce and remarriage, variation in age of first marriage and increasing life expectancy have all been central to the de-standardisation of the life course:

> Middle age, which previously has been associated with a stable marriage and a houseful of children, had become a period of painful divorces and empty nests, no longer a timeless state but a period of frantic changes (Gillis, 1999: 117).

Moreover, as in earlier periods, economically and politically driven patterns of migration have fractured communities and domestic groupings, and different patterns of employment have triggered the making of new choices among individuals entering adulthood. As a result, by 1995, 34 per cent of children were being born outside marriage, compared with only 8 per cent in 1971 (Wasoff and Dey, 2000).

Such processes of de-institutionalisation and de-differentiation within the life course are, it is argued, currently destabilising the age-bound categories of childhood, adolescence and adulthood and working to overturn the notion that identity is produced within the process of 'scheduled development' (Featherstone and Hepworth, 1989: 144). This raises the question of power and leads us to ask to what extent the hierarchical and generational relationships which once juxtaposed childhood and adulthood and adulthood and old age are collapsing? And, if so, what does this mean for the authority of the meta-narratives of ageing? Is the current cult of youthfulness, for example, a sign that generational differences are dissolving and that the social marginalisation of young people, first postulated by Eisenstadt (1959) no longer applies?

This evidence that a fuzzying of life-course categories is taking place can, however, be countered by other data. Blaikie, for example, suggests that despite changes in demographic patterns, increasing longevity and the cult of youthfulness and leisure reaching out across a wider and wider age range, 'retirement for the mass continues to be an economically dependent phase, characterised by poverty, material deprivation and a dwindling quality of life' (1997: 16). Similarly, the supposed disappearance of childhood (Postman, 1982) can be countered by strong evidence which points, instead, to an intensification of the many social and legal parameters of control over children's lives. In the name of protection, these are having the effect of further separating children from adult life and confining them to an even more institutionalised child's world (James and James, 2001; Qvortrup, 1994). How, then, might we understand and account for these two somewhat contradictory standpoints?

Non-standard lives?

In delineating the characteristics of a postmodern life course, Featherstone and Hepworth are careful to acknowledge that they are describing an 'emergent cultural tendency' rather than an everyday reality (1991: 373). When considering the potentialities and the limitations of postmodern perspectives, this point is important. If postmodern theories come under critical fire, is it because they imply a world which has yet to materialise? Or, indeed, is postmodernity little more than the pipe dream of an exclusive avant-garde who have corralled resources to resist the constraints of social 'structure'? Certainly there *is* evidence of resistance to age-based social categories.

Therapeutic initiatives exemplify this point. The UK Child Death Helpline, set up in 1992, received calls from 'parents' whose 'children' had died at ages which ranged from 22 weeks gestation to 58 years of age (Simons, 2001). Similarly, if childhood extends from pre-birth to late middle age, the years which modernism has segregated as 'childhood' are no longer immune to 'adult' behaviours. An extreme, and yet telling, example of this is the growth in popularity of child beauty pageant contests in the United States, despite a simultaneous growth in awareness of child sexual abuse. Estimated to involve more than 100,000 children at any one time, with entrance fees of between $250 and $800 dollars, and innumerable offshoot industries, this is now big business. However, though the age span of contestants can run from two years old up to twenty-four, as Giroux notes, there is a common aesthetic:

> The makeup, pose, smile and hairstyles of the six-year-olds are no different from those of the much older contestants. All of the images depict the same cool estrangement and sexual allure (1998: 272).

Whereas in the 1970s, children participating in such pageants 'wore little-girl dresses, ribbons in their hair, and embodied a kind of childlike innocence as they displayed their little-girl talents', the entrants of the 1990s are more likely to be sporting 'tight-off-the shoulder dresses, bright-red lipstick, and curled, teased and bleached blond hair', striking the pose of alluring sex kitten rather than displaying their singing and tap-dancing talents (1998: 272–4).

This so-called disappearance of childhood (Postman, 1983) finds other less eroticised forms of expression; from Elkind's (1981) concern that children are growing up too fast to Winn's (1984) somewhat tautological assertion that children now talk and act in ways which do not seem very child-like! However, these anxieties are mirrored by a paradoxical *welcoming* of the apparent collapsing of age-based distinctions at the other end of the life course. As 'grandmothers start to dress like their daughters do and grand-fathers to jog with their sons' the chronology of age which traditionally bound people into age-appropriate behaviours is, seemingly, beginning to crumble (Blaikie, 1997: 18). Retirement has been reinvented as a time of transition to a new life, rather than simply the end of an old one.

A further example of the supposed destabilisation of the life course would be the replacing of the stigmatised concept of 'middle age' by that of 'mid-life', a broad-band category now encompassing everyone between the ages of 35 and 60. Envisaged as a process of ragged transition, Featherstone and Hepworth argue that

> the use of the term 'mid-life' should not be taken to imply a complete break with the past on the part of a new generation of 'mid-lifers' but is a rather loosely arranged collection of ideals which intersect around the concept of youthfulness and its capacity for personal and social change . . . (1991: 384).

It is epitomised, for example, by individuals who actively resist age-based categorisation such as Tom Jones who still makes hit records in his sixties and the Rolling Stones who include grandfathers and still go on tour.

The new 'mid-life' is, demographically speaking, the key period for grand parenting, yet stereotypical representations of 'grannys' and 'grandpas' remain. Though fifty is the *average* age for first becoming a grandparent, the National Childbirth Trust fronts its advice booklet for new grandparents with a photograph of a white-haired elderly woman who appears to be in her late seventies, if not early eighties. Such images of grandparents, comfortably retired people with time on their hands to indulge small children, their ageing bodies easily falling into step with a toddler's ambling pace, are however at odds with the look and lifestyle of the fortysome-things who are *actually* grandparenting today. Hummel *et al.*,'s (1995) comparative study of children's drawings of their grandparents in six different countries provides evidence that children themselves perceive their grandparents as active and engaged. However, this is heavily gendered, in that it was grandmothers who were most often depicted carrying out an activity (50 per cent to 70 per cent of drawings), with only 5 per cent of grandfathers represented in this way. This suggests that earlier gender stereotypes of the domestic division of labour persist across the life course and across time itself.

However, if the idea of 'mid-life' *has* begun to displace the nega-tivity which traditionally surrounded the idea of 'middle-age', and now incorporates thirtysomethings into a plateau phase which extends as far as the 60s, then arguably it is the transition to 'deep old age' which has now become the key marker of ageing which all people are at pains to avoid. Higgs argues that the forms of state surveillance which accompany consumer citizenship for older people create a target group of 'fourth age' older adults whom 'active seniors have purposefully to separate themselves from, but live in fear of' (1995: 548).

The resulting rift between adulthood and old age could be said, then, to be one which resembles the relationship which formerly divided adults from their children. And if, similarly, the distinction between children and adults has now become blurred, then perhaps that between infants and children has been sharpened? This would appear to be the case. Whereas, at the beginning of the nineteenth century, infancy, the first of the seven stages of man, was divided into two with 'Puerita' identified as a new period between 7 and 14

years, by the mid 1950s, the first *year* of life had become subdivided
into smaller and smaller units – stillbirths, perinatal, neonatal and
infant deaths (Armstrong, 1983b). And by the turn of the century,
medical technologies are refining these still further through ensuring
earlier and earlier survival times for premature babies: the official
age of foetal viability is legally set at 24 weeks gestation (Department
of Health, 1990).

Arguably, then, such changes in perception do not, in themselves,
obscure or fuzz age-based identities across the life course; they
simply reposition the boundaries and dichotomies between them.
Indeed, as Blaikie notes, the effect of a more positive discourse on
ageing may, ironically, be leading to the increased stigmatisation of
the very elderly, with the result that 'final decay and death take on
a heightened hideousness since these will happen, regardless of
whatever cultural, economic or body capital one might possess'
(1997: 19).

It could be argued that postmodern perspectives on ageing have
arisen from the necessity of accounting for the immense variation in
individual experiences of ageing across the life course, which is
rendering the idea of fixed, chronologically-based categories meaningless. That mid-life, for example, is now extended for as long as
possible implies, 'a flexible, individualised, biographical approach
which takes into account human diversity', one which is able to build
on what Bourdieu describes as as the 'cultural capital' of a youthful
appearance and the capacity for social reciprocity (cited in Featherstone and Hepworth, 1991: 386).

Evidence for this contemporary variation is often drawn from the
growth of a new consumerism of the middle aged, where concerns
about growing older are addressed by products and services which –
or so it is claimed – hold back the years through diet, exercise and
other forms of body modification. Likewise, consumption practices
feature in arguments which represent childhood as disappearing.
Television, computer technology and other media, it is argued, play
a critical role in giving children access to the previously separate
world of adulthood and to the knowledge which it contains. This
phenomenon, remarked on in the 1980s by Postman (1983) and
Meyrowitz (1985) is, however, now being problematised as a new set
of moral panics about the extent to which children should be
shielded from access to sexualised adult knowledge or the depictions
of extreme violence now freely available on the web (McRobbie and
Thornton, 1995; Valentine, Holloway and Bingham, 2000). It is

a concern which centres on threats to childhood through the loss of childish innocence, which is seen as one possible outcome of children's unlimited and uncontrolled access to the media. This means that 'ICT is a tool some parents use to exercise care and control over their children while simultaneously also being a tool some children use in negotiating their autonomy and independence from their parents' (Valentine *et al.*, 2000: 16).

Qvortrup's (1994) work on the changing face of childhood develops this point. He argues that contemporary children spend more and more time outside the family home in institutional settings such as schools, after-school centres, nurseries and leisure clubs of various kinds. Children are therefore increasingly living lives separated from their parents. This, he suggests, questions the conventional wisdom that dependent childhood is becoming an ever longer period in the life course.

This theoretical position finds some resonance with Harper and Laws' (1995) focus on the changing use of space in relation to the life course and recalls the importance of movement through space within the social construction of identity, already noted as central to rites of passage (see Chapter 3). Harper and Laws argue, for example, that space is no longer governed by a linear temporal regulation, organised according to the pre-determined chronology of ageing. Instead, people now enter, leave and re-enter the classroom, the private home, the university, the factory, the sheltered home and the nursing home, as their *individual* life circumstances dictate. Mature students sit alongside eighteen-year olds in university lecture halls and children who left home to study may now return, after an absence, to live once more with their parents in the family home, while their grandmother is, instead, moved into residential care.

Preferring to explain this in terms of the power of images and representations to both produce and reflect particular social realities, rather than the structuring roles of the state, work, class and gender, Harper and Laws argue that 'identities are created according to consumption practices in which the form of one's body is all important' (1995: 214). They cite images of older adults in either sun-drenched holiday resorts or greying institutional armchairs as powerfully promoting particular collective representations of later life.

That there are increasing numbers of individuals who flout the traditional expectations of life course categories, spearheading the breakdown of any clear boundaries between them, might lead us to ask, therefore, whether 'age' and 'life course passage' are any longer useful terms for addressing the questions of social identity – and therefore whether a project such as the present volume is worth undertaking! Rather worryingly, Featherstone and Hepworth, for example, refer to the growth of 'a more informal uni-age style' (1991: 372).

However, it can also be argued that the body-focused and consumerist strategies, out of which such suggestions have grown, reflect the *centrality* of the body and mind to the ageing process and therefore that age remains an important marker of identity. That is to say, while shoring up arguments that the new designer life course is *socially* constructed and open to choice, consumerist practices also, paradoxically, intensify our focus on the determining role which biology and chronological age have in conceptualisations of ageing. Even though it is suggested that, with sufficient resources and personal commitment, resistance to growing old may be achieved for a while, this is *in spite of*, and set against, the materiality of bodily ageing. Notwithstanding the cult of youthfulness in social behaviour, organically we *do* maintain a steady progress from childhood towards old age and death, however extended the social construction of mid-life becomes.

Lifestyles and life strategies?

In support of the argument that there is indeed a shift occurring in the experience of the life course, Featherstone and Hepworth identify two drivers of change. The first is the state, which continues to promote an ideology of personal responsibility in the areas of health and welfare. Health-promotion strategies enjoin individuals of all ages to develop a 'healthy lifestyle', the benefits of which will reduce the toll of an ageing population on central funds, both now and in the future. Secondly, they point to the cultural sphere. Here the possibility of designing one's own life is promoted through patterns of consumption now straying well beyond updating the three-piece suite, into the more creative and exploratory realms of theme parks and post-tourism where new vistas and alternative identities are imaged. Echoing this view, the social geography of ageing describes postmodernism as 'an approach...concerned to deconstruct categories, to celebrate diversity rather than seek universal laws and to explore other than dominant meta-narratives' (Harper and Laws, 1995: 212). Contrasting with the rigid stages of the modern life cycle, the fluid postmodern life course perspective opens up the possibilities of multiple lifestyles and identities which can be combined or exchanged across time and space.

Giddens (1991) argues, for example, that self concern or reflexivity has become a core feature of high modernity. He is not persuaded that people ageing during other eras engaged in comparable practices of self-reflection. Thus he refers to, 'a process of "finding oneself" which the social conditions of modernity enforce on us all...[as]...one of active intervention and transformation' (1991: 12). Citing macro-level political, economic and social change during the twentieth century, he celebrates a continuity of transformations which extend into the personal, intimate lives of families and individuals. With the loss of traditional meta-narratives of morality and social conduct, individuals are set free in high modernity within cultural milieux which lack a single authoritative code. The resulting 'freedom' is, in fact, an experience of risk. Nothing can be taken for granted and the riskiness of all options has to be assessed in everyday lived reality.

Within this changed environment, individuals, necessarily therefore, become anchored to the project of the self. There is an imperative to fulfil one's potential within the context of new life and family styles, choices which have become available as a result of a greater flexibility within relationships. Rather than economic obligations or community involvement, individual fulfilment is the guiding rationale – or vocabulary of motive – for choice and decision-making. Giddens sums up his account of new, reflexively-organised self identity as follows:

> The reflexive project of the self, which consists in the sustaining of coherent, yet continuously revised, biographical narratives, takes place in the context of multiple choices as filtered through abstract patterns... The more tradition loses its hold, and the more daily life is reconstituted in terms of the dialectical interplay of the local and the global, the more individuals are forced to negotiate lifestyle choices among a diversity of options (1991: 5).

Less positively than Giddens, Gergen echoes this perspective in his notion of the saturated self, engulfed by possibilities and connections:

> filled to overflowing, the self loses any distinct meaning. It can no longer distinguish itself from all that it could be (cited in Horstein and Gubrium, 2000: 58).

Giddens' vision of personal agency, and indeed empowerment, set against a backdrop of structural change has, however, been challenged.

Featherstone and Hepworth, for example, argue that, with respect
to ageing, this process is one largely confined to middle-class sections of the population, members of the post-Second World War
baby boomer generation, who grew up during an era of political
radicalism and consumer growth. This experience has left them
empowered with both the vision and the resources to redesign
successive life course phases as they age. This reinforces the observation made in the previous chapter that historical time has to be
taken into account when exploring individual biographical trajectories of the life course. Blaikie agrees:

> better health statuses and higher life expectancy may allow a sharper gradient to
> emerge between the fit and active ('use it or lose it') majority and a minority
> group sans teeth, sans eyes, increasingly sans NHS, but most older people are nei-
> ther affluent nor infirm: they are both poor and relatively fit and well (1997: 16).

Indeed, in 1991–2, men over 74 had an average weekly income of
£81.07, compared with £173.70 for men aged between 17 and 59.
Women of the same age had an average weekly income of £58.65,
compared with £80.59 for women aged between 17 and 59 (General
Household Survey, cited in Vincent, 1995: 22). Giddens, however,
adamantly claims that the greater freedom to negotiate one's lifestyle is a phenomenon which is evident among the members of all
social classes – even if modern global transformations do act to
produce or underline gender, 'race' and class-based inequalities.
For Giddens, the lack of resources may simply make it harder to live
out traditional family forms and social relations.

Core to this theoretical potential for the realignment of self are
changes in the nature of production which, from the political economy perspective described in Chapter 4, once underpinned the social
construction of age-based dependencies. Within the conditions of
postmodernity, however, it is argued that patterns of consumption,
rather than production, predominate. As markers of social identities
for elderly people, it is precisely goods and services which promise
a more malleable passage through the life course (see Chapter 10).

Here the health club and its entailments – diets, exercise machines
and sunbeds – have an iconic status. But, additionally, Featherstone
and Hepworth (1995) suggest that, since the 1970s, other goods and
services associated with an active lifestyle – particularly those to do
with the travel and leisure industries – have also been harnessed for
the promotion of positive images of ageing. Their analysis of these
changes is based on evidence to be found in the magazine for

retirement planning, significantly entitled *Choice*. Featherstone and Hepworth describe how, through its articles and advertising, it has worked to reconstruct the 'image of aging as a vigorous, lively and above all enjoyable pathway to self-realization' (1995: 40). However, they also note the persistence of less positive traditional images of ageing – such as retirement as social disengagement – and note that the imagery which such magazines promote is targeted at the 'young old' rather than those whose ageing has carried the body beyond repair. The dominant image is of 'the body as a machine which can be serviced and repaired, and the array of products and techniques advertised, cultivate the hope that the period of active life can be extended and controlled' (Featherstone and Hepworth, 1995: 44). Finally, they note that the absence of adequate income may also inhibit many elderly people from pursuing the consumer values central to such a new vision of ageing, a point echoed by Sawchuck:

> When marketeers talk about a seniors market they're talking about a small privileged sector of that age group with money to spend, a segment who have had the opportunity to build up assets and equity, savings and bonds (1995: 182).

Thus the 'choice' and agency promised by postmodern accounts of ageing must, we suggest, be tempered by the social inequalities of income and of health. These continue to produce considerable variation in the experience of ageing and thus offer rather different prospects for individuals with respect to the changing social identities which accompany the ageing process.

The age of the body

The paradoxical privileging of the tyranny of the flesh within an era which promises choice and freedom from material constraints is, as we have seen, a consistent tension within postmodern accounts of ageing, whether in relation to childhood, mid-life or old age. Featherstone and Hepworth, for example, have made the postmodern preoccupation with the body as the creative site of social identity a core feature of their work (1982, 1989, 1991, 1995), but, nonetheless, note that the postmodern promise of multiple lifestyles and identities may result in *fractured*, body-based identities. Resistances to age-bound social categories can, for instance, produce a divergence between the body's surface – read off within social interactions to yield 'interpersonal age' – and the 'inner' experience of the individual whose private 'personal age' is experienced as far younger, perhaps fixed at a defining life stage in their late twenties. During adulthood, the two ages may mesh in 'consensual age', but as people grow old the slippage between the two is exacerbated; the body's 'look age' skips ahead of a youthful 'feel age'. Here, social interaction and social context are important. Those who have aged alongside the individual for many years may be better placed to share in the 'feel' age of someone they have known intimately as a younger adult. However, to a stranger, someone's 'capable mother' or 'sexually attractive wife' may be just another 'little old lady' – to be ignored, spoken to patronisingly or indeed infantilised (Hockey and James, 1993).

Nonetheless, this divergence between 'exterior' and 'interior' understandings of age opens up the possibility of agency or resistance to the macro-level structures of ageing which are buttressed by notions of 'natural' stages of development. Though the body cannot be moulded to represent a desired chronological age, it can at least be referred to as something which belies the 'true self' which remains 'young at heart'. Conway reports an elderly woman's representation of herself as ageing:

> The thing is that bits of your body wear out, but inside, the essential me is still the same. The physical me is the envelope in which the letter is, and the envelope gets worn out (2000: 91).

Featherstone and Hepworth (1991) describe the ageing body's outer surface as a mask which can act in at least three different ways: as a useful shield; a constraining cage; or a separate sphere to which one's apparent 'ageing' can be distanced. They refer to Stephens' work among elderly people living in a 'single room occupancy' hotel in urban America (cited in Featherstone and Hepworth, 1991: 378) which reveals a deliberate 'masking' of private habits such as sex and drinking, activities which their unsuspecting children might respond to negatively if they found out. But alongside the convenience of an outward appearance which masks one's private pleasures can be set other evidence of older people's unwillingness to step out from behind the 'mask' of their outer bodies to reveal feelings which younger people would prefer not to know about. Caged in by the assumptions of others, even older people's choices of dress and their public presentation of self can be limited by their juniors. Lurie, for example, describes how dress codes powerfully constrain older women – and indeed older men – with the shawl and long nightshirt marking out generational difference (Lurie cited in Featherstone and Hepworth, 1991: 379). The cultural demand that hemlines of women's skirts should lengthen over the life course similarly reminds women that their now ageing knees and dimply thighs no longer possess the sexual allure they once did (Lurie, cited in Featherstone and Hepworth, 1991: 380). Finally, the 'mask of ageing' is an experience of fractured embodiment which can empower those individuals who refuse the age-based social category imposed upon someone with a wrinkled face by permitting them to choose to locate their sense of identity elsewhere – in their social roles as wife, teacher or voluntary worker.

Whereas older adults disclaim the age which might be read off their bodies, it can be argued that young people, in contrast, actually use their bodies to 'mask' their age. They may wish to disguise their youth, despite the positive discourse which surrounds the cult of youthfulness in the modern life course, since it is age which confers rights to adult license presently denied to them (James, 1986). Thus, early and legally forbidden sexual encounters or illicit drinking may be masked by girls wearing clothing and make-up to enhance their age, although boys have less scope in this respect. Younger children may similarly choose to maximise the chronology of their age, replying to the question, 'How old are you?' with an exactitude which takes account of *all* the time that has passed en route to adulthood. They are ten and a half or nine and three quarters. Alternatively they may refuse to disclose their age at all, saying that they are as 'young as as my tongue but older than my teeth'. As James and Prout argue, adult questioning of a child's age 'denies time present in the life of the child, focusing as it does on the inter-relationship between time past and time future' (1997: 235).

Diverse lives?

The mask of ageing therefore refers to the body and its appearance and to the ways in which the social cost of *looking* old or young is managed by elderly and young people alike. But, despite these possibilities, we can still ask how useful the notion of the 'postmodern life course' might be for making theoretical sense of the relationship between ageing and identity for, as noted in relation to old age, class-based inequalities remain important. Changes in the nature of the life course have occurred mostly among more affluent rather than poorer sections of the population.

If, however, we turn to Giddens work on self and identity we find far less of a distinction being made between social classes. Giddens is committed to a belief in the historical specificity of the kinds of practices which go to make up the postmodern life course, but adheres to the view that 'we are, not what we are, but what we make of ourselves' (1991: 75). Like Featherstone and Hepworth, Giddens evidences his case in forms of popular and consumer culture, particularly the self-help book. This, he argues, is the text which both reflects and drives the project of the self. Adrift among competing 'expert' narratives, the individual reflexively assesses the diversity of the knowledge claims made, bending to the task of choosing a life course which represents a coherent narrative that links features of their past life with the anticipated future. Though flexibility, recursiveness and fragmentation are the characteristics of the postmodern life course which Harper and Laws (1995) work also foregrounds, Giddens' represents a more linear, coherent and forward-looking life course passage, albeit one which the individual constructs reflexively for her or himself. Life-course passage, a concept reminiscent of Van Gennep's model of age-based rites of transitions, is still required, but this is not viewed as a constraining structure. Rather, it is a necessary part of the process of self-actualisation. Giddens sees the individual as prepared to free themselves from externally-imposed 'safe-bet' life strategies and to risk passages or changes in the pursuit of a more authentic body of self knowledge which they have been able to generate via the injunctions of self-help books.

But to what extent is this borne out in everyday practice? Giddens is insistent that we cannot act without making choices of some kind. With the demise of tradition in high modernity, nothing can be taken for granted, believed or enacted simply because 'this is the way we do it'. Even if we follow traditional patterns of, for example, the gendered division of labour or the family holiday, we can no longer remain unaware of alternatives. Our adherence to tradition is therefore, itself, a choice we have made, a focus on the self as project. This perspective also informs Bauman's work on postmodern life strategies. Like Giddens, Bauman notes spatial and temporal disjunctions as the hallmark of postmodernity. He uses the images of pilgrims and nomads to highlight differences between the project of self in high modernity, the era in which Giddens grounds his discussion, and the postmodern. Speaking of 'life course as pilgrimage' during the modern period Bauman says:

> Everything one did was serious and important, since everything in the present weighed heavily on everything still to come: the future fate of the project hung on the deeds of today. No void, no momentary lapse; no opting aside from the unstoppable and *continuous* march of time ... (1992: 166).

Bauman differentiated the 'life course as pilgrimage' with its series of meaningful and *connected* markers, from the pre-Reformation, traditional model of 'life course as confessional'. Here the image was of a less linear and more repetitive life course, one sliced into alternating and repetitive segments of sinning and confessing (cf. Chapter 2). With the Roman Catholic notion of confession and forgiveness of sins, the individual life unfolded, not in the form of a linear route across a map, but a fan which doubles back and forth between identical, repeating pleats, each act of confession and penance cleansing the sinner and granting them a fresh start, a clean sheet. Protestantism, however, with its rational, account-book balancing of sin and salvation, eroded this possibility. Instead, it set up the requirement for a self-monitoring accumulation of worthy life course achievements: 'Pilgrims select their destination early and plan their life-itinerary accordingly' (1992: 167).

With the destabilisation of what Bauman refers to as connexity – the interconnections of times and spaces – the contemporary life course, however, more closely resembles a period of nomadic wandering. Choices are made contingently by nomads. The future extends no further than the next 'caravan site', any sense of connection being attributed retrospectively. These images thus powerfully point to the existence of different life-course strategies, the notion of the nomad capturing very effectively the essence of the postmodern life course. As Bauman says,

> the nomads, like the pilgrims, were all along busy constructing their identities; but theirs were 'momentary' identities, identities 'for today', until-further-notice identities. Nomads do not bind the time/space they move through it; and so they move through identities (1992: 167).

Yet in bringing us back, once more, albeit metaphorically, to spatialised conceptions of the life course, Bauman's notion of nomadism implicitly invites us to re-consider the materially-grounded dimensions of ageing and identity, which is the theme of this volume. From this perspective, then, we can ask whether the life course has indeed become fragmented and whether identities are now inhabited simply in the moment?

Adulthood in prospect

To explore these questions in detail we turn now to Kenyon's (1999) account of the categorical movement from adolescence to adulthood which is exemplified in student housing choices. As she says:

> very often an independent dwelling away from the childhood home is seen to be both a physical manifestation of independence and citizenship, as well as the arena in which other adult emotional and social developments are most likely to occur. Leaving home is therefore viewed as one factor associated with the complex movement from childhood towards full adulthood (1999: 84).

Drawing on data from interviews within 32 households in Sunderland, where students aged between 18 and 23 were living, Kenyon's data do show the persistence of 'connexity' among this group of individuals. Personal, temporal, social and physical dimensions of the meaning of 'home' for students are all in evidence. When describing their parental and their present student homes the young people identified mismatches between ideals and experiences. Having registered at university, and anticipating future paid employment, the parental home no longer provided them with the prospect of an appropriate long-term stable living space. Further, it was an environment where the autonomy and independence they felt they needed was curtailed. However, student accommodation also failed to match up. This involved sharing a space which lacked communal living areas; it was dirty, insecure and and intrinsically impermanent. For these students, the meanings of home would be realised only when they had graduated and secured paid employment, as one interviewee described:

> [After graduation] you will have more respect for everything. You will be more choosy about everything. You will be choosy about the type of neighbourhood that you want to live in, and the house you want to live in (1999: 91).

Sharing a living space with immediate family members was also integral to concepts of the 'real' home and, as Kenyon says:

> students therefore stated that close family groupings would eventually form the social units of 'real' future homes. As Mark told me, 'I'll get a job, hopefully, and then I will settle down, you know, probably get married at some point, have a few kids. That's what we all really expect isn't it?' (1999: 91).

Thus, despite the constraints on choice it represents, the parental home continues to occupy an important place in students' lives –

"'It's the only stable thing in my life at the moment...I always know that home-home will be there and still be the same when I go back"'. Kenyon's account therefore reveals the importance of the homes they have left and the homes which they envisage as aspects of their future lives for students who think of themselves in transition between categories. Their provisional student identities are predicated upon the comfortable but constricting category of 'childhood' which continues to remain open to them on their return to the parental home. However, the more desirable future-focused category, 'adult', is the taken-for-granted future to which they aspire.

For these 18- to 23-year olds, therefore, the life course remains unreservedly modern. It is time-bound and chronologically defined. It is not the postmodern condition in which the future is collapsed into the present and social identities only woven into a narrative retrospectively. Or as Bauman puts it:

> All competing narratives are invited to test themselves in the yet-unwritten chronicle of the future, to prove themselves in tomorrow achievements. No more point in looking back, brandishing birth certificates and meticulously composed charts of genealogical trees (1992: 162).

Such a postmodern view seems alien to these young people's experience.

Staying with this example, what we need to recognise also, however, is that education is no longer the prerogative of the young. Students combine full-time participation in higher education with parental and occupational roles. Some complete degrees by distance learning which might mean only the minor spatial re-organisation of a dining-table being made available for study. Similarly, as the introduction of tuition fees hit home for UK students and employment opportunities shrank, the 'progression' from school to university to independent adulthood ceased to represent the key life course transition which it used to for many 18 year olds.

Conclusion

Examples such as our case study of the transition to adulthood therefore challenge arguments for the postmodern fragmentation of the life course. They show that a chronologised, modernist life course project remains in place for many young people. As Kenyon's interviewee said of his plan to enter paid employment and start his own family: 'That's what we all really expect isn't it?' (1999: 91).

Thus, although throughout this chapter we have considered evidence which points towards a withering away of 'age' as a structural feature of the life course, its role remains ambiguous. Individual choice and innovation is everywhere apparent: among six-year old contestants at beauty pageants; the new informed 'consumers' of university education; 'mid-lifers' and jet-setting, executive grannies and grandpas. However, alongside this proliferation of freedom and choice there is considerable evidence that the chronologised body continues to be a source of constraints. The new consumerism simply compounds the demands of the flesh as desperate and increasingly futile attempts are made to remedy the impact of ageing through face-creams and vitamin intake. Linked with this are the structural features of poverty, unemployment and inadequate pension provision which debar many people from the free exercise of personal agency.

Does this diversity of material mean, therefore, that we will continue to trail back and forth between competing sources of evidence in our search for a sound theoretical basis for exploring the contemporary life course? Perhaps not. Jencks (cited in Walter, 1994: 42) provides one way of bringing this discussion to some kind of closure with his notion of double coding. Using this idea, postmodernism might be defined as neither the rejection of the modern nor the traditional, but rather an unconstrained mixing of styles borrowed from different eras. As Walter notes, modernists oppose themselves, by definition, to traditionalists. The postmodernist however characteristically *combines* features of different eras and, as the following chapters go on to explore, it is this approach which offers the most potential for making sense of the diversity of life courses unfolding around us.

PART III

Embodying the Life Course

7

Revitalising the Life Course

Introduction

This volume began by outlining some of the ways in which the experience of ageing and the negotiation of identity across the life course have been theorised. As noted, the predominance of the Durkheimian legacy within both the sociology of the recent western life course and the anthropology of non-western societies has meant that accounts of the external, nominal, categorical and socio-structural aspects of identity have traditionally been privileged over those which have stressed a more individual, virtual and actor-oriented perspective. Before suggesting a new kind of account, let us recap the argument we have outlined so far.

In Chapter 2, we showed how the early explorations of ageing via rites of passage confronted the materiality of the ageing body by emphasising the supremacy of the social in ordering and regulating the passing of time in an individual's life. Indeed, as we described, in many cultures, age-based *social* identities, are literally carved upon the body's surface through bodily mutilations such as foot binding, circumcision or scarification. In Chapter 3, we noted how particular ethnographic accounts of the structuring and ritualisation of life course categories paralleled the broader structural explanations of processes of identity ascription across the life course offered by social historians. Thus, we explored the role which the macro political and economic processes of the nineteenth and early twentieth centuries played in shaping rites of transition from childhood to adulthood and thence to old age. It was argued for example that, within British society, the rapid progress of industrialisation released young bodies from the drudgery of the factory system through the imposition of aged identities as 'children', only to enclose and contain them in different, but similarly excluding, ways within the walls of the school room.

Bringing structure-oriented perspectives to bear on historical material, we noted how the social identities of child, youth or elder seemed to be imposed upon the individual as they aged. This, as Jenkins notes, suggests that 'social identity' is somehow more real and more enduring than 'individual identity' – more robust, less vulnerable. The legacy of such a theoretical tradition has meant that 'social identities are thus liable to reification as solid or hard-edged, as phenomena which exert influence "above our heads" or "behind our backs"' (Jenkins, 1996: 16). Aged identities are visualised as being imposed on social actors in the form of a combination of the roles and positions which are institutionally or organisationally ascribed for different phases of the life course. This Nicholson (1995) terms the 'coat rack' approach to explaining identity. But such theorising tells us little, we argued, about how individuals themselves experience transition between aged identities across the life course.

Thus, in Chapters 5 and 6, more agency-focused theories were explored. Here, we developed our historical perspective, again drawing largely on British examples. Chapter 5 argued that the determinism of structural accounts of the life course has to be tempered by acknowledgement of the fact that life-course passage may be differentially experienced by individuals. This may be in terms of the impact that structural factors have on a person's life course in practice and with regard to the precise shape which any individual's biography takes. This idea was developed further in Chapter 6 through exploring recent postmodern theories of ageing where agency perspectives predominate. Arguing that there has been a withering away of structure in postmodern society, these postmodern perspectives suggest that the taking on of aged identities is now almost entirely within the individual's gift. Such a view operates both at the theoretical level of agency-focused analysis and at the descriptive level of an account of changing social conditions. It is argued, for example, that consumerism has permitted aged identity to become increasingly less prescriptive and is now much more a matter of personal choice and preference, realised through the lifestyle decisions which people make. Thus, within this view, the relentless biological base of ageing is rendered less powerful, subject as it now is, within industrial cultures, to a new concern with health and fitness regimes and to alteration through technological and medical interventions. In such a model, 'social identity' becomes seen as that which individuals pick up and discard as they age across the life course. This view does not move us much further forward, however. It still does not provide an adequate account of human *experience*. Nor does it engage effectively with questions about how individuals come to know that they are ageing. It conjures up, instead, a calculating, performing and curiously selfless self which negates our commonsense and our everyday appreciation and consciousness of the self (Cohen, 1994).

It would seem therefore that, despite a great deal of progress in studies of identity and ageing, at the start of the new millennium, theories of the now radically altered western life course remain ensnared within the structure and agency debates which have traditionally bedevilled social scientific explanations of change and social reproduction. In addition, 'biology' has now been largely barred from any determining role in human behaviour by the dominance of social constructionist perspectives within the social sciences; yet at the same time we also seem reluctant to understand cultural variation merely as different elaborations of a set of bodily 'givens'. In these circumstances it has become increasingly difficult to assess the relative merits of arguments about the body's corporeality on the one hand and discourses about the body on the other. Discussing the impact of technological interventions in the flesh, Shilling says:

> In this time of uncertainty, knowledge about what bodies are increasingly takes the form of hypotheses... [t]his situation is not inconsequential for the modern individual's sense of self identity (1993: 4).

Accounting for ageing and identity across the life course would therefore seem to be mired in a theoretical impasse. In the following critical discussion of the work of theorists who have addressed issues of the body and social identity we explore ways of moving beyond this potentially circular debate, however, by revitalising contemporary theorising about identity with insights from the sociology of the body.

Towards the embodiment of identity

Contemporary work within the sociology and anthropology of the body offers, we suggest, a way forward to revitalise our understanding of ageing across the life course by permitting the bodily materiality of the ageing process to be radically reconceptualised. In this, the ageing body emerges neither as a canvas upon which aged identities are sketched, nor as an organic imperative. Rather, it is simply the site and source of the process of human ageing itself. Turner (1992), for example, argues that the corporeality of human existence is a fact of life. It cannot be ignored. But in arguing this, Turner is not beating a hasty retreat to an old biological determinism. Instead, he views corporeality itself as eminently social. Thus he writes:

> as a consequence of their embodiment, all human agents are subject to certain common processes which, although they have biological, physiological and organic foundations, are necessarily social in character (1992: 35).

Thus, though conception, gestation, birth development and ageing are indeed 'biological' processes, they are also fundamentally social affairs in that they involve the embodied interactions of individuals. Conception, for example, whether it occurs as the result of love, mishap, IVF, rape or ignorance, is contextualised by the social; by the inter-actions of individuals in particular social circumstances, involved in particular social relationships with one another; and it is also bound by the particular moralities of particular social conventions. Similarly, though birth is certainly a biological event, it is also firmly embed-ded in the social: a child's birth restructures the family; it shapes descent systems and inheritance patterns; birth changes women into mothers, men into fathers and mothers into grandmothers; and, over time, the event of birthing itself has moved between the realms of the 'natural' and private and those which are more public and tech-nological. Such examples give very practical illustration, therefore, of the ways in which bodily events and processes are firmly embed-ded within, and indeed inseparable from, the social realm.

Developing this notion, Shilling eschews the nature/culture binary within social theory entirely. Instead he posits a view of culture as being intrinsic to, rather than irreconcilable with, natural biological processes. In his view, culture is the necessary context for the 'finishing' of an inevitably incomplete state of human embodiment:

> the body is most profitably conceptualised as an unfinished biological and social phenomenon which is transformed, within certain limits, as a result of its entry into and participation in society (1993: 12).

In thus bringing the body back in to social theory, Shilling acknow-ledges that 'as we get older our faces change, our eyesight deteriorates, our bones can become brittle and our flesh starts to sag' (1993: 12). Yet, at the same time, he recognises that the ways in which these changes occur – how they are managed, interpreted and socially classified, what meanings they convey and what consequences they have for the individual – vary across and between societies. However, the *particular* ways in which our bodies in themselves age testifies to the bodily experiences which we, as individuals, have undergone through out lives.

> In later life an entire social history can be read off the old body – in the lines of the face; in scarring from childbirth, accidents and surgery; and in the way clothing is worn and everyday tasks are performed (Hallam *et al.*, 1999: 46).

Turner and Shilling both suggest, therefore, that the 'structural' and 'social' aspects of the environment in which any individual finds themself act to complete the body in different, culturally unique ways. In exemplifying this, they draw out the implications of Mauss's (1934) work, who, in his descriptions of the 'techniques du corps', shows that even our unconscious bodily movements – ways of sitting, eating, walking, standing – are shaped by the social and cultural contexts in which we find ourselves and through which we relate to others. However, neither Turner and Shilling choose to privilege the social. Indeed, they reject the implicit opposition between what they call foundational and antifoundational views of the body and argue instead for a synthesis of these approaches or, at the very least, a way of mediating between them (Turner, 1992). In Turner's view, foundational approaches to the body endeavour to understand the body as a lived experience. They explore the ways in which corporeal existence impinges on people's everyday lives; the body is given, as it were, 'out there' as a constraint on individual social action. Anti-foundational approaches, by contrast, construe the body as an effect of social discourse. In disregarding the lived experience of the body, such research focuses instead on the ways in which the body is used, for example, as a source of power or as a medium through which social relations are displayed.

Rejecting this opposition Turner calls for recognition of the process of embodiment and for simultaneous acknowledgement of the experience of both 'having' a body and 'being' a body. Drawing on the work of Max Scheler, he advocates the useful distinction to be made between the objective fleshy body (*Korper*) which might be classified and described in particular ways through discourse and (*Leib*) the sensations and the lived experience of the inner body. For

Turner, 'the body' is 'both simultaneously discursive and animated; it is both *Korper* and *Leib*, socially constructed and objective' (1992: 57). Such a perspective is also central to Lyon and Barbalet's depiction of the process of embodiment:

> the body is a subject of (and subject to) social power . . . it is not merely a passive recipient of society's mould, and therefore external to it. The human capacity for social agency, to collectively and individually contribute to the making of the social world comes precisely from the person's lived experience of embodiment. Persons do not simply experience their bodies as external objects of their possessions or even as an intermediary environment which surrounds their being. Persons experience themselves simultaneously in and as their bodies (Lyon and Barbalet, 1994: 54).

The usefulness of such a perspective for understanding ageing and social identity across the life course is immediately apparent for as Turner goes on to note,

> the very identity of social agents cannot be easily separated from their embodiment within the interactional situation. In everyday life, in interacting with other social agents, we have in principle to be able to recognise and distinguish between different social agents. At the level of everyday life, therefore, the ongoing identification of other social agents depends fundamentally on their embodiment (1992: 36).

This process of identification involves 'putting together context, biography and the body' and is ongoing and recursive (Turner, 1992: 76). The body, as both an objective and discursive object, thus mediates identity through the process of embodiment. Its very materiality provides the conduit through which identity comes to be ascribed and taken on by people in the course of their everyday day lives.

Like Turner and Shilling, Frank (1991) also rejects the opposition between foundational and anti-foundational approaches to the body. He suggests that 'the body' can be best 'constituted in the intersection of an equilateral triangle the points of which are institutions, discourses and corporeality' (1991: 49). He illustrates this by looking at the ascetic practices of fasting among women in the mediaeval period, arguing that the bodies of those women – their corporeality – both reflected and was shaped by their positioning between the institutional practices of the mediaeval church and discourses about the particular place of women and marriage in mediaeval society. Though apparently advancing a structural argument, Frank (1991) goes on to insert an agency-focused perspective. He argues that by assuming the identity of 'holy women', an identity taken on through the adoption of strict fasting practices, these women actively exploited the opposition between two very different and powerful discourses of the period. Many fasting women came from wealthy families, where marriage and re-marriage represented strategic political alliances made within a patriarchal system which rendered women submissive. By fasting, and thus using their bodies to intervene between these discourses and institutions, women were able to challenge their subordination within the family. However, this of course meant complying with the discipline of another, albeit similarly patriarchal, system – the Church. Nonetheless, through demonstrating bodily purity and gaining veneration for their piety, these women, though not necessarily breaking free from the dominance of patriarchy, nonetheless managed to create a greater freedom for themselves within the relatively closed and ordered world of mediaeval society.

Theories of embodiment and of the preeminently social nature of bodily practices help us, then, to begin to map out the relationship between action and structure and to explore the internal – external dialectic of the process of identification through which age across the life course can be represented and understood. Critically, it is the materially-grounded positioning of embodied individuals within social space – and in relation to one another – which allows us to understand how time and its passage is apprehended. It is, as it were, through spatialised locatedness that we come to know that we are ageing. As we have remarked before, earlier models of rites of passage indeed emphasised the movement of individuals through space. They used material metaphors of the threshold to develop theoretical perspectives which helped make sense of time passing. Ethnographic accounts of such rituals described individuals and groups being moved out of the spaces of everyday life, often to be segregated in marginalised places, separate huts or the countryside outside the village, for extended periods of time – before being allowed to return to the village with a transformed, socially-aged identity – as man rather than boy, woman rather than girl. This spatial mapping of age category transition in traditional societies, in many ways, reflects modernist spatial segregations which likewise produce the separate spheres of the home, the workplace and the school to accommodate changing age-based identities.

However, as the historical and ethnographic evidence drawn upon throughout this volume demonstrates, an agency-focused account of identification reveals the fragility or arbitrariness of many of these body-focused boundaries; individuals may sometimes only 'grow up' when their fathers have the money to pay for a rite of passage; ties between space and category may therefore not be clear-cut. It is such nuanced readings of the embodied self as it moves within space which take us therefore to the heart of age-based identification. However, though we now move on to discuss Battersby's (1993) explanation of the problematic *linkages* between misleading 'frozen moment' conceptions of both 'social structure' and 'the body', we must nonetheless acknowledge our debt to those early theorists who first persuaded us to think about the body *via the social domain*.

The body as the site of identification

If the experience of the self as it ages is produced through direct engagement with the body, how has embodiment been theorised in the history of social science and in theories of identity? Referring to the phenomenological work of Merleau-Ponty, Turner (1992) discusses the notion that our perception of the world is always sited in a particular experience of embodiment. Radical alterations to that experience, such as the amputation of a limb, will be manifested in shifts in that perception. Thus he cites Langer's argument that, 'the body is not an object for itself; it is in fact "a spontaneous synthesis of powers, a bodily spatiality, a bodily unity, a bodily intentionality, which distinguish it radically from the scientific object posed by traditional schools of thought"' (Turner, 1992: 43).

This perspective is important given the limited role of embodiment within theories of identity (Craib, 1998) which in different ways, as du Gay *et al.* (2000) show, challenge the concept of the person as an individual subject. Despite sharing the same *critical* perspective on unitary conceptualisations of the individual subject, there are, du Gay *et al.* (2000) suggest, three different ways of understanding identity. The first, the 'subject-of-language' approach, foregrounds the capacity of discourse to produce its own subjects. Within this framework, identities are constituted primarily through alterity and difference. The second, and psychoanalytic, approach critiques the abstract quality of identities produced simply through discourse. Instead, it calls for greater recognition of the affective dimensions of identification. Third, the genealogical approach, examines the ways in which human beings acquire 'limited and specific forms of personhood ... in their passage through social institutions' (du Gay *et al.*, 2000: 4). While psychoanalytic theorists of identity tend to operate with a relatively 'thick' view of human material, genealogists have a much 'thinner', contingent and historically specific sense of that which constitutes human being. Thus, if we take the work of Foucault as an example of poststructuralist theories of identification, we find that, in Shilling's words, 'the body is present as a topic of discussion, but is absent as a focus of investigation' (1993: 80). Such theorising fails, therefore, to come to grips adequately with embodiment. As Craib argues:

> sociological approaches to identity of the self tend to assume that the world is peopled by normotic personalities, by people who have no subjective or inner experience. ... [but] when sociologists lay claim to talking about identity, the self and emotions we need to know what we are talking about and experience, the subjective inner world, is a vital part of that discussion (1998: 9).

Thus, it is in contrast with the cognitively-based theories outlined above that the feminist philosopher, Battersby, tackles the subject of identity. She suggests that the way in which we understand and experience our bodies is in fact intimately linked with the way in which we think about identity. In this sense, she is not therefore discussing how we *produce* our identities through embodied social interaction; rather she is taking issue at a theoretical level with the way we conceptualise identity, suggesting that effective re-formulations of this concept need, in fact, to be grounded in our experience of embodiment – especially if we are to understand how it is that we come to know that we are ageing.

She begins by critiquing the notion of classification, the allocation of things to categories. She argues that its implicit basis is located in a universalising model of human embodiment as being 'contained' within the body's boundaries. Here self/inside are clearly demarcated from other/outside. Our understandings of systems of cognitive classification assume that all human thought is primarily a process of categorisation, an assumption which also obeys the logic of this containment: 'just fitting things into categories relies on the fundamentally human experience of embodiment' (1993: 31). Against this, Battersby argues that the body is not, in fact, universally experienced as a container. As a woman, this notion is, for example, foreign to her. For women embodiment may be a fluid experience, since the body's 'boundaries' continuously admit and expel external matter and indeed the other selves of mothers, lovers and children. In her view, our conception of identity and identities as fixed reflects a masculinised model of the body: the body as a bounded container.

They do not admit the mutability of bodily experience which, at times, is bounded and, at others, open and intersubjective. As social scientists, we often forget that forms are simply 'structurally stable moments within the evolution of a system' (Battersby, 1993: 35). In other words, following Battersby, we need to view identities as contingent, relational moments within a dynamic matrix or social system (cf. Harris, 1987). As we have demonstrated, however, accounting for the life course does not *just* mean tracing the passage of individuals through age-based stages. It also involves recognition of the inherent instability of fundamental life course categories, such as 'childhood' and 'old age', and indeed the enormous diversity of institutional arrangements through which one's ageing may be apprehended. As Harris argues, social structure itself is 'merely a moment in a process of societal change of which the choices of subjects are constituents' (1987: 24).

Battersby concludes by arguing that we need to conceptualise social structure, the body and identity as open systems with 'leaks of energy into and out of the system' (1993: 35). This position more accurately reflects the heterogeneity of conceptualisations of the self in western thought, each one representing a 'singularity' or 'moment' within a labile system. Thus, the bounded self, Battersby argues, is not in itself a false conception. It is misleading only when treated as a *closed* bounded entity with its own, permanent autonomy. Instead, she suggests, selves move into and out of boundedness, identity taking form contingently and temporarily, in relation to the other moment-ary identities which together make up a dynamic social system.

The embodiment of age

The changing boundedness of the body is illustrated well in Christensen's (1993) discussion of the cultural meanings of vulner-ability in childhood – the idea that children are weak, vulnerable and in need of protection. In her analysis of children's playground acci-dents and illness episodes, Christensen shows how the transformed surface of the child's body becomes an identifier of children's age-based vulnerability. Drawing on Battersby's (1993) notion that the body is both bounded and unbounded at different moments, Christensen situates this within a life-course trajectory. In the case of children, she argues, their bodies are 'in continuous action and connection with other features of the social world' (2000: 46). Illness or injury is not distanced from the person as something external which happens to the body, but as something embodied and continuous in their everyday social experience. Reflecting on her field data, Christensen says that:

> it became apparent that children's concern was with the interruption of their body and their connections with the social and material world, not with, for example, the penetration of the body skin or naming the body part that hurt. They experienced the situations in which they were involved and the associated interactions as an integrated process (2000: 47).

Thus, Christensen argues, children are rather differently positioned from adults with regard to their attitudes to the body and its ailments, a difference pivoted around the body as somatic (as observable object) and incarnate (as subjective experience). While adults might rush to the aid of a child bleeding from a cut in their concern with the body's objective health status, the child might be calmly engaged in the subjective experience of watching blood seep out through the body's boundaries. What the child thus learns to take on through such encounters with adult carers is a western re-framing of their body as both bounded and objective.

Such re-framings of the flesh have a history. As described in detail elsewhere (Hockey and James, 1993), over time within western societies the bodies of children and elderly people have come to be invested with a particularly powerful signifying potential when it comes to identity ascription. Thus, childhood, for example, is now commonly envisaged as the literal embodiment of change over time, a perception made explicit in the often repeated phrase 'when you grow up'. Not being 'big enough' or 'old enough' both excuses and sets limits on children's actions, the growing body seen here as central to changing the parameters of constraint. Older people, on the other hand, may be regarded as 'too old' or to 'too frail' to undertake certain tasks. The ageing body is seen to impose rather than free the individual from constraints.

Thus, apparently 'natural' bodily differences become a trope which spiral into a whole variety of social, political and educational ideologies which by turn control and govern the embodied actions of the young and the old. In the case of children, Steedman, for example, argues that:

> The building up of scientific evidence about physical growth in childhood described an actual progress in individual lives, which increased in symbolic importance during the nineteenth century, whereby that which is traversed is, in

the end, left behind and abandoned, as the child grows up and goes away. In this way childhood as it has been culturally described is always about that which is temporary and impermanent, always describes a loss in adult life, a state that is recognised too late. Children are quite precisely a physiological chronology, a history, as they make their way through the stages of growth (1992: 37).

Thus, she shows that, during the nineteenth century not only was the rapidly developing conceptual space of childhood within the life course being supported by a variety of philanthropic and political reforms, as described in Chapters 4 and 5, but, increasingly, an understanding of the child's body became central to the firming up of the social identity of 'the child'. As James notes:

> Progressed and popularised through contemporary physiology the child's body was seen as one characterised by change and growth, a process of biological development which was increasingly in need of measurement and monitoring. To grow up as an adult was to out grow (or, more precisely, to grow out of) the body of a child (James, 2000: 24).

This example, therefore, confronts us with questions about the relationship between the materiality of the body and the socially produced nature of human cultures. On the one hand, it would seem that the ephemeral nature of the flesh has the incontrovertible status of 'the real'; we can document the changes wrought upon the flesh by age, via photographs and memories. On the other hand, as we have seen, historical and anthropological evidence demonstrates the socially constructed nature of human ageing. It shows how experiences of growing up and growing old emerge out of culturally specific assumptions about the shape and nature of the life course. Here, when we speak of the social construction of the life course, we do not, therefore, envisage a split between the materiality of the body and particular social and cultural elaborations of the flesh. We see the body as neither a passive slate upon which 'culture' is written, nor an automaton which society programmes; nor indeed as a force of nature which determines the possibilities of human social interaction. Rather than thinking in terms of a power struggle between two opposing forces – 'culture' and 'biology', we recognise a participatory, spiral process whereby the bodied beings who constitute society are themselves producing and giving meaning to their own experience of embodiment. Thus, as Wright has argued, to demonstrate the socially constructed nature of the body does not mean that we have to de-materialise its flesh and bones. He says, 'far from social construct-ivism regarding the objects that it studies as illusory, it grounds them yet more firmly in reality, by basing them on the foundation of all meaning: the lived and shared experience of human societies' (Wright, 1987: 104). He goes on, 'all human knowledge...is the product of human social activity and is used by human beings to bring into existence their own lives and experience' (1987: 104).

This interrelationship is given historical illustration by Foucault who reminds us that the apparently unproblematic biological knowledge through which we now understand our organic make-up was *itself* the social and cultural product of a late eighteenth-century discipline. Thus, it was the invention of a biological gaze that constituted the conditions of possibility within which the specialisms of anatomy and medical science emerged (see Armstrong, 1987). It was through these 'knowledges' that the body, as we now understand and experience it, was produced, their disciplinary power being manifested, for example, through normalising conceptions of 'hygiene', 'health' or 'pathology'.

When it comes to understanding ageing, for example, a process of what might be called medical pathologisation can be identified therefore in the post-war attempts to develop a specialism of geriatrics which could mirror the successful, autonomous status which paediatrics had achieved in an earlier period. In attempting to mark out later life as a separate sphere of medical knowledge and skill, geriatrics promoted the view that: 'age made multiple pathology the rule rather than exception and age altered the resistance of the old to disease processes. Management, too, had to be different as defects accumulated with age...' (Armstrong, 1981: 253). While all medicine is concerned with the identification of pathological processes, geriatric medicine distinguished itself by claiming that 'in geriatric patients the ageing process constituted a vital dimension of the medical problem' (Armstrong, 1981: 253). Armstrong notes, therefore, that geriatric medicine had an uneasy status caught between social gerontology's emphasis on old age as a time of 'normal' bodily decline and 'natural' death and medicine's commitment to differentiating between natural processes and pathologies. Thus, it can be argued that illness and ageing are by now closely intertwined as a direct result of the professionalising practices of geriatric medicine. We now *expect* old age to be accompanied by ill health and celebrate as exceptions those older people who manage to elude this process and who remain fit and active.

As noted in Chapter 3, in the case of children, an explicit link was made between the welfare of children's bodies and the future welfare of the state such that children's bodies became the object of intense concern. This meant that infant mortality declined from 148 per 1000 live births in 1841–5 to 50 in 1941–5 (Woodroffe *et al*., 1993); the incidence of tuberculosis in childhood decreased from the 1930s onwards, following the discovery of the importance of vitamins and fresh air (Bryder, 1992); the average weight and size according to age increased for children following state intervention to improve food provision, housing and sanitation and, through an education policy which encouraged physical exercise within the school curriculum (Mayall, 1996: 25–6). But these structural conditions did not, in and of themselves, alter children's levels of morbidity or childhood mortality rates. There was not a 'natural' or inevitable follow-on from an increased scientific knowledge about nutrition or legislation for better housing. Rather, as Steedman (1990; 1992) and Urwin and Sharland (1992) have shown, it, was through the active participation of individuals – of parents and their children – in new forms of child-rearing and parentcraft practices, through their acceptance of a particular envisioning of the importance of child health, that changes in patterns of childhood morbidity were produced. Parents and other family members, including children themselves, were engaged, through their everyday family practices at home, in fostering physiological changes in children's bodies.

Evidence such as this belies arguments which suggest that individuals have no say or control over the ways in which their bodies are 'finished' and that aged identities are therefore simply the outcome of society's strictures. On the contrary, as Shilling (1993), emphasises, it is not simply the body's entry into society but its *participation* in society which is important. Citing the work of Bourdieu and Elias, Shilling suggests that individuals are able to capitalise on their bodies in ways already exemplified in this volume. Through different actions, through access to different kinds of resources, an individual's sense of self identity as this or that kind of a person arises out of the ways in which that participation takes place.

Sites of ageing

To illustrate the theoretical argument outlined above we now consider some of key sites within which the experiences of time and ageing can be produced. Here, the geography of home and workspace and the landscape of the body become significant. Furman (1997), for example, in an ethnography of ageing among American women, investigates the space of the beauty salon within which the ageing body is 'finished' as an important site. She opens her work with field notes which begin: 'What about Julie's International Salon makes me feel that I move into a different psychological space?' (1997: 1). She recognises that this space operates upon her experience of time, making her remember the safety and comfort of her childhood, the positive moments spent with grandmothers and aunts. Despite this sense of crossing a spatialised boundary into a different quality of time, Furman fears that the beauty salon frequented by older women is a less than serious focus for an academic project. She needs the reassurance of Evans and Thornton's argument that, 'the practices which a culture insists are meaningless or trivial, the places where ideology has succeeded in becoming invisible, are practices in need of investigation' (cited in Furman, 1997: 4).

Her aim, then, is to investigate the meaning of the older body for women in a society where the youthful body is promoted everywhere. Importantly she carries out this project precisely in the segregated space in which women physically engage with the effects of time upon their flesh. Through the maintenance of sets of lifelong beauty practices, they work on and with their bodies as sites of identification. The women quite literally create and recreate their identities and, when Furman asks them to show her photographs of themselves at earlier ages, her informants used these as starting points for retelling the stories which account for particular kinds of identification across time. Thus, while photographs associated with illness, death and divorce are radically excluded from family albums (Spence, 1986), the historio-biographical image of the past self at particular points in time may nonetheless still require explanation and interpretation when viewed through the lens of the present – the mini-skirt, the bouffant hair-do, the ill-chosen boyfriend have to be accounted for.

Another example of the significance of the body as site for age identity making can be found in the free paper *Mature Tymes* (sic). As its name suggests, the paper addresses an audience of people in the later part of the life course, those over 50. Alongside articles on finance, travel and entertainment, adverts for holidays and financial planning vie with those for body maintenance. Vitamins 'unlock the pain in your joints' and the deluxe version of a reclining chair comes complete with 'double arm storage, modem access, 10 motor adjustable massage, handsfree phone, privacy handset, heat system in seat' (November, 2000). One advert stands out, however. A large black-and-white insert for a company calling itself 'Independence Ltd' offers a range of products aimed at enabling the individual to cope with or disguise the impact age is having on their bodies. These products include: arch supports for the feet, big toe straighteners, toe relief pads and incontinence pads. A 'helping hand' claims to assist those who have difficulty with reaching or bending, hold-up stockings give comfort to women with poor circulation and ward off thrush or cystitis, while for men, support belts for lumbago sufferers and hernia trunks provide relief from the ageing process. In addition, the availability of single-leg tights, which allow women to only replace one leg of a laddered pair at a time, ensures that the clothed body can always be properly maintained, even in times of economic hardship.

What view of old age does such an advert evoke for the reader? On the one hand, the reader is presented with a view of ageing as a process of relentless physical decline, wherein the body, willy-nilly and without let or hindrance, will begin to ache, creak and leak. On the other, it is suggested that products are available to cope with the body's new demands which, should the individual choose to purchase them, offers older people a degree of choice. Literally, they can buy their physical, and therefore also social 'independence' via low-tech counterparts of the miracles of medical science: knee and hip replacements, cataract surgery and colostomies.

Encapsulated here, then, in this single advert, is the argument we are advancing in this book. If, as Jenkins (1996) argues, individual identity can only make sense in relation to social identity then the reverse is also true. Social identities only come into being through their embodiment or animation by *individuals*. Thus 'the social is the field upon which the individual and collective meet and meld' (Jenkins, 1996: 17). We therefore come to know that we are ageing through our embodiment. And, in the social, this experience conjoins with ideological and economic structures.

Thus, in the advertisement, the expectation is that 'disorderly' organic processes and weakening bodily boundaries will be kept under control; and that older people will invest resources in the prolongation of their physical independence. In this way, the advertisement represents ageing as a threatening social and physical process to which the individual then responds. In that it is accessed by individual members of an ageing readership, however, *Mature Tymes* is of course a social document which interpellates the elderly consumer. It reminds them of the exclusions as well as the inconveniences they risk, should they fail to regulate their bodily appearance and functions.

At the other end of the life course, a similar process of identity-making can be identified through the use of the medical technique of ultrasonography during pregnancy. This scientific invention allows the foetus – the child yet to be born – to take on a social identity pre-birth. Medical images produced on a screen represent the body of the growing child to its parents and such images have now been appropriated in ways which afford it social, rather than just medical significance. Photographs of the foetal image may be passed around within families and even included in the family album. Further, as Layne (2000) has argued, in North America, through the rituals of baby-showers and gifts from relatives, the baby-to-be is made to take on a social identity before birth, the beating heartbeat and movements of the foetus which are experienced by the mother become translated and embodied through material objects, even for those babies who are still born and will not become 'real' babies:

> Through the buying, giving and preserving of things, women and their social networks actively construct their babies-to-be and would-have-been babies, real babies and themselves as 'real mothers', worthy of the social recognition this role entails (Layne, 2000: 321).

This expansion of the life course temporal envelope back into the pre-natal period in western societies can be compared with ethno-graphic accounts of its opposite: the *deferral* of social identification until well past the time of birth in many societies, entry into society requiring ritual, rather than technological processes, for this to be carried out (see Chapters 2 and 3).

Embodiment and identification

As the above examples have demonstrated, in the process of age identification there is an ongoing tri-partite relationship between social environment, human agency and the body. Indeed, this is the processual form through which, over the life course, we come to know that we are ageing and this is how we get to take on age-based identities. Jenkins sums up this perspective as follows:

> Individual identity – embodied in selfhood – is not meaningful in isolation from the social world of other people. Individuals are unique and variable, but selfhood

is thoroughly socially constructed, a product of the processes of primary and subsequent socialisation, and in the ongoing processes of social interaction within which individuals define and redefine themselves and others throughout their lives.... An understanding emerges of the 'self' as an ongoing and, in practice simultaneous, synthesis of (internal) self-definition and the (external) definitions of oneself offered by others (1996: 20).

For Jenkins then the '*internal – external dialectic of identification* [is] the process whereby all identities – individual or collective – are constituted' (Jenkins, 1996: 20, emphasis in original). Working from this view therefore, although individuals *are* unique, their identities are constructed in and through embodied interaction with others.

However if, as Hall (2000) argues, identification also concerns a lack of fit with what one might be, as well as an experience of distance from what one tries or hopes not to be, then it is the identities of *other* people which allow this process to be engaged with. Thus it is embodied *interaction* which is described by Rapport as 'the synthesising phenomenon whereby private, individualised meanings and public cultural forms intersect' (1993: 164). Unlike a structure-based conception of age-based identity therefore, which gives rise to timeless, empty categories, this notion of ageing as embodied – rather than biologically driven – acknowledges the dynamic, processual and creative nature of the everyday experience of growing up and growing old. In that it captures the transience integral to human existence, it revitalises theoretical perspectives which either freeze the scope of the moment within 'structure' or shrink it down to individual 'choice'. That which we would commonly call the individual, what Cohen (1994) terms the irreducible organic self which traverses the life course, is thus in a state of endlessly becoming rather than being.

A significant but unremarked consequence of such an understanding of identity formation, and one which is central to our understanding of social identities across the life course, is that the categorical and cultural identity of, for example, 'child', 'adult', or 'old person' only acquires its meaning from the ways in which it comes to be embodied by individuals in social space and across time (James, 2000 and James and James, 2001). These empty, age-based social categories can therefore be seen as aspects of a world of 'cultural objects' which are animated only through the actions and interactions of individuals (Rapport, 1993). As Rapport argues:

Individuals then use these objectified forms and make them subjective. They 'consume' cultural objects, incorporate them into their daily lives and, in personalising them, use them to develop a subjective world-view. In this way they also maintain them. Thus, in any social phenomenon form and content constitute one reality (1993: 164).

Following Rapport, therefore, we can argue that cultural ideas of what childhood is or what old age means are produced through their enactment and embodiment by individuals. It is this process which can account for change over historical time in conceptions of what children, adults or old people are or should be. Our ideas about life-course categories – our popular images of 'the child' or 'the pensioner' – are, in effect, the cultural sediment or product of the very process of dialectical identification – that is, the ways in which society's embodied members reflexively live out those categories at any point in time. This explains why life course categories are merely contingent and why they vary both in time and space. Thus, exploring identity as a process which involves the internal – external dialectic of identification not only challenges our view of the 'individual' and 'society' as separate entities; it also provides a way of mapping out the implications of embodied social interactions for 'social structure'. As a result, the fine detail of the very processes of identification can themselves can be investigated.

Conclusion

In earlier chapters, we referred to the ways in which aged identities have been quite literally carved upon the body within the institution of a rite of passage. From footbinding, scarification and circumcision through to school uniforms which act transformatively to age the body, the flesh is the vehicle through which identities come to be known. However, as noted, such accounts play up the influence of social structure as a force which imposes itself upon the bodies of society's members. Their own experience and indeed their agency is downplayed.

Though this inadequacy might seem to have been redressed through later postmodern, agency-focused perspectives which highlight choice and diversity, this is not the case. Indeed there is a danger, as we have suggested here, of simply following the path of the pendulum, 'structure'- and 'agency'-focused accounts of identity complementing the other's partiality. Thus, in this chapter we have sought to break free of this pattern by addressing more recent work on the body and we have endeavoured to move the debate forward by refusing the structure/agency binary. In its place we have argued that those other binaries – culture/nature or discourse/materiality – also need to be collapsed. The body has to be re-cast as the undissolvable product of both nature *and* culture and *the fact* of human embodiment seen as integral to the *process* of identification.

Drawing on Battersby's work on the body, which sees it as a fluid and dynamic element in a complex system of identification, it becomes possible to see how a focus on embodiment will allow both structural and agency perspectives to be brought together as a set of integral and integrative modes through which it becomes possible to know that we are aging. In the following chapters, we explore this proposition through three empirical arenas within which age assumes importance in terms of the contemporary western life course: gender and sexuality; the family and work and consumption practices.

8

Gender, Sexuality and the Body in the Life Course

Introduction

We have been arguing that the body is simultaneously a material object or possession and the site of human experience. Only by inhabiting the flesh, via the processes of what Turner (1998) calls bodily enselvement, can social identity be acquired. The site within which this process or practice takes place is, as noted, the social. This is a milieu made up, of course, of the similarly enselved bodies of others.

Thus, while structure-focused and discursive accounts highlight sources of power which are external to the individual, we return in this chapter to our key question – how do we know we are ageing – by focusing on the actual workings of systems of power with respect to the assumption and allocation of aged identities and their embodiment as elderly men or women, young boys or girls. Agency and choice imply an empowered and embodied individual. Yet, as personal experience reminds us, our access to power and control *is* often constrained. Since we negotiate, acquire and practice our identities within social milieux, that process inevitably brings us up against other individuals who themselves also exercise agency and choice. They are thus making choices which are potentially counter to our own interests.

Certainly, as Rapport (1997) argues, such a model of the workings of power, at this level, escapes the dangers of positing totalitarian, ideological systems which unfold haphazardly to structure identities regardless of the choices and actions of individuals. However, it nonetheless side steps the question of how the agency of one individual may, in practice, constrain that of another. Within the liberal tradition, as Rapport notes, individuals [are] expected to seek to make the 'best selves' for themselves that they can, not allow this potential to be curtailed by cultural, social or linguistic norms (whether this curtailment is self inflicted or imposed) and grant others the space to do likewise (1997: 188).

For Rapport, this is not however sufficient as an explanation of how the agency of individuals is played out in practice. Dalley (1988) similarly explains that the value of freedom is interpreted differently within different political traditions. Freedom to act without external constraint – for example from the state – is as necessary as freedom from oppression: 'the freedom of one individual must not be paid for by the denial of freedom to other' (1988: 42). Clearly, this is a problem which many liberal democracies have tried to address through political strategies which might 'level the playing field' and enable each individual to operate from the same starting point. The net effect of this, however, as Rapport observes, is that 'in the actual workings of most (if not all) of the world's societies and cultures, it is not a "politics of individual rights" which is being played out, so much as a "politics of common good"' (1997: 189). Working towards this common good may, within communitarian regimes for example, end up impoverishing and over determining individuals, rather than as was intended, freeing or empowering them (see James and James, 2001).

Thus, the postmodern theoretical perspectives on age and identity, depicted in Chapter 6, which emphasise flexibility and creativity across the life course, often downplay the fact that, in practice, individuals vary considerably in the extent to which they are able to exercise choice. And, in this chapter, we consider the extent to which gender and sexuality might differently enable or constrain the choices made by men and women as they age across the life course.

Drawing on the theoretical discussions which have been unfolding in previous chapters, we take up here this key dimension of identity difference to ask how ageing intersects with gendered, sexualised identities. Do men and women age differently? Or is the biology of ageing tempered by society and their respective embodiment therefore differently experienced? This chapter thus grounds our question – of how it is that we come to know that we are ageing – by discussing how, within the contemporary western life course where the age of the body is seen as key, same-aged bodies may nonetheless display marks of difference which become a focus for gendered and sexualised classifications.

For example, how and to what extent are aged individuals constructed as sexually active or available? Or, alternatively, as sexually unavailable? What is the nature of appropriate partnerships between aged individuals thought to be? Is this, in large – or small – part, determined by position or stage in the life course or indeed by the materiality of the body? Or do individuals have and make choices about the ways in which they express themselves and their identities as gendered or sexualised beings? Sexual practice and indeed sexual identity is in many ways difficult to legislate for. Since these constitute areas of life conceived of as both the most 'private' and the most individual, people, potentially, have considerable scope for agency and choice. Yet often, ironically, their sexual lives unfold in a highly constrained, structured or preordained manner and one which is, as we shall explore, often age-related.

As a case study, therefore, gender and sexuality require us not only to explore the ways in which age intersects with the other aspects of identity, but also to reveal the existence of subtler systems of power which operate covertly as a form of moral and structural regulation over individual agency via a micro-politics of discipline (Turner, 1987). And, in later chapters, we follow through this discussion by exploring other empirical examples – how the family, the workplace and consumption practices similarly provide a framework for the embodiment of aged identities.

One of the central questions to be addressed in this chapter, therefore, is how in practice does modernist moral regulation intersect with postmodern fluidity and flow? Both remain very much in evidence. Is it through flexible processes of identification – identities being imposed, resisted and found to be untenable – that individuals draw upon, animate or sidestep the aged personae available? Or, is such freedom and choice only rarely able to be exercised in practice? Through taking a life-course perspective, which emphasises the temporal and spatial dimensions of this process, we begin here to plot the movement between identities which individuals undertake or experience, across time, with respect to gender and sexuality.

Constructing sexual identities

As noted, previous stage models of the life course often relied heavily upon contrasting sexual identities as a way of demarcating one social category from another. However, the so-called puberty rituals discussed by Van Gennep in relation to traditional societies represented, as we suggested, transitions in *social* status, rather than the ritualisation of physical puberty per se ([1908] 1960). Nonetheless, male and female initiations *would* be separately conducted. Thus it was not just the transition from childhood to adulthood which was being socially marked and celebrated, but also the movement from boyhood to manhood and, less commonly, from girlhood to womanhood.

Accompanying such age-gendering of social status is also its sexualisation. Thus, for example, within the western tradition the absence of sexual feelings, and most particularly sexual practice, is constituted as core to notions of childhood innocence. Adulthood, by contrast, is partly constituted through sexual activity. Considerable importance is attached to the frequency and intensity of desire put into practice with, ironically, both too little and too much sexual activity rapidly regarded as key pathological conditions of adulthood (Irvine, 1995). During old age, by contrast, and in line with childhood, sexual quietude and unavailability are key markers of identity (Hockey and James, 1993). Sex in old age is viewed far more equivocally than it was during adulthood. Moreover bodily changes, such as loss of skin tone and the reduction in the capacity for penetrative or reproductive sex, make it much harder for older adults who wish to resist an ageist desexualising to live up to hegemonic media images of sexual practice. These seem, so often, to be narrowly focused around delimited genital contact between slim, fit mid-lifers. Thus, while the postmodern life course may admit child beauty pageants and third-age sky diving, which suggest that 'one is as old as one feels', at the same time a modernist moral regulation continues to bite hard in the area of sexual practice and to limit and constrain individual agency.

This modernist discourse of age-based sex emerged in the late nineteenth century. It was an aspect of other systems of discipline and control which sought to differentiate between 'normal' and 'deviant' sexualities, bodies and mental states, and all three were connected via the emergent medical science of that period:

> fin-de-siècle anatomists of sex ... were involved in attempts to shore up cultural order by reinforcing sex-roles and middle-class morality in the teeth of the unnerving perils and affronts of modern life: streetwalking, child prostitution,

domestic violence, incest, and all the other festering moral scandals of the city of dreadful night – to say nothing of sexual anarchy amongst 'new women', Bohemian artists, intellectuals and other 'degenerates'. Sexology was also proffering a practical toolkit, the classificatory and diagnostic expertise required to administer the asylums, hospitals, reformatories and gaols charged to cope with the chronic masturbators, simpletons, child molesters, rapists, pregnant teenagers, prostitutes and other sex offenders who terrified nineteenth-century elders and legislators (Porter and Teich, 1994: 13–14).

This sexual regulation via life-course categories coincided with the chronologisation of the life course in other social arenas – such as the registration of births, the introduction of compulsory schooling and the trend towards excluding older adults from paid work on the basis of age rather than infirmity. Medicalised health care, coupled with health promotion, became seen as a key component of moral regulation, age being used as an important source of legitimation for biomedical classificatory systems and giving rise to the specialist disciplines of paediatrics and gerontology (see Chapter 7).

However, gender is particularly salient here since the emergent structural regulation of sexuality across the life course was brought to bear more upon girls and women, than upon boys and men. From the nineteenth century onwards, medicalised framings of women's health, for example, focused on their sexual and reproductive systems while marginalising life-threatening illnesses such as heart disease which remains today a major killer of women. The degree of sexual desire experienced by a woman was, for instance, medically regulated. So-called 'excessive' interest in sex, said to be revealed in masturbatory practices, was pathologised. It was seen to be associated with mental instability. 'Cures' were sought through bodily interventions of all kinds and often taken to extremes through clitoridectomy (Showalter, 1987: 75–8). An example Showalter cites is of a twenty-year old girl who

> had suffered 'great irregularities of temper,' had been 'disobedient to her mother's wishes,' was sexually assertive in sending her visiting cards to men she liked, and spent 'much time in serious reading' (1987: 77).

A clitoridectomy performed, the girl was later married and became pregnant, proof indeed of the dangers of sex for women! As Showalter observes, wryly, such women 'with their sexuality excised . . . gave up their independent desires and protests, and became docile childbearers', thus swapping one kind of female identity for another (1987: 77). The regulation of the growth of sexual awareness in childhood was followed by its further gender-based regulation in the transition from girl to woman. Thus, both historically worked together to control girls' agency as sexual beings, a pattern which persists today.

It is apparent, for example, that the developing gender and sexual awareness and agency of children, and of girls in particular, was always and still remains in tension with conceptions of childhood innocence. The persistence of this view contemporarily has meant that, within the UK for instance, the provision of sex education in schools has become a highly politicised area of social policy. Plans for the distribution of contraceptive advice for younger teenagers, and most recently the plan to make the morning-after pill available from school nurses, are all subject to heated debate. In comparison with other parts of Europe, for example Holland and Denmark, what sex education is available in the UK often constitutes a set of warnings, rather than practical advice and information and is rarely suited to the needs of individual boys and girls. Thus, as Holland *et al.* (1998) argue, gendered patterns of inequality are in such ways shored up, with boys often being represented as active desiring agents and girls as simply the victims of male desire. And, as the fierce debates of the late 1980s revealed, the issue of homosexuality remains explosive with regard to the 'inappropriate' age at which it can be practised and even talked about. This is testimony to the persistence of nineteenth-century pathologising definitions of sexual practice and the sexualising of, usually, male social identities. In the rest of this chapter, we consider examples of the ways in which individual agency is both suppressed and/or empowered by such structural forces in the constitution of gendered identities across the life course through the medium of the body.

Gendering sexual inequality across the life course

As argued earlier, age-related activities and processes have implications for the ways in which identities unfold across the later life course. Here we begin by discussing the sexual education of girls in the UK. This continues to be seen as far more problematic than that of boys, often consisting largely in filtering, if not concealing, information and, as Scott *et al.* (1998) point out, public anxiety about girls' access to the information about sex contained in teenage magazines may be misguided for preserving ignorance is no way to preserve purity. This can be seen from the continuing high rates of teenage pregnancy in the UK. For girls, teenage magazines may ironically be one of the few sources of information and help that is available to them in a culture which fails to empower them with sufficient knowledge through other media.

The wider ramifications of this social construction of girls' need for protection are pointed out by Katz (1993) who suggests that they are constrained in their access to public space. In societies as diverse as the Sudanese village of Howa and the cities of Stockholm and Baltimore, 'many of the restrictions on children's movements were concerned primarily with access to girls' bodies', she argues. A New York based study (Blakely, cited in Katz, 1993: 102) identified parental prohibitions on entering physically 'unsafe' and socially 'dangerous' areas for both boys and girls. Yet these apparently age-based conceptualisations of risk were recast in gendered practices. The management of boys' movement in space was often far more lax than that for girls. Thus discourses of sex and gender intersect differentially with age to impinge on the everyday lives of children. In childhood, then, can be found the seeds of patterns of inequality and identity difference which will work to either empower them or restrict their choices later in the life course when children grow into adult women and men. Thus, it is as these restrictions begin to bite that children come to know that they are ageing.

Many studies (for example James, 1993; Thorne, 1993; Connolly, 1998; Kelley *et al.*, 1999) have established that the ways in which boys and girls reveal their awareness of gender is through demonstrating rather different kinds of sexual knowledge and behaviour. As Thorne (1993) observes, in public, boys actively brag about and demonstrate their awareness of sexual matters with an emphasis on genital sexuality. Girls, by contrast, share 'talk focused less on actual sex than on themes of romance', differences borne out consistently by other research (1993: 144). Connolly's (1998) study of five- and six-year olds goes further, suggesting that the aggressive and highly sexualised talk of the 'bad' boys objectifies girls as sexual conquests. It is, he suggests, one of the ways in which concepts of masculinity are learnt and perpetuated within the boys' peer group. Connolly describes, for example, how the girls would complain to the teachers that the boys had been spoiling their game by 'making groaning noises while thrusting their pelvises up against them' (1998: 142).

Young girls who overtly display sexual knowledge, on the other hand, put their femininity at risk, the polarising identities of 'good girl' and 'slag' drawing upon the 'virgin'/'whore' dichotomy of earlier nineteenth-century thinking (Thorne, 1993). Given the expectation that boys will and do not only exchange sexual knowledge, but also circulate information among themselves about particular girls and their willingness to participate in sex talk and practice, it can be argued, therefore, as Lees (1986) does, that girls are subject to powerful surveillance on the basis of the reputations which boys build for them.

Such observed differences raise questions therefore about children's awareness of adult sexual practices and what significance the taking on of these kinds of gendered and sexualised identities during childhood might have in terms of their future adult lives. Worryingly, for example, Plummer argues that stories of rape have become such a common feature of everyday life that 'no self respecting soap opera can now afford to ignore' them (1995: 73). No longer the 'crime in the closet', rape is increasingly portrayed as bound up with ordinary life. Though of course not all men are rapists, the institutional expectations of male and female roles remain consistently imaged, he suggests, through, respectively, 'active dominance and passive compliance' (1995: 73). These are exactly the kinds of behaviour which are exhibited by children in their performance of sexualised and gendered identities.

Thus, despite the rise of feminism and the supposed sexual revolution of the second half of the twentieth century, it seems that girls remain distracted and absorbed by the complexities of selecting the hair-styling, clothes and make-up from which an appropriate feminine identity may be read off the body. This is the filtered knowledge of sex vouchsafed to girls and therefore, arguably, girls' potential to embody different kinds of sexualised identities remains limited and rooted in men's, rather than women's, desires. Thus, as Holland *et al.* (1998) demonstrate, through interviews with 148 young women and 46 young men in Britain, both girls' and boys' sexual practice is subject to surveillance by the 'male-in-the-head' which represents sex as penetration. Aimed at male orgasm, such a representation remains silent on the topic of women's desires. Indeed, female bodies were experienced by young people as sites of embarrassment, rather than desire. Being 'always material, hairy, discharging, emitting noises, susceptible to pleasure and pain', embodiment for young women meant feeling that they 'had to discipline their unruly bodies into conformity with male desires' (1998: 8–9). In addition, contraception could not easily be put into

practice by girls. They believed the carrying of condoms would com-
promise their femininity, making them be seen as inappropriately
'knowing' and at risk of the label 'slag'.

Among boys and men, however, the presence of a condom confers
the honourable status which derives from active male sexuality.
Heterosexuality, Holland *et al.* (1998) therefore conclude, is not
constituted through a balanced opposition between femininity and
masculinity. Rather, they suggest, the 'male-in-the-head' drives the
behaviours of *both* young women and men, rendering heterosexuality a thinly-veiled form of masculinity. They conclude that 'femininity
is constructed from within heterosexuality and on male territory', a
formulation which, as we show later, may continue to shape
women's pleasure and sexual health across the life course, albeit in
rather different ways as the ageing process takes hold (1998: 11).

Gendered bodies across the life course

From childhood onwards, then, girls and boys negotiate a heavily
sexualised path which is oriented towards the present and future
management of their own bodies throughout their lives. However,
as Thorne (1993) observes, sexual dimorphism means that a girl's
developing sexuality is, unlike that of boys', not only more visible
and obvious, but also occurs earlier. In Prendergast's (1995) study,
girls offered a set of narratives about the difficulties of managing
menarche and menstruation in the mixed-sex environment of
school, ranging from stories of accidents and public embarrassment
when things go wrong, to stories of the power of the male gaze and
the failure of the school to provide adequate sanitary facilities. She
sums up their experience as follows:

> this social mapping of gender and difference around menstruation and the body
> in school is the naming and disguising of what are in fact *social processes, material
> circumstances, ideological forms* as 'biological', and therefore, natural, legitimate
> and inevitable. When girls speak so eloquently of the onset of puberty as a 'blow',
> about being 'hit', 'clobbered' I suspect that this is partly what they comprehend,
> a metaphor for what is to come, the unfairness of being a girl, inexorably bound to
> a body that's treated as, and feels unequal, about which they can do very little
> (Prendergast, 1995: 362, emphasis in original).

As Laws (1990) reveals, girls' concern with their bodies is intensive.
Through data drawn from interviews with men, she articulates the

notion of an 'etiquette' of menstruation which requires that girls and women be consistently vigilant, not only about the sight and smell of menstrual blood, but even about the products which allow them to hide it. Techniques learnt during adolescence, such as the double concealment of tampon cases which masquerade as lipsticks, reflects this etiquette which, like the rigid practices imposed within Victorian social life, testifies to a hierarchy of power in which girls' and women's sexual identities and procreative potential must be concealed. Indeed, only as the twentieth century drew to its close was the advertising of sanitary protection at last permitted on television.

During childhood and adolescence, the body is therefore the site and vehicle of and for the articulation of the broad-ranging social practices and institutional structures through which masculine and feminine identities are reproduced. However, this experiential grounding of the adult-gendered identities which will be later taken on can be disrupted during childhood by the very materiality of the body itself. Thus, as Thorne (1993) describes, when 'heavyset Latina with full breasts and rounded hips' arrived in a fourth-grade classroom of an American school, her appearance and thus her child-identity was constantly scrutinised and discussed for, at nine years old, her body was regarded as more like that of a woman than a child. And well-developed, big-breasted Lenore, who wore tight-fitting jumpers and flirted with the boys was deemed in need of parental guidance so that her body and behaviour might be better brought into line with her age. Most recently, in the UK, the refusal by doctors to consider a 15-year old girl's request for breast implants reflects a similar conceptual disjunction with respect to age and social identity: until she reaches the age of adulthood, 18, the girl's body must remain child-like.

This latter example is highly indicative of the relationship between age, body and identity. It underscores the body as a key site for identification across the life course in that it mediates the demands of both structure and agency. The request for implants had been made by the girl herself, with her parents' permission. It was a request which focused on a claim that big breasts are, for adult women, the passport to fame and fortune. Thus, to have an implant at 15 years old would, the girl argued, enable her to take charge of her future adult life. She envisaged her new breasts as a source of personal self esteem and confidence, as well as serving to attract the attention of men. The doctors refusal was, however, on grounds of age alone. They ignored the gendered symbolism of the breast as a powerful identity marker and route to adult social status in western cultures. This role of the body is something which was, however, clearly articulated by adolescent boys who were later interviewed about the matter:

> big breasts, hips, all the curves in the right places but not fat – you've got to try to get her number, because that's the type of girl you want to be seen with. But if you've got a girl with no breasts people are going to think it's because you're not a man enough to get a real girl (*Guardian*, 8 January, 2001).

As we have argued, such forms of gender and age-based moral regulation can be traced as far back as the nineteenth century, working to shape and order identities and processes of gender identification across the life course. But, as adulthood approaches, the medical profession comes to play an increasingly prominent role in the production of gendered identities. While employment represents an important transition to adulthood for young men (Willis, 1977, and see Chapter 10), it is motherhood which contributes significantly to a mature feminine identity and conception, antenatal care, delivery and childcare are all aspects of women's lives which have been consistently medicalised (Oakley, 1979; Martin, 1987; Foster, 1995). As Jordanova (1989) has argued, women's bodies played a core role within the professionalisation of medicine itself. The post-enlightenment fostering of a world view which saw 'nature' as a focus for control by science provided a context within which knowledge of the inner workings of the female reproductive system occupied an iconic role. Moreover, as Turner wryly observes, 'since in the medical literature both menstruation and pregnancy are regarded as "medical problems", there is a basic logic to the medical view that women are, as it were, natural patients' (1987: 102). By contrast, men's sexual needs are privileged without them being required to subject themselves to regular interventions by members of the medical profession.

Thus, for example, as Foster (1995) shows, the attention now paid to pre-conceptual health means that even the most everyday aspects of women's lifestyles must be made subservient to the needs of those family members yet to be conceived. Thus, women are urged to limit their consumption of certain foods and alcohol *before* conception as well as during pregnancy and to pay attention to their own health for the well-being of the foetus. Similarly, advances in foetal medicine – particularly developments in ultrasonography which allow the foetus to be represented in motion and independently of the mother – mean that its interests, as a future person, may gain priority over those of the mother. Thus, to return to our argument made in Chapter 7, though during mid-life a woman's self identity may indeed become fragmentary and shifting, this may not be through lifestyle choices of her own making. It may simply be a function of her gendered and chronologised position in the life course. Indeed, those women who do exert their right to choose, as debates over abortion suggest, may be held morally responsible and stand accused for choosing to assert their own self identity over that of the identity of their unborn child. Here then, chronology is disrupted by science in relation to the rights of citizenship.

On the other hand, it is important to recognise that femininities and masculinities are not fixed. They emerge, instead, as moments within the flow of individual choice and agency and across the life course. Indeed, as Holland *et al.* (1998) cited above suggest, it is precisely through individual women's participation and collusion that heterosexuality becomes so firmly embedded within the discourse of masculinity. Furthermore, what their data also show is that within the privacy of one-to-one sexual relationships young women do exercise some degree of power and agency, or at least engage in a process of empowerment:

> men can resist masculinity by allowing communicative, trusting and loving rela-
> tionships to develop and taking responsibility for their own behaviour. Women
> can resist femininity by defining their own situation, and developing a more active
> agency than conventional femininity allows' (Holland *et al.*, 1998: 146).

Similarly, Martin (1987) shows, despite such constraints, as they grow older, women may be able to redefine the terms of their embodiment and, in relation to birthing practices, she argues that 'as a result of many individual acts and many activities of organisations, doctors and hospitals have changed their practice' (1987: 189).

To develop this idea further, let us therefore now look at the consequences of processes of gender identification for men across the life course with respect to choice. If heterosexuality privileges an aggressive masculinity within a discourse of predominantly penetrative sex what, if any, choices and freedoms are open to men as they mature? By contrast with older women, whose recent access to new reproductive technologies and post-menopausal pregnancy has attracted scathing criticism, the persistence of a sexualised identity into later life among men has been endorsed by viagra. Indeed, this extension of a sexualised identity, including the capacity to procreate, is seen as a cause for celebration rather than concern, even though children born to men at the very end of their lives are unlikely to receive their social or emotional support as death may quickly intercede. But what if, in mid-life, a man's body can no longer be identified with the fit and active masculine body of his youth, honed into shape, as Watson (2000) suggests, primarily through physical activity and sport?

Watson (2000: 96) argues that middle-aged men look back to youth to sustain their present self-identities. This backward-glancing man, reluctant to acknowledge the bodily changes he regards as negative, may partly explain why men resist the injunctions of health promotion. In addition, and more charitably, their pragmatic interpretations of culturally appropriate scripts such as the 'bread-winner' 'the guardian' or the 'sturdy oak' may contribute to their inability to acknowledge the failings of their own bodies (2000: 142). But, with respect to sexual function, this slippage between body and self-image across the male life course is less stoically embraced – namely, the financial dilemma now faced by a National Health Service confronted by an ageing male population wishing to recapture youthful potency via a chemical remedy.

Drawing on interview data with middle-aged men, Watson says that 'it is the known body, the developing physical body through which these informants, as boys, recall experiencing the world', with the body being subject to abuse and testing through exercise and excess, through 'squeezing 25 hours into 24' (Watson, 2000: 96).

> It is a mental thing. A man can live like a couch potato, he can drink 5 or 6 pints every 2 or 3 nights, he can eat all the unhealthy foods, but inside his head he ... believes that he is ... Rambo ... he will try and do 20 or 30 press-ups and will probably damage himself (Watson, 2000: 97).

Thus, a focus on masculinity and age across the life course returns us to the proposition that processes of identification do arise in the flow of time. They are not fixed coat-racks for the self (Nicholson, 1995). Structure melds with agency over time to produce particular and particularised embodied and gendered identities.

Gender in longevity?

To explore further our tri-partite model, it remains then to consider the role of the body in the production of gendered and sexualised identities during later life. It is this period in the life course where ostensibly the body provides the most marked indications that ageing has taken place. Grey hair, sagging, wrinkly skin, hair thinning and hair loss, arthritic joints and deteriorating vision are taken as irrefutable signs of the ageing process. But how are these highly visible signs of bodily decay and old age experienced and embodied and to what extent does this vary for men and women?

Fairhurst (1998) challenges the long-held view that there is double standard of ageing in later life, whereby women, but not men, must remain vigilant about their physical appearance. Instead, from her empirical research among late middle-aged people, she argues that both women and men strive to 'make the best of themselves' and to avoid the accusation that, through their behaviour or appearance, they might seem like 'mutton dressed up as lamb'. Interestingly, she argues that it is children who are important moral guardians of this endeavour. They 'call upon typifications of appropriate dress for specific life stages in order to inform parents of their transgression of the acceptable' (1998: 263). Such power to constrain the bodily expression of another is normally exerted by parents over their offspring. Chronologisation is thus once more disrupted by the body, such practices prefiguring those more humiliating processes of infantilisation which in deep old age work to give young carers a more totalising control over older people's bodies (Hockey and James, 1993). In middle age, therefore, as Fairhurst argues, to 'grow old gracefully' was important to both men *and* women, as a way to ward off criticism from those who are younger.

Thus, during late middle age the body serves as a continual material reminder of the ageing process, pushing the self relentlessly towards the identity of an old-aged person. One of the ways in which people of 50 and 60 years old strove to avoid this reclassification of their selves was, therefore, through the separation of the self from the materiality of the body – they reminded themselves, for example, that 'you are as old as you feel'. In this way, as Fairhurst comments, though 'the body is subject to change with the passing of time, the self, if not totally untouched, is less likely to be affected by such chronological issues' (1998: 268–9).

One consequence of this dislocation of self from the body is that the steady effects of time upon the body may no longer signify the ageing process. Instead, it is the interruption of this gradual process which is taken as a sign that ageing has taken place. Thus, for example, for both men and women, the onset of sudden illness episodes served as more significant benchmarks for conferring meaning on the process of growing older than bodily changes per se since the former prefigured death and the end of life.

The diminution of the significance of gender differences in later life, with regard to the experience of the body in everyday life, is further evidenced in one man's account of the declining importance of sexuality in relationships between men as well as those between men and women:

> on the other hand, another way it [growing older] doesn't upset me is that when I'm at work and meet men of my age I am talking on the same level because all this jousting, the sexual bit, those sexual overtones have gone now. I don't have to do that anymore. There's no to-ing and fro-ing that there used to be. So that's gone and you find that you can have a conversation with a man it means exactly what it is – a conversation and you can be friends (Fairhurst, 1998: 270–1).

Gone is the youthful bragging and banter associated with the expression of masculinity and, taking its place, is a new and less competitive style of friendship and masculine identity.

Choice and identity across the life course

Chapter 6 explored arguments for the emergence of a postmodern life course, flagging up the centrality of consumerism as a vehicle which secures greater individual flexibility when it comes to life course stages. With regard to the part played by gender and sexuality within the negotiation of age and identity across the life course such consumerist trends, especially within healthcare, are important. Indeed, the implications for sexuality and sexual identity of a consumerist society are core to our argument that the body is often a site for struggle between proliferating identity options and provides important ways in which the ageing process is managed, its chronology being either disrupted, interrupted or postponed.

Cosmetic surgery provides an example whereby identity might seem to be facilitated by life-style choice and individual agency. Reaching its apogee in transgendering surgical techniques, the body becomes the potential vehicle of a whole newly gendered self, but, for older women, breast reshaping, liposuction or face-lifts help obliterate or disguise the changes wrought by age. And, for middle-aged women, the chemical magic of hormone replacement therapy (HRT) prolongs and extends a symbolic youthfulness beyond the chronology imposed 'naturally' by the body. Davis (1995) suggests that women who opt for such body modifications may not simply be the victims of patriarchal beauty myths. Her data suggest, instead, that women choose surgery not as part of a blind search for sexual attractiveness but as an informed choice which will bring their bodies into line with more acceptable versions of the middle-aged body and so render them *less*, rather than more visible. Much the same might be said of men who, through body-building exercises, chemical treatment and dietary regimes, choose to reform their bodies and through so doing rebuild their sense of self and maintain the vigour of youth (Bloor *et al.*, 1998).

Thus, though feminist theory and medical sociology have challenged the apparently altruistic motivations of the medical profession and the ideologies of health, such examples require us to rethink arguments which locate power *solely* within the remit of large-scale institutions. Not only is it important to recognise the role of individual agency, but, in the growth of consumer power and opportunities for consumption, we find evidence of individuals themselves taking control of the processes of identification which connect age, gender and sexuality.

For example, via new reproductive technologies, individual men and women now have alternative means to build families, potentially offering the possibility of flexible patterns of childbearing for those for whom a parental identity might otherwise be denied – single, lesbian, older and post-menopausal women or gay men through surrogacy. As Franklin (1997) argues, NRTs also offer new choices for the future to the child-less, albeit ambiguously, given the likelihood of their continual failure to conceive. Thus, critiques that cite IVF as intrusive to women's lives and see women as simply colluding in the medicalisation of their reproductive control are confounded by women's own acceptance of the possibility of both successful and unsuccessful outcomes and their decision to continue treatment.

Similarly, though medical interventions in childbirth such as induction are often critiqued as simply serving the interests of the medical profession, there is evidence that they are being made use of by women whose professional commitments require them to give birth at more predictable times (Foster, 1995: 38). Finally, Diane Blood who fought for access to her dead husband's semen in order to have his baby showed the capacity of the individual to overthrow institutional power and to challenge the 'normative structures and values of family and kinship...that currently shape and direct the social organisation of reproduction (Simpson, 1999: 30).

Conclusion

These examples therefore contrast with other arguments presented in this chapter. They show the body to be a far from rigid vehicle which constrains the production of gendered and sexualised identities and that, within a consumerist society, the ageing body is rendered infinitely more elastic and flexible than we have hitherto allowed. Through IVF, childbirth can now take place at a much later stage in women's lives, even post-menopause, thus potentially reordering traditional generational relations within families. Pre-natal ultrasonography and other medical tests allow women and men to make choices about giving birth to children with disabilities or permit foetal sex selection, unleashing both a positive and negative commentary about the ethics involved in the fashioning of so-called designer babies. Drugs such as viagra and HRT allow the progression from mid-life to later-life sexuality to be deferred, opening up the potential for new kinds of sexual relations to take place between partners of rather different ages and thus overturning the more traditional preferences and practices within the western tradition for sexual relations to be between co-eval age mates. Though, currently, the political and ethical debates which these possibilities throw up are far from resolved, and it is within this arena that issues of identity are often central to competing claims to citizenship, nonetheless, there is clearly some scope for individuals to transcend what have previously been seen as the 'insurmountable' constraints of a chronologised life course.

This chapter has thus explored the ways in which the ideas of gender and sexual practice work to differentiate identities across the life course, intersecting variously with age-based classifications and the materiality of the ageing body itself. It has revealed the complex ways in which, even within this one arena, identity is both ascribed, assumed and re-ascribed. In some quarters, therefore, we find claims that the body is indeed infinitely malleable and the aged identity which it encompasses and produces is correspondingly flexible. Such a view points to the importance of seeing the scope for the exercise of agency, even within strong regimes of power. Thus, although choices might be said to be removed, *choice* remains.

Citing Sartre's views on the necessity and unavoidability of freedom, Craib argues, 'If I am clapped in irons and suspended upside down in a dungeon, I still have to choose how I will suffer' (1998: 34). Genetic research, transplant techniques and the possibility of cloning as a way of growing new body parts for old bodies would seem, therefore, to support this possibility with the result that death itself – the final threat to identity at the end of the life course – seems to be receding.

Nonetheless, such freedoms for the individual, as Turner (1992) and others argue, may curb the choices of others. Within this dynamic and shifting context, the ageing body will continue to represent both a strong constraint, as well as a possible resource. Indeed the limits of the body are perhaps already being felt increasingly powerfully, the financial motivation for research in medical science being fed by a growing refusal in some quarters to accept the particular body and indeed the period of the lifespan with which the individual has been allocated.

If following Battersby (see Chapter 7) we see body form, and by extension social identity, as 'not something that is imposed on matter, but which erupts in matter or is a state of matter' then what she offers is useful in helping us make sense of the simultaneity of the modernist and postmodernist framings of the embodiment of age, gender and sexuality across the life course which have been explored in this chapter (1993: 263).

9

Family Sociality across the Life Course

Introduction

In his memoir, *Out of Place*, Edward Said argues that 'all families invent their parents and children, give them a story, a character, fate and even a language' and he describes how his own family's invention had led him always to feel out of place (1999: 3). Said attributes this to the different ways in which a range of social identities were not only bestowed upon him but also refused for him during his childhood. He links this process firmly to the familial patterning of his life course across different times and spaces.

In Said's recollections we find ample and vivid confirmation, therefore, that if, as we have been arguing, one's sense of who one is arises in and through processes of social interaction then it is the family, traditionally regarded as the primary site of socialisation, which can be seen as one of the key contexts within which we come to know who we are as we age. While 'work' represents another primary site of identification across the life course as Chapter 10 will demonstrate, it cannot be separated out from family. Instead, it needs to be recognised as a time and space within which family continues to make itself felt in different ways at different points in a person's life. The data presented here, for example, show family events intruding upon the workplace, family space constituting a site for alternative or hybrid forms of work, and, in the case of family businesses such as farming, family structures providing the organising principle for work itself.

Thus, while we have chosen to make 'family' and 'work' the focus of two *separate* chapters, our discussion in both cases hinges upon their engagement and indeed intermeshing with one another. Structurally separated out within legislative systems and academic specialisms, when investigated from an agency-focused and life course perspective, we uncover the fluidity of work-based life course categories and their close association with the creative work of family-making.

The idea that family-making constitutes a form of 'work' shines through, for example, in Weeks *et al.*'s (1999) accounts of non-heterosexuals' 'everyday experiments' in making relationships and families. The authors point out that despite the 1960s' questioning of many traditional institutions, the concept of the family has recovered its currency as site for intimate relationships across the life course. When, for example, the 1988 Local Government Act legally enshrined the term 'pretended family relationships', it made the relationships of non-heterosexuals 'somehow not real' (1999: 83). And yet, in the 1990s, there remains a desire among non-heterosexuals for 'alternative families' or 'families of choice', for as Weeks *et al.*'s data show, non-heterosexuals draw on the metaphor of 'family' to describe relationships, friendships and other experiences of intimacy: 'I think the friendships I have are family'; 'we call each other family – you know, they're family... I have a blood family, but I have an extended family... my friends'; 'for me [family] means the gay community' (1999: 86–8). Thus 'family' can be seen not just as a site which bestows identity, but also a vehicle through which individuals seek to *create* identity. And, though arguably this happens most in childhood, as we age, so 'the family' works in different ways to locate us conceptually in the life course chronology of family life.

From this starting point, the present chapter therefore explores some of the ways in which family sociality works – or is made to work – to shape and contextualise particular aged identities across the life course of its members. Discussing 'the family', Morgan argues that, 'the mixing of ages and generations is a central and not accidental feature of family relationships' and, as we suggest, it is through this that a range of social roles and identities are both brought into being and cast aside, identities which both reflect and refract the ageing process (1996: 155). But this begs the question as to what is meant by the term 'the family'. Morgan notes that it has proved a continual subject for academic debate, being variously brought into focus and differently illuminated through its linkage with ideas of community, social class, sexuality and gender. The result is that a concern over definition has become 'one of the main factors contributing to a sense of fluidity and flux in family studies' (1996: 11). Noting this history, together with the powerful ideological roles which the concept of 'family' also has in policy and practice, in this chapter we take up Morgan's point that the family should therefore be seen as a topic to be explored in all its usages; it is not a resource to be used uncritically. Political controversy throughout Europe and America about issues such as adoption, surrogacy, divorce, partnerships rights and same-sex marriage (Neale, Wade and Smart, 1998; Weeks *et al.*, 1999), attest to the competing imperatives of different interest groups. All of these privilege potent conceptions of something called 'family'.

For our purposes, here, Morgan's concept of 'family practices' is particularly useful:

> If we talk about 'family practices' we are referring to certain practices which participants tend to think as being in some way 'different' and which may colour other practices which might overlap with them. Thus 'family practices' might overlap and interact with 'gendered practices'. This strategy should serve to underline the argument that 'family' is not a thing, without denying that notions of 'family' are important parts of the ways in which people understand and structure their lives (1996: 11).

In this definition, we find therefore more evidence to suggest that social identity is always in process, that it is never settled and fixed, but arises in and through the flow of social interactions of all kinds across time and space. This chapter will go on to ask, then, how it is that *aged* identities emerge through different kinds of family practices in order to explore the role of the family in shaping our experience and conceptions of the ageing process. First, however, we examine some of the ways in which identity has traditionally been understood in relation to ideas of 'the family' within sociology and anthropology.

Family structures and social roles

In his classic account of the workings of the social system, Talcott Parsons (1951) outlines the ways in which social order is maintained through the different layers of social life. Drawing on the Durkheimian concept of collective representations, Parson's analytic model represents social integration as a state achieved by cultural norms and values being voluntarily taken on by individuals. Through social interaction, individuals develop and reinforce these expectations about one another's behaviour which, over time, come to orient and routinise their actions towards each other. Collectively, such expectations are sedimented out as institutionalised roles and status positions in society and these social roles were, in Parsons view, central for explaining how it is that society endures. For Parsons, 'the family' was a key institution within which such processes took place. Within the family, young children learn their roles as 'children' and take on, through the socialisation process, the moral blueprint of social norms and values which, as adults, they will go on to reproduce when forming families of their own.

Notwithstanding the persuasive critiques of Parson's functionalist account – its determinism, its overemphasis on conformity and consensus and its neglect of social inequalities (Layder, 1994) – his identification of the significance of familial roles is not unimportant. It is precisely notions of, for example, 'mother' and 'good mothering' which, as we shall explore, constitute the common cultural stock of knowledge through which identities are helped into being. Becoming a 'mother' is only in part a function of biology for identification as a parent at particular points in the life course is also formed through sets of social expectations about what that identity entails.

Such expectations are socially constructed in and through particular social contexts and practices, forming the backdrop against which everyday life unfolds. For example, in the wake of the publication of the UK Government's Green paper, 'Supporting Families' (Ministerial Group on the Family, 1999), the National Family and Parenting Institute conducted an enquiry into attitudes towards the parenting role in 1999. It concluded that a large majority of people believe that 'parenting does not come naturally but is something that you have to learn'. This encouraged the Institute to mount a government-backed programme of support for developing 'positive parenting' roles and attitudes amongst the British public, and for the introduction of parentcraft classes for immature parents. And, as the post-war cohort of baby-boomers come of grand-parenting age, this role too is no longer a taken-for-granted aspect of later life, the outcome of 'natural' chronology. It is now, instead, attracting academic and media interest about how to do it properly. Citing the family as the location for the learning of age-specific identities, Farmer (2001), for example, argues that the earlier age of death among previous generations means that baby-boomer grandparents often grew up as children in families which lacked role models for grandparenting. Thus they did not come to learn the generational shifts in families which the birth of grandchildren initiates. In addition, medical and technological innovations have made the parenting practices they learned in the 1960s outdated, while the growing involvement of fathers in childcare supplants the practical and emotional support which older family members once gave automatically. On the birth of her first grandchild, Farmer therefore realised that, 'in reproductive terms, things had moved. I was now firmly in the back seat. This I had to work out, painfully, over the coming days of cooking and cleaning at my daughter's house' (*Guardian*, 18 January, 2001). And in the absence of this familial knowledge, learned at a grandparent's knee, Farmer's 'work' of learning to be a grandparent included consulting manuals with additional help from Grandparents Plus, a lobbying group launched in 2001 to 'achieve fuller recognition of the social and psychological value of what grandparents do' (*Guardian*, 18 January, 2001). In the context of widespread anxiety over the declining state of the family in Britain in the twenty-first century, such externalised sources of 'knowledge' about family chronology are held to be necessary if the UK Government's vision for the millennial family is to be realised – for such a family is envisioned through sets of specific role expectations linked to an age-based chronology.

In traditional formulations of social roles within the family, however, individuals are positioned within a static framework of familial identities, with associated roles and expectations being defined primarily in and through their positional relationships vis-à-vis one another. Thus 'father' becomes meaningful in relation to 'child', 'husband' in relation to 'wife' and 'brother' in relation to 'sister'. While such formulations may be at odds with changed family practices, in setting out these relationships, role theory did underscore the multiple roles which any individual family member might have at any one time and the many role-others with whom an individual interacts through the course of their life time. Role theory thus began to depict, in part, the complex ways in which, over time, 'the family' and a person's identity as a family member come to be constituted through different and changing forms of age-based sociality across the life course. Though hampered by its functionalist framing, as Morgan (1996) notes, role theorising nonetheless already pointed to the fluidity and variation which contemporary theorists recognise as fundamental to processes of self identification across the life course. An individual who is a son to his father, later in life, becomes a father to his own son.

Traditional anthropological studies of kinship have similarly laid some important groundwork for how family sociality might contemporarily be understood to contextualise aged identities across the life course. Though the highly schematic and abstract modelling of traditional kinship theory has largely been abandoned by contemporary anthropology and vigorously challenged in its claim to represent the reality of everyday kinship relations, some of its insights are not without merit. For example, a central practice of traditional kinship studies involved the identification of role identities through the schematic plotting of Ego's kinship relationships. This was achieved by tracing out biological links from one person to another, a methodology which, theoretically, enabled every individual within a network of kin to be located and positioned – as Father's Father (FF), Mother's Brother (MB), Father's Sister's Daughter (FZD) and so on. Over this abstract schema, the social pattern of expectations for behaviour and familial roles was laid. These expectations might be connected with patterns of marriage, lines of inheritance, systems of political allegiances or, more mundanely, the expectations a nephew might have for support from an uncle or other relative. Thus, in certain African societies, though there might appear to be a structural equivalence between Ego's cousins in terms of their genealogical positioning, only the MBD (Mother's Brother's Daughter) is valued as a potential spouse; in other societies, such as those of the Middle East, the FZD (father's sister's daughter) would traditionally be preferred. This system of abstract notation established through emphasising biological relatedness, ironically however, also assisted in demonstrating the ways in which 'biology' might, in practice, be glossed or ignored. In many societies, special naming systems enable whole groups of people to be classified together, with regard to expectations about their behaviour and roles towards Ego, even though they might be differentially located genealogically, and even generationally. For example, within an English genealogy, the term 'aunt' is used for both mother's sister and father's sister and can also be extended to friends of the family who have no biological link to it whatsoever. On the other hand, the assumptions and expectations of 'auntyness' become potentially problematic when strict age accounting means that a niece is older or the same age as her aunt!

As Carsten (2000) notes, academic interest in such formal studies of kinship began to fall away from about the 1970s onwards as 'part of a general shift in anthropological understanding from structure to practice, and from practice to discourse' for such ideal modelling of kinship structures frequently failed to match up to the realities of people's everyday kinship practices (2000: 2). However, the emphasis on ideas of relatedness, which has now found favour within kinship and family studies, does have its roots, we suggest, in the concerns of these earlier studies. Despite their deficiencies, these studies were already pointing to the importance of the social construction of age-based processes of identification across the life course for an understanding of the nature of kinship and the process of family life.

Thus, though concentrating primarily on structural issues in relation to family and kinship, such early theorising about familial relations from within sociology and anthropology are important in two ways for our contemporary understanding of how in the family we come to know we are ageing. First, they highlight the importance of social roles as forms of identity-markers and second, they underscore the ways in which cultural ideas of relatedness differentially combine biological/genealogical/generational relationships, or indeed sometimes ignore them altogether (Strathern, 1992), to produce a *social* account of kinship, as it is experienced. Thus, within sociology, attention is no longer focused on trying to define what 'the family' is, but rather as Bernades has indicated, on exploring when and how people 'begin to regard themselves as members of 'a family' and when they cease to use the term' (1986: 601). Finch and Mason's (1993) study of family practices, for example, shows that within a wider network of genealogical relatedness, in practice individuals choose to activate some kin links rather than others. They do this, not simply on the basis of familial obligation, but also according to principles of friendship and geographical accessibility. Similarly, within anthropology, by shifting attention way from the formal properties of kinship systems, contemporary studies are able to 'offer new possibilities of understanding how relatedness and ideas of kinship may be composed of various components – substance, feeding, living together, procreation, emotion' (Carsten, 2000: 34). Thus, it is through explorations of practice and social action that we may begin to see how age-based social identities are brought into being across the time and space of family life.

Familial roles and familial identities

Returning at this point to the Parsonian model of the family, we can recognise in it a variety of traditional familial roles and identities. Located in terms of kinship positions, such roles are primarily temporal classifications in terms of ideas of generational identity. Thus, for example, a traditional generational age hierarchy might be inscribed as follows: a first generation of grandparents, great-uncles and great-aunts; a second generational level of mothers and fathers, uncles and aunts; and the third generation as composed of children, cousins, and siblings. Onto this schematic model might be inscribed sets of power and authority relations, such that, traditionally, power and authority is assumed to descend through the generations, with relatively little authority and power being attributed to children who are perceived as 'dependents'. Indeed, in the traditional functionalist account of the family, socialisation *can* only work if power and authority are understood to be distributed in this way. 'Growing up' entails the movement towards the achievement of independent personhood, a transition mapped onto the move from 'child' to 'adult' status, from being someone's child to having the potential to bear children of one's own.

And yet, as a way of describing everyday family practices, or capturing the experiential and affective context of family lives, such a model is limited in the extreme. First, the chronology of the aging process cannot be assumed to map directly onto familial roles and generational positions. Post-divorce marriages, for example, may lead to the reconstitution of 'nuclear' families into what Simpson (1998) terms the 'unclear' family, where traditional family and generational structures are disrupted. A second marriage, later in life, may in some instances, lead to there being a near age equivalence between a wife and a daughter; the early marriage and procreation of siblings in a large sibling group can result, genealogically speaking, in an aunt being approximately the same age or younger than her niece or nephew.

The five wedding photographs featured in one edition of a local newspaper, the Craven *Herald and Pioneer* (November, 10 2000), bear testimony to this. Only two of the weddings featured might be regarded as traditional. At one wedding the bride was attended by a bridesmaid who was the bridegroom's daughter; in another, the couple's wedding was immediately followed by the christening of their daughter; in the third, the best man was the bridegroom's son. Such examples force us to think carefully, therefore, about the ways in which concepts of 'age' mesh with those of 'generation' in relation to familial identities and the consequences this has in terms of everyday social practices within the family. And, while a child may in terms of 'age' become adult, they remain genealogically the offspring of their parents however old they are. This factor, as we shall see, often has considerable significance for the ways in which family practices are performed. As Falmer, the apprentice grandmother, describes, 'When (my grand-daughter) is playing me up and wails, "I want my mummy", I wail back: "And I want my little girl". And I watch her stop, think and realise – with all the implications – that her mother and my little girl are one and the same person' (*Guardian*, 18 January, 2001).

What Falmer experiences can, in some ways, be described as a 'generation gap'. Her maternal family practices fail to match the requirements of her daughter as she finds her own place among the next generation of mothers. Yet this 'generation gap' – that is said to signal an increasing difference between the worlds of the young and old, and especially between children and their parents – has, in industrial societies, only been naturalised as a phenomenon since the 1960s' rise of sub-cultures. As family historians have pointed out, the idea of generational difference is relatively new and, as Gillis notes, was not common before the start of the nineteenth century. Pre-nineteenth century, the concept of generation implied sameness, rather than difference, and simply referred to the idea of common parentage:

> [B]y this definition all generations occupied the same capacious present. The young were not necessarily identified with the future, nor the old with the past. In the pre-modern economy of time all ages were conceived of as equidistant from death and the age differences we make so much of today mattered much less (1997: 17).

Thus, when discussing the concept of the life course in family history, Hareven makes clear the distinction between 'generation' as a kin relationship and genealogical lineage that encompasses a thirty-year or more age span, and the concept of 'cohort'. The latter she sees as a more specific age grouping, one that shares an historical experience. It is the cohort which interacts with historical events. This means that each 'generation' may therefore consist of several cohorts, 'each of whom has encountered different historical experiences that have affected the life course' (2000: 134). Thus for example, as she suggests, families with many children may have had two age cohorts of children, who differed markedly with regard to their historical experiences.

In many parts of the world, contemporarily, it is still possible to identify different cohorts of children among larger sibling groups. Such cohorts may not only have different histories, in the manner described by Hareven, but, more importantly for our purposes, they can occupy rather different positions with respect to the distribution of patterns of care and authority in families. For example, in rural Africa, while the parental generation may wield ultimate authority, practical day-to-day supervision and care of young children may be invested in the hands of older siblings, numerical age here being superseded by social practices. As LeVine *et al.*, note, at about five months old, infant siblings may be given into the day-time care of older sisters, a practice which can be argued to be beneficial in terms of developing the older children's 'pro social skills and values, helping to prepare them for becoming parents' and for the babies 'in providing social stimulation and easily imitated models of competence' (1994: 39–40). And the impact of Aids (acquired immune deficiency syndrome) in Africa has destroyed an entire generation of parents, such that grandchildren and grandparents now encounter one another in rather different roles (Nyambedha, 2001). In the West, by contrast, compulsory education excludes children from much of this kind of everyday social participation, and it is therefore children's segregation through schooling which, in part, helps maintain age-based models of child and parental generations within families.

Thus, the theoretical model of generational power and care-giving, ascribed on the basis of designated age-based familial identities may, in practice, not be adequate to describe the wide range of different social and familial realities which exist cross-culturally, nor the ways in which 'child' and 'adult' identities are socially constructed with regard to ideas of competence (James and Prout, 1997). Comparable examples of the disruption of this model of generational power and control in western industrial societies would be the caring work performed by children who look after sick or invalided parents; or, as noted elsewhere (Hockey and James, 1993), the infantilisation of very elderly people which is still common to everyday caring practices. In such instances, the generational seniority traditionally vested in old age is disregarded. Elderly people may be made to take on a child-like identity in terms of the social roles and expectations which are allocated to and for them. Thus, 'age' may articulate variously with 'generation' to shape the ways in which ideas of the family and familial roles come to be constituted in practice.

Dependency, independence and interdependence

As we have suggested elsewhere (Hockey and James, 1993), within western industrial societies the family is a key site through which aged identities are brought into being in relation to ideas of independence and dependence and, as a byproduct of the growth of individualism, adulthood is held to represent the pinnacle of independence. Childish dependency on parental care is expected to give way at a certain age to independent adulthood, a pattern inscribed most readily through familial role expectation. Describing the shifting and varied patterns of father – daughter relationships over the life course, Sharpe (1994) cites the words of 54-year-old Richard who describes the changing relationship he has had with his daughter over the course of their lives together. Significantly, he has to invoke a wide range of 'familial' identities and genealogical positions in order to portray the complex changes in their relationships. But, rather than numerical age, these changes centre on the practices of care and protection through which the idea of 'the family' is held to be enacted:

> I suppose you could argue that our relationship has gone through a series of changes. To begin with I was the father and she was the daughter. Then we were like brother and sister really. And I suspect now it's gone right round and she's more like a mother to me, because she tends to keep an eye on me, tried to steer me in the right direction. She is inclined, probably because in some respects I am somewhat of a child, to be be a little more mature than I am. So it has gone through this metamorphosis from father and daughter to mother and son almost (1994: 151).

Whilst in this example the reframing of a 'father – daughter' relationship as one of 'son – mother' is not portrayed as particularly problematic, once physical dependency becomes extreme in deep old age such shifting identities and roles may become more so, because they appear to project very elderly people back into a childlike state. But through drawing on the positive childhood imagery of growth and development, we suggested (Hockey and James, 1993) that the decline and loss of independence towards the end of the life course is rendered conceptually less problematic and disturbing for those who fear old age as degradation. The wrinkled and arthritic body's manifestation of new dependency is reframed. A new identity is produced through treating such physical dependency as if it were akin to that exhibited by children. But this process can, however, be experienced as deeply humiliating by both carers and very elderly people themselves. One daughter describes her own ambivalent feelings about this role-reversal:

> I looked after him quite recently . . . He was like a child. He is quite happy for me to wash him, etc. He has no embarrassment. I find my feelings are very confused

now. He needs me to help him. I look at his face and find it so hard to believe
nothing is happening behind his expression. I keep thinking how appalled he
would have been at the thought of my doing what I am now doing with him
(Sharpe, 1994: 160).

Though such strategic re-identification of very elderly people as
childlike may in some instances enable those adults who are in their
middle age to offer more effective care through distancing the
emotional context surrounding the loss of ability and competence,
the moral and ethical consequences of such a perception is profound.
And not only for very elderly people themselves. There is, for example,
considerable leakage of this child-metaphor from its usage for very
elderly people to the wider community of older people, embracing
those who still lead active and independent lives. As noted, this
leads to a subtle but wide-spread age-based discrimination within
western industrial societies such that the adjective 'silly' often
accompanies that of 'old' and that a person may be already considered
'too old at 58' (Hockey and James, 1993; Bytheway, 1995).

However, ageism does not just affect the lives of older people. It
manifests itself in various forms of social exclusion on the basis of
age across the life course for, as Bytheway notes, 'it is an age-specific
society in which we live' (1995: 9). Thus young people, as well as
those who are very old, may experience ageist attitudes which relegate
them to the status of non-persons on the assumption of a presumed
incompetence and dependency derived from their age-based identity:

ageist prejudice is based primarily upon presumptions, sometimes about chronological age and sometimes about different generations. It is by linking age to such
presumptions – that 'five year olds' are incapable ... and that 'young people' are
unable to cope – that young people suffer from the ageist prejudice of their elders
(1995: 11).

Brannen *et al.*, show, for example, that children experience 'the
widespread practice of adult disrespect' and feel that their rights
and opinions are not worth pursuing in the face of adults' greater
power and resources (2000: 33). Thus, though acknowledging that it
is adults' job to protect them, many children draw attention to 'the
double-edged aspect of adult protectiveness and [see] a need to balance
protection with providing children with the space to develop some
autonomy' (2000: 33).

Within the family, however, this simplistic mapping of dependence
and independence onto the status categories of 'child' and 'adult'
becomes further complicated in the everyday practices of families.

As we have already observed, a unidirectional flow of power authority from adult to child cannot be assumed. Children, for example, while having conventional ideas of what proper parents are – those 'who will provide them with love, care and respect in their own right' – do not necessarily link these qualities to any particular or conventional family form (Neale, Wade and Smart, 1998: 22; see also Morrow, 1998). Rather, as these authors show, the qualitative dimension of practice is crucial: what a child thinks a family *is* depends on 'not only who children include as members of their family but how much time they want to spend with them' (Neale, Wade and Smart, 1998: 22). Moreover, as other research has suggested, children do not regard themselves as passive dependents on their parents' care:

> from a children's perspective this experience of 'being parented' – of being cared for and cared about – is part and parcel of the act of parenting. Regarded by children as an interdependent relationship their own active experience of receiving such 'care' is . . . seen as fundamental to the proper enactment of parenting (James, 1999: 192).

Age-based relations of dependency and independence are therefore sometimes subtly translated within the family context across the life course. This is most obviously the case in families where the pattern of the child – parent relationship, set down in early childhood, continues to shape the affective and/or practical aspects of their kinship relationships even after the child has grown into adulthood and has children of their own. Thus, within some families, simply achieving the 'age' of adulthood may not lead to independence, despite the transition to independent adulthood having been made through, for example, gaining financial independence through employment. As one of Sharpe's respondents noted:

> even as adults my dad feels that he has to provide for us in some way. Getting him to receive anything from us, since we have been in a position to give, has been very difficult (1994: 154).

The persistence of the social patterning of age relations and kin identities in the context of 'the family' may be particularly pronounced in families who own and manage their own business. Here, affective and moral age-based familial obligations become overlaid and entangled with the social and economic ones of the workplace. In a study of farming families in the Yorkshire region of the UK, Christensen, Hockey and James (1998) describe how marriage does not necessarily lead to independence in adulthood. The farm and the farming way of life must come first and the farming way of life is mapped onto cross-generational familial relations. They relate 52-year-old Lucy's account of her early years of marriage to Dick, a highly successful farmer:

> if she complained that her husband did not spend enough time at home or they had other disagreements, Dick would simply leave the house and go to his mother who lived close by. She would then provide Dick with his meals. In this way Lucy's mother-in-law succeeded in keeping 'the family' together. Thus, rather than taking Lucy's part in marital conflicts, she made Lucy realise that if she wanted to keep her husband at home she had to accept his work demands and 'get on with the farming way of life' (Christensen, Hockey and James, 1998: 22).

And now, as a mother-in-law herself, Lucy repeats the pattern with respect to her son and daughter-in-law. This is one of the ways in which the farming way of life is to be maintained. As Christensen, Hockey and James note, the main day-to-day responsibility and control of family farms is usually with the middle-aged or younger members of the family. They will live in the main farmhouse, with the older parental generation living in an adjacent bungalow or nearby cottage. However, retirement in old age is not part of the farming way of life. Old farmers maintain an active interest in the farm by 'providing a source of intimate knowledge of the farm and the land and helping out by undertaking less physically demanding farming tasks, such as fetching spare machinery parts' (1998: 21). Thus, in this family context, age-based dependency is recast as a relational concept, constituted through mutual and reciprocal exchange, rather than in terms of the more hierarchical age-based relations traditionally noted between an independent and a dependent person. Farming lives have to be understood more complexly, therefore, in terms of sets of interdependent relations constituted over the course of a life in which age does not necessarily have the kind of determining role which it does in other economic sectors and social environments.

What this example underlines is that dependency is not therefore a fixed attribute of persons. Nor is it a quality which can be assigned, necessarily, to aged identities. Thus, as Christensen, Hockey and James go on to note in another example of family practices within the farming community, though farmers may see themselves as highly independent, self-employed people, their lives and work are grounded in sets of highly dependent relationships with the members of the older and younger generations of the family, as well as with members of the wider local farming community. Indeed, as these authors remark, 'it is this very interconnectedness which makes farming a way of life and not just a job' (1999: 178). Citing the case of Tom, a 'self-made man' and local agricultural entrepreneur, they write:

> without his wife's social, familial and domestic support, without his son's financial dependency on him, without the loyalty and admiration of every member of his immediate family and without his farm and factory worker's dependency on him for employment, Tom's representation of himself as 'independent' could not be sustained: it is precisely these dependent relationships – economic, social and material – which provide the context for his own experience of 'independence'. ... Without his family Tom would have remained a small-holder with a produce delivery round. Now, as his arthritis worsens, he could be entering a restricted and impoverished social life beyond the realm of the working world. But for Tom this has not happened, precisely because of his interconnectedness with others. Family connections, land, pigs, weather, the rugby club, the shooting fraternity have all sustained his claim to 'independence' and yet, at the same time, in their close and binding proximity they have worked to temper it (1999: 186).

The negotiation of family responsibilities across the life-course in relation to ideas of dependence and independence is not, of course, restricted to members of the agricultural community. As Finch and Mason (1993) have described, it is the ongoing work of all families. In a study of intra-familial relations of support, Finch (1989) pointed out that genealogical position did not determine concepts of family obligation. Instead, she argued that the moral rules which are traditionally held to pertain to kin-based obligations might be regarded more as guidelines for behaviour, than rules, to be seen as open to interpretation and dependent on context. In this sense, familial responsibilities are created within families rather than automatically ascribed and thus Finch and Mason reject the notion of fixed-age and kin-based identities in relation to notions of dependency (1993: 167). Their data show that,

> it is not simply elderly people who want to maintain independence from their relatives, and strive hard not to rely too much on them – it applied to young adults, to people in middle age, to both men and women, every bit a much as it does in the case of elderly people. All try to ensure that they do not get into situations where they are 'beholden' to relatives (1993: 179).

In familial contexts, therefore, the agency of individuals can work to mediate the fixity of age-based status and relationships which the ageing process threatens to bring with it.

Homes and families

This final section extends our focus on family practices by foregrounding their spatial dimension. It looks more closely therefore at the ways in which aged identities come to be constructed and embodied within the family. Allan and Crow (1989) argue that ideas of 'the family' and 'home' have combined together to lay the foundations for the modern domestic ideal so that, in contemporary industrial societies, they conceptually reinforce one another. Citing Oakely's observation that 'the home is the family ... [and that] "home" and "family" are now virtually interchangeable terms', Allan and Crow argue that it is the home which contextualises familial experiences (Oakely, quoted in Allan and Crow, 1989: 2). Indeed, such is the ideological role of the 'home' in helping constitute 'the family' that as James (1998) notes, children's identities within the classroom as able or weak pupils are often held to be a direct reflection of their home background and great significance is attached to familial influences and experiences. And in TV advertising, it is in the home, often in the kitchen, that family life unfolds and its members assume their 'naturalised' roles as father, mother and children.

And yet 'the family' is not always the site of homely domestic harmony that such imaging might suggest. The family home can be the site for the most abusive of social relationships, the context within which identities and ageing selves can be shattered and torn apart. Within the black and private box of the family, inside the home, domestic violence, psychological terrorising and child sexual abuse occurs away from the wider gaze. Here, then, the home and the family present rather bleaker contexts within which a sense of self identity develops across the life course. Goldsack (1999), for example, brings out the dangerous dimensions of the normally highly-valued association between home and privacy: 'Privacy acts as a shield against public scrutiny, and is generally believed to be important for the maintenance of private dignity and intimacy. However, to be private can signify deprivation as well as advantage. For women in the home, privacy can mean confinement, captivity and isolation. In such circumstances the home is less of a castle and more of a cage' (1999: 121). How, then, is ageing experienced and invented in such contexts? They seem to present radical contrasts to the idea of the 'home' as an environment within which we can 'safely' age.

Lorna Sage's (2000) memoirs drew a large readership partly because of the *failure* of her home life, both within her grandparents' and parents' homes, to conform to prevailing social norms. Marital tensions between her grandparents were marked out in intractable spatial divisions of their vicarage living space, 'shared' between grandparents, parents and grandchildren. Overcrowding in the council house her parents later moved into led Lorna, then, to exploit opportunities to avoid family life, even while living at such close quarters to other family members. The doctor's edict that her insomnia be treated by allowing her to spend her nights reading with a bedside light on granted her a place of retreat, as did the accepting welcome of a neighbouring farmer who let her help with the work of the farm. Growing up, she relished too any opportunity to escape her family's 1950s' models of an appropriate feminine identity for an adolescent girl; for example, as her mother's 'little shepherdess'. And, as the later years described in her autobiography reveal, Sage's withdrawal from 'growing up' as framed by the experience of family extended into other age-based inconsistencies within the chronology of her life course: she becomes a mother during adolescence and she marries before becoming an undergraduate, thereby radically disrupting the prevailing norms of 1960s' university life.

Sibley offers a way in which such personal memories and insights might be accounted for in terms of social theory. He argues that the very physical environment of the home may well help shape a child's identity, both in terms of a self and the self's role and position of 'child' in the family for, Sibley argues, generational power relations are enacted through the familial patterning of space and time in the home. He suggests, for example, that some families may work to separate out generational roles and positions by a fierce concern to keep 'children out of rooms and spaces decreed as adult spaces and...with the temporal regulation of children's activities' (1995: 131). In other families, by contrast, the distinguishing features which separate out 'child' from 'adult' identity may be less well marked, meaning that 'the uses of space and time in the home are negotiable... [and]...the mixing of activities is encouraged' (1995: 131). Thus, children get to know their 'age' and place through being allowed access to certain times and spaces. Indeed Chapman's (1999) account of the idealised family lives which are mapped in show homes suggests that among those within the range of upmarket, executive homes, it is the separation of generations which constitutes a power-ful selling point. The provision of separate bathrooms for parents and children provides not only generational separation but also points to the importance of the body as a way of marking out age-based categorical distance. In the show home, the master bedroom offers a double ensuite shower, mirrored wardrobes and a draped, canopied four-poster bed. It is blockaded off from the children's bedroom by fitted storage which acts as a baffle board. According to Chapman, show homes thus promise the buyer 'the kinds of sexual opportunities in the marital bedroom that were for several decades only available in hotels' (1999: 53–4).

Such spatial mapping of age-based identities within the home is of course most obvious in the shift from dependent child to independent adult status. This is represented contemporarily by young people moving out of the parental home into a home of their own, a practice which, however, is of relatively recent origin. Kenyon (2000), for example, shows how, for young people, the move out of home into other kinds of shared, but non-familial-based, households marked a significant biographical moment in the development and refinement of their own identities. For instance, it may signal the assumption of a gay identity or record a person's partner as the younger sister in a strong sibling pair. The symbolic significance of this life course transition is, of course, remarked in the traditional imagery of 'the key to the door' which accompanies twenty-first birthday celebrations. Until recently, the age of 21 has been regarded as the age of adulthood and signified by its status as the legal age of majority, the right to vote and hence the status of full citizen (see Chapter 4). However, before 21 such cross-cutting status was denied and this conceptual binding of young people to their natal homes was, for example, confirmed in the 1980s in the UK by New Right legislation. This succeeded:

> in getting unemployment benefit withdrawn from 16 and 17 year olds and prevented young people from moving to seaside towns in search of casual work while continuing to claim the dole; school-leavers were thus immobilised in areas of high employment, made absolutely dependent on family support (Cohen, 1997: 282).

Not yet full citizens with regard to age, their continued dependency on their parents was assumed or reinstated. The net result was that many young people who did not receive financial support from their parents were forced to leave home and live on the streets.

However, as Allat (1996) notes, the process of leaving home is more often a ragged transition, than an abrupt and final departure, movement back and forth generally signalling the shift from child to adult age. Young people may leave and return home a number of times, before finally leaving to establish an independent home. During this drawn out process of transition, they may find themselves in a somewhat marginal position between dependence and independence. For some families this can lead to tensions:

> to treat the parental home as a lodging, with the instrumental, tenuous relationships that this implies, transgresses the idea of a home which by its essence is rich in affective bonds. It is to treat the home as mere accommodation, as a utility devoid of obligation to other occupants, where it is acceptable to come and go as one pleases, to be out all the time apart from eating and sleeping, and to take others for granted (Allat, 1996: 133).

However, the commonly held idea of home as a fixed space, often used synonymously with 'house', has recently been challenged through the suggestion that the definition of home be expanded to a view that home is simply 'where one best knows oneself' (Rapport and Dawson, 1998: 9). Taking up John Berger's suggestion that home is 'no longer a dwelling but the untold story of a life being lived', Rapport and Dawson are keen to demonstrate the various ways in which identity unfolds across the life course (Berger, 1984: 64 cited in Rapport and Dawson, 1998: 27). They argue that it cannot be seen as stable and fixed but as continually changing and that 'home' – in this broader definition – is where and how identities come into being. Using the idea of narrative – or what might here be termed life story – they argue that

> human beings conceive of their lives in terms of a moving-between – between identities, relations, people, things, groups, societies, cultures, environments, a dialectic between movement and fixity. It is and through the continuity of movement that human beings continue to make themselves at home; seeing themselves continually in stories and continually telling the stories of their lives, people recount their lives to themselves and others as movement (Rapport and Dawson, 1998: 33).

Such a perspective moves then away from the stability of the built environment of the home as a geographical space within which people come to know they are ageing through the taking on of particular roles and familial identities, to a much broader approach. This focuses, instead, on the mobility of roles and identities within the family across time and in space and raises again therefore the possibility that individual agency can intervene to redirect the ageing process as a matter of choice. An increasingly prominent example here are the later-life north European migrants who overwinter in mobile homes and camper vans in countries which border the Mediterranean. The 'grey nomads' who monopolise many campsites in Australia, and their US equivalents, the 'snow birds', similarly exemplify a practice which not only challenges age-based conceptions of leisure, but in addition disrupts notions of home-based family life as an increasingly and necessarily sedentary practice towards the end of the life course.

Conclusion

This chapter has argued that Parsons' insights into the conceptual-isation of the family and its constitutive roles, though developed within the context of 1950s' American conservative, white home-based family life, continues to have relevance for understanding the experience of members of a far more diverse range of social categories. Drawing on Giddens' (1992) notion of the pure relationship, Weeks *et al.* (1999) suggest that a search for satisfactory, affirmative personal relationships is now a cornerstone of personal identity, a reflexive project currently undertaken within the highly politicised national and local territory of the family and its conceptualisations: 'increasingly, it can be argued, identities are not pre-given; they have to be articulated in increasingly complex social circumstances' (1999: 84). This would seem to suggest that the family persists as a set of core 'practices' through which life-course passage is relationally negotiated and that, despite a breakdown of traditional narratives of family, there is nonetheless a 'logic of congruence' within the diversity of partnering and family-making practices still to be found in contemporary society.

The range of data incorporated within this chapter therefore speaks to the more active model of identification which, following Hall (1996), one can argue is centrally important to an understanding of identity and change across the life course. 'Family' can be recognised as a repertoire of roles and relationships which resources the inter-personal negotiations of individuals whose embodied relationships with one another are both traced through the biological connections of 'blood' and 'genes' as well as being lived out in the everyday, materially-grounded activities of sleeping and eating. Encountered often on a daily, indeed hourly basis, the imperceptibly changing bodies of family members may not easily be recognised as 'ageing'. Yet, as this chapter has demonstrated, it is precisely within the flow of family practices oriented towards the projects of childcare, the management of domestic space and the support of elderly relatives that ageing comes to take on particular features across the time and space of the life course.

10

Production and Consumption across the Life Course

Introduction

This chapter draws on the sociology of the late nineteenth and early twentieth century which made work a key basis of social differentiation. It asks whether the variety of work-based explanations for differences of social *class* can help us make sense of ageing across the life course. Whether, as in the Marxist tradition, theories were oriented towards economic differences or towards the kinds of cultural differences identified by Weber and Durkheim, it was work which was seen as producing different kinds of class-based identities. Later, Oakley (1974) set out to research what we now think of as a particular form of work – domestic labour. She discovered that the nineteenth-century separation of work from home, with pay as its defining characteristic, had been blindly reproduced within the categories of sociological theory. Her choice of topic uncomfortably straddled the separate sub-disciplinary areas of 'family' and 'work' and failed therefore to find an adequate theoretical base in either. This problem led to a re-framing of the notion of work and the inclusion of gender as an important differentiating factor in accounts of the ways in which work might be thought about and the different kinds of identities a working life makes possible.

If work has thus been seen as so central to our understanding of modern forms of social differentiation – and therefore to processes of social identification – this chapter asks whether paid work might also constitute one of the primary activities through which we experience ageing? Is work an important means through which age-based identities are brought into being across the life course and thus one of the ways in which we get to know that we are ageing? Although Bauman (1997) has argued eloquently that it is time, rather than work, which sets us apart from one another – individuals experiencing either a problematic poverty of time or an equally problematic over-abundance – his distinction nonetheless still stems, largely, from people's relationship with employment. It is, for example, now overwhelmingly the case that those in paid employment are working very long hours. This daily practice effectively separates them socially from the members of other age-based social categories – 'schoolchildren', 'old age pensioners' and 'unemployed adults' – and leaves precious little time for generational sociality or reciprocity.

Similarly, 'What do you do?' remains a key question through which a fix on individual identity is sought. And despite feminist and anti-ageist initiatives, 'housewife' and 'retired' are answers which still risk the individual being categorised as socially inferior to an employed interlocutor. Thus, for example, while women have been at pains to insist upon the distinction between 'working' and 'working outside the home' as a way of challenging negative perceptions of 'housework', recent British government policy has taken an unpopularly heavy-handed stance in requiring women who are lone parents to return to paid work (*Guardian*, 10 October, 2000). This initiative thus reveals the continuing valuation of paid work as core to social and personal identity, as well as to economic security. 'Retired', similarly, is an identity which not only continues to undermine the individual's social status, but simultaneously produces a feeling of being old. Hence, the proliferation of schemes to train older people in how to make the best of the transition from work to retirement. Negative perceptions of age would thus seem to remain inextricably tied up with exclusion from the labour market.

However, as Slater argues (1998), categories which resemble the work:leisure binary are not just a nineteenth-century invention, as is often held to be the case. As he points out, ancient Greek thought also differentiated between forms of work – those which allowed the material necessities of life to be secured and forms of leisure which enabled body and speech to be perfected and justice to be promoted. These separate sets of practices, however, mapped onto the opposed social categories of slaves and citizens, rather than being linked to a chronological life course.

Structural factors are not unimportant when we consider the contribution of the sociology of work. Within contemporary western societies, for example, unemployment has separated the concept of 'adulthood' from its assumed underpinning in paid work, which as

Willis (1977) noted, used to constitute the primary symbolic life course transition for young men. Social stigma therefore follows the loss of this symbolic transition, rather than simply the poverty incurred by being 'out of work', which highlights the centrality of paid work for a positively perceived identity. Thus, homeless unemployed young people in the UK take on the job of selling the newspaper *The Big Issue*, which raises awareness about their situation, a form of work which is seen to hold in abeyance the stigma arising from unemployment at the start of the adult life course. Retirement *from* work, on the other hand, has undergone a whole sequence of different re-framings with older adults being encouraged to participate in the labour market, either at times when there are labour shortages or as a reflection of health promotion strategies. These more recent strategies equate 'keeping active' with good health and thus, it is hoped, lead to a diminished demand upon health services (see Chapter 6).

Retirement itself, as noted in Chapter 4, is a twentieth-century invention, an aspect of the chronologisation of the life course. Yet, in its short life, it has been subject to a series of contrasting rhetorical representations. As such, it exemplifies the processes which we now go on to explore, across a longer time trajectory, in our investigation of the changing nature of work and its role as a site for identification across the whole of the life course. In this chapter, we will argue that an exclusive focus on macro-level socio-historical accounts tends to produce overly simple accounts of the 'structuring' of the life course. These give little insight into the experience of ageing and its embodied relationship with work. As a result, we may gain only limited understanding of the processes whereby work-based identities have been negotiated, resisted or incorporated as part of the process whereby we come to know that we are ageing. Through a series of empirical examples, therefore, this chapter seeks to document, but also to problematise, the part played by work as a key institution through which the life course takes shape.

Becoming modern

As Chapter 4 demonstrated in considerable detail, the way we know that we are ageing has changed across time. Work has not always been central. Hareven, for example, has argued that 'historically the family was the locus for life course transitions' (cited in Kohli and Meyer, 1986: 145), particularly during the early modern period when the modern division between the spheres of production and reproduction was not in place. Thus, events such as leaving home, marriage, childbirth and the handing over of property and productive work to younger family members constituted the key distinctions between different life stages. But these markers were not determined on the basis of chronological age, but rather as a result of factors such as the changing makeup of the individual's family and the national and the local economic situation. As Hareven has argued, during the nineteenth century, we also find a lack of any ordered sequencing of transitions out of childrearing and household headship, and into widowhood. As she says, 'the 19th-century pattern of transitions allowed for a wider age-spread within the family and for greater opportunity for interaction among parents, adult children, and other kin' (1986: 173).

Early modern life-course transitions were therefore unique to particular combinations of circumstances, rather than being informed by large-scale, institutionalised and bureaucratised systems which operated according to chronological principles. The more individualised choices of the late twentieth and twenty-first centuries, made largely on the basis of age – for example, leaving the education system, becoming a parent, retirement – were simply not in evidence. Thus early modern life-course transitions took place as an aspect of the changing life of the family as a whole.

This period between 1600 and 1850 is often seen, therefore, to contrast starkly with the later nineteenth-century drive towards the regulation and chronologisation of the life course which went hand-in-hand with urbanisation and industrialisation. Indeed we cannot overlook the considerable social impact of the very rapid shift towards urban factory labour which displaced a predominantly agricultural way of life. In the course of the nineteenth century, time ceased to be experienced in relation to the natural cycles of seed-time and harvest, and the traditional, often religious, calendar of feasts, fairs, saints days and market days. Thompson (cited in Slater, 1998: 394) describes the clash between factory managers and workers over 'Saint Monday' when employees would choose to take time off, just as they had within the more flexible system of rural labour. The mechanised time of the factory drove a schedule which was constructed around a measured working day, with only the main religious festivals earning workers some free time. Time, work and money thus came to be inextricably conjoined for those in employment during the nineteenth century. As Slater says:

> Getting to work on time, keeping a steady rate of work within that time, reducing to a minimum those activities which do not contribute to productivity (socialising, eating, resting, going to the toilet): these are central to what is known as 'labour discipline', which in turn is deemed essential to modern forms and relations of production (1998: 393).

The history of the trade union movement and its conflicts with employers testifies to the binding connection between time and paid work, issues such as the length of the working day and the allowances for meal breaks having been fought over intensely.

The centrality of timetables and timekeeping to the development of a modernised, capitalist economy in late nineteenth-century Britain was mirrored in the gradual firming up of the life course into age-based social categories. This system of differentiation occurred in close association with a series of other radical spatial transformations that reflected new sets of relationships between social classes and genders. Thus, a core theme in all of this was the emergence of social life organised around separate gendered spheres. Space therefore began to play a significant role within the production of much more firmly demarcated social categories, with age being prominent among them as a base for social difference. Thus, just as space has been shown to be integral to rites of passage, in an albeit condensed and symbolic form (see Chapter 3), so too, in the historical development of the life course in relation to work, movement between different spheres has proven to be a significant marker of age-based identity. This emphasis on movement between spaces, or the significance of a person's location and position in social space, thus serves to reinforce the embodied notion of ageing and identity which we have been concerned to draw out and develop in this book.

For example, in ceasing to be a sphere of production, the home, as the site of human reproduction, gradually came to be thought of as separate and differently oriented from 'work'. The new middle classes, whose economic base lay in money earned from industrial sources, rather than wealth inherited from landed, aristocratic lineages, recognised the limitations of financial status. They sought cultural capital – and therefore a more elevated social identity – by aping the social mores of the upper classes. In urban villas, the wives of industrialists played out a new, symbolic role as lady of the manor, angels of the hearth who provided a haven for men returning from the 'satanic mills' of production (Davidoff *et al.*, 1976). The growth of public health measures, coupled with urban forms of private philanthropy, meant that theirs was a lifestyle which was soon rapidly extended, to be imposed upon working-class women. They were enjoined to leave the work force and provide care for children and older people, who were themselves now also barred from paid employment. Thus, nineteenth-century formulations of class and gender-based social categories were therefore not only strongly work-related, but also reflected the shifts in categorisation underway with respect to the life course. A raft of new employment laws, for example, excluded children and older people from work. Though ostensibly introduced for welfarist reasons, other structural reasons can be identified. Trade pressure from within Europe, for example, was a key motive for restricting older people's access to employment on the grounds that they were less productive (Thane, 1983). Similarly, the mass of legislation introduced to forbid the employment of children within the factory system from the 1830s onwards, although certainly reflecting new sensibilities around 'childhood', only achieved a real effectiveness with the introduction of compulsory schooling in 1880 (Fyfe, 1989; Hendrick, 1997). Thus, the law, though beneficial in many respects to children and older people, also worked to strengthen the chronologisation of the life course by cementing the relationship between work and adulthood and barring members of the other life-course categories from taking on legitimate employment.

For the individual, therefore, entry into and exit from work became key experiences through which life course passage was experienced in the UK by the end of the nineteenth century. At the level of social policy, therefore, we can note a series of changes which had profound effects in that the exclusion of children and older adults from paid work contributed to the production of major divisions within the life course. Being eligible or ineligible for paid work became *the* major age-based form of social differentiation and the time of working lives began to be played out and reflected in a series of spatial divisions and transitions: between home, school, workplace and retirement 'home'.

However, the danger with this structurally-based historical account is that dominant models of employment – hinged on men's full-time work histories – provide only a partial, overly simplified representation of the emergence of the modern life course. Though as a generalised account of social change it suffices, its schematic nature works to exclude other aspects of ageing across the life course such as concepts of citizenship and personhood.

Citizenship and work

Central to industrialisation was the commodification of labour which had a profound effect on citizenship status for, as Twine notes, 'what is distinctive about complex industrial societies is the way in which our material life-chances and social relationships are crucially affected by our need to sell our labour power as a means of life' (1994: 17). Then, as now, those who for various reasons could not sell their labour were faced, therefore, with the prospect of potential marginalisation and exclusion from one of the central social institutions – the workplace – through which identity and citizenship are accrued. As a result, both childhood and old age became more clearly differentiated from adulthood, once the potential to have 'a working life' became the key signifier of full adult citizenship. Significantly, though, the biographical consequences of this social exclusion for children and older people were, and are, rather different. Children, although excluded from the labour force, are on a trajectory towards a working life and full citizenship status. By contrast, older people, having left work, may face the prospect of filling in their time with work-like, leisure activities; being 'encouraged to engage in handicrafts such as basket weaving, embroidery, knitting, and sewing – activities that are not often only foreign to them but are perceived as demeaning' (Hazan, 1994: 42).

To look more closely, then, at some of the more subtle implications of industrialisation for the emergence of age-based social identities across the life course we return briefly to the history of children's working lives within the factory system of production. E. P. Thompson's (1968) now classic account of the making of the English working class depicts some of the changes which the introduction of the factory system wrought on the life course when it describes the changes in child labour accompanying the shift from cottage and home labour to industrial manufacture within the textile industry. Noting that child labour was nothing new in the eighteenth century, Thompson observes, however, that what the shift to the factory system did in the nineteenth century was to 'inherit the worst features of the domestic system in a context which had none of the domestic compensations' (1968: 370). Thus, ironically, the move to a factory system led to an increase, rather than decrease, in child labour between 1780 and 1830 due to the special-isation and differentiation of economic roles which this involved. As with contemporary child labour in parts of the developing world, children's small bodies gave them some advantage: they could get inside machines to free up tangled threads and manipulate small items within the production process. Children thus continued as workers within factories, but in conditions less conducive to health and welfare than those at home had been: 'in normal circumstances, work [at home] would be intermittent: it would follow a cycle of tasks, and even regular jobs like winding bobbins would not be required all day unless in special circumstances ... No infant had to tread cotton in a tub for eight hours a day and for a six day week' (Thompson, 1968: 368).

In addition, however, children were also employed as cheap labour in other kinds of work. They frequently undertook those monotonous and repetitive jobs which adults would not do, at piece-rates, and outside the factory gate: 'little toddling things of four years old were kept hour after hour at the monotonous task of thrusting the wires into cards with their tiny fingers until their little heads were dazed, their eyes red and sore and the feebler ones grew bent and crooked (cited in Thompson, 1968: 370). Thus, when the Factory Acts came into play in the mid nineteenth century, Acts designed to exclude children from the workplace through decreas-ing the hours they could work and raising the age at which work could start, the *contemporary* pattern of children working in low paid marginal jobs outside of mainstream economic life was set in place (see Fyfe, 1989). Thus, although one of the most significant markers of childhood and child status became, and remains, chil-dren's exclusion from the world of work, not all children were or still are barred from selling their labour. They simply did it – and still do it – in less obvious spaces.

For both children and older adults, however, the loss of the *right* to sell their labour power fostered the grounds of their dependency and their potential for social exclusion. As Twine (1994) notes, in an industrialised society the commodification of labour goes hand-in-hand with the rights of citizenship. If a person is unable to sell their labour power then they are excluded from social participation. This occurs even in the context of the welfare state where, ideally, 'the basis for a social right ... needs to relate not to a person's unequal and insecure relationship to the labour market but to his or her equal status as a citizen' (Twine, 1994: 21). Although the existence of the welfare state therefore potentially modifies processes of social exclusion, in the case of Britain, this has not happened. Though democratic political rights for all were established by the mid twentieth century, in practice the existence of free education and free healthcare has not removed social inequalities, and especially those which are age related. The opportunities for full social participation, in practice therefore, still rest largely on the social right to sell one's labour, a right only acquired fully on reaching adulthood.

Rethinking modernity

As noted, work provided the base for theories developed by the founding fathers of sociology – Marx, Weber and Durkheim. These emerged within the new science of society at the beginning of the twentieth century, itself arguably a reflection of the notions of work which were dominant in an ideological sense at that time – even if not necessarily pervasive as a social reality. The sociology of work which has subsequently developed repeatedly demonstrates, however, the breakdown of the work/family/leisure distinctions which were seen to characterise modernity and were basic to a political economy perspective. Industrialisation and urbanisation did not therefore have a straightforward or monolithic impact upon the life course. Rather, we need to unpack their effects in a more nuanced fashion if we wish to tease out their implications for those who actually inhabited the reformulated age-based social categories of the nineteenth century. Here we find a more complex picture emerging.

Gender, for instance, differentiates the way in which a work-based identity was and is experienced by adults. During the hundred years between 1860 and 1960, entry into paid employment represented a far more central aspect of adult status for men than it did for women. Marriage was core to the realisation of women's adult status and, writing in the 1980s, Westwood (1984) suggests that this remains important. Describing the scheduled chaos of the marital rites of passage which took place in the hosiery factory where she conducted an ethnographic study, Westwood's data demonstrates that, for women, models of the life course grounded in family transitions persist and, moreover, that these underpin practices which unfold in the workplace. Not only were many of the employees members of the same families, but in the days prior to a wedding, the company's time and materials were redirected towards a set of complex ritual behaviours. For the young women, these marked a symbolic transition from the innocent freedom of the single life to the sexualised bonds of marriage. Thus brides-to-be were dressed up in suggestive, sexualised outfits made by female employees during their working hours, taken out for extended drinking sessions during their lunch 'hour', tied to railings outside the factory and, when released, were brought back in to be spun round the factory in trolleys.

Containing many of the elements of a traditional rite of passage, such as the humiliation and disorientation of the initiand, these behaviours symbolically draw on the work/leisure distinction. This binary is, however, symbolically inverted through practices which in economic terms are markedly unproductive and indeed cock a snook at 'labour discipline'. Yet, these highly public goings-on were accepted by management, an example therefore of the conjoining of family time and work time in the marking out of life course passages as one way in which ageing is also experienced via economic structures. In contrast, therefore, with generalised structural accounts of work-based class and gender divisions, agency-focused, micro-level sociological accounts such as Westwood's show how family life and age identities can unfold *within* the context of work. Alongside these data we also have evidence of the continued centrality of some forms of paid work to the culture of family and community life during the twentieth century. Heavy industries and male-dominated occupations such as mining, fishing and farming provide the base for a collective, as well as individual, social identity, which expresses itself in domestic and leisure activities as well as the time and space of work across the life course (Dennis *et al.*, 1969; Christensen, Hockey and James, 1999). As such, the culture of occupations such as the police, the medical profession, the clergy and the diplomatic service transcends what are seen as the separate spheres of work and home in that the process of family life itself is made to take on or is shaped by the characteristics of the job (Callan and Ardener, 1984: 1).

Where the family itself constitutes the workforce, as in family-based businesses, the links between ageing, life course transitions and work is even more pronounced. In their study of farming families in the north of England, Christensen, Hockey and James (1997; 1999; 2001) discuss the indicators of the ages and stages of family members which are ingrained into the agricultural landscape: for example, death could result in holdings being divided between brothers, or in property being left to deteriorate visibly if a will could not be agreed; and marriage could lead to land being bought or rented at a distance if men wished to assert their independence from a dominant father. It could also lead to increasing prosperity if a man married a woman from a farming family because she would provide him with support in his economic activity by minimising the family's demands upon his time.

The fixity of the family and the work in space is central therefore to the ways in which ageing across the life course is experienced and lived out in such settings. Occupationally mobile urban dwellers, by contrast, often experience only a transitory relationship with their material environment. Life-course transitions such as entry into education, employment, marriage and widowhood all provide triggers for spatialised shifts, sometimes between towns, but increasingly between countries and continents. Among the members of farming communities, however, the built and the natural environment are experienced *in terms of the life course*, families seeing themselves as contributing towards not only the establishment of a family business but also the creation of a wider network of local amenities which will endure for their children and grandchildren to come. Tom, a farmer, describes the local landscape through reference to past work and work relationships, now seen by him as imprinted on the land which his family owns:

> That barn over there that belongs to one of my friends. We bought the land together and shared the large fields between us. This wood I planted up . . . when I came here it was all briars, and we cleared it. Four hundred and twenty nine acres here and I bought it seven years since. We've just bought as we have been able to buy (Christensen, Hockey and James, 1999: 176–7).

This sense of belonging which transcends the individual life course and incorporates it into the sequencing of generations remains an important principle of identification. Individuals are at pains to achieve a sense of personal continuity within their own life course, as Grace a farmer's wife reflects:

> We have spent money on the house because we think we are going to be here for a life time . . . we can plan that we are going to be here for a lifetime or until we are retired. And then maybe some of our children will live here (Christensen, Hockey and James, 1997: 637).

The localised sociological and anthropological studies described in detail above therefore problematise many of the spatially and temporally located boundaries which might otherwise be seen as inexorable markers of age-based transitions: exit from school, entry into employment, getting married, retirement. They also reinforce the argument that identification is an ongoing process which persists *throughout* life, and is not limited to certain age-based, symbolic transitions. Work is not a fixed basis of age-based identification but, instead, for the individual, shifts across time and in social space, disrupting any formally institutionalised chronology.

What we now move on to consider in more detail in the next section, therefore, are the implications for life course identities of contemporary changes in the nature of work, both as an institution and in terms of how it is experienced. As Held argues 'if the account of the institutionalisation of the life course describes social reality rather than a bureaucratic norm, it is obviously limited to certain segments of that reality' (1986: 158). Thus, although failure to turn up for work on 'Saint Monday' may have been a flash point within nineteenth-century industrial relations, the demands of domestic and leisure activities remain, and may still intrude upon work time. Adults in employment, for example, may take advantage of the twenty-first century institution of 'Poets' Day' (Piss Off Early, Tomorrow's Saturday). Similarly, despite a well-established system of institutionalised education, children continue to truant, either to set their criminal careers in motion, to engage in seasonal agricultural work or to generate wealth by setting up dot.com companies. And many retired people also continue in paid employment, whether in high-status roles as writers, artists or politicians, or in more menial jobs such as night watchmen, domestic cleaners and newspaper 'boys' and 'girls'. The ties between age, work and leisure are not, therefore, as clear-cut as a political economy perspective might represent them to be.

In the bureaucratic age, work-based chronologisation is challenged by such embodied acts of resistance across the whole of the life course. This denies simplistic assumptions about the ways in which work, in practice, confers aged identities. Working children, unemployed men, employed adults of pensionable age are all examples which force us to recognise that the supposed structuring of identity across the life course is made less rigid and constraining, through the more mundane and everyday negotiations individuals make in the course of everyday social lives.

Postmodernity, work and consumption

What we have suggested so far, therefore, is that many of the spatial and temporal boundaries which divide home from factory, leisure time from working hours, women from men and the young and the old from the age-based social category 'adult' are largely figurative or symbolic. In practice, these boundaries are *always* open to negotiation and often transgressed by individuals. For example, many occupations – particularly high-status professions such as medicine or the diplomatic service or 'callings' such as the Church, acting, writing, music, painting or sculpture – appear to transcend the times and spaces of work altogether and are not chronologised. As such, they constitute something more than an occupational identity, seeping into every aspect of the individual's life, and indeed that of their family. Often they have no official retirement age in that they are inseparable from the self. For those employed as ministers of the Church, for example, the notion of a self divided into 'I' and 'me' is especially problematic since the 'I' is understood to have the capacity to stand aside from and reflect upon the 'me' (Hockey, 1992). Called by God, for them the notion of a dimension of self which can stand apart from that vocation implies religious doubt and a fundamental instability of faith. Clergy who do indeed find themselves reflecting on their professional role often experience this as a generalised life crisis rather than work-specific role strain.

As argued above, farming can similarly exceed the boundaries of an age-specific 'working life', instead constituting a family-based economic activity which reflects a continuity of pre-modern organising principles. While women contribute largely by freeing men up from domestic and childcare duties, they may also provide important backup as unpaid secretaries or as 'gofers' when a spare part needs to be fetched for a piece of farm machinery. Importantly, age-based divisions are less in evidence too. In this setting, boys grow up – or 'evolve' – into farmers through participation in productive labour from an early age:

> My father being a frustrated farmer wasn't so very far away from a farm and so, because I used to run along at his heels and he just used to go and talk to farmers and he knew them and I used to go with him and I mean, I just soaked it all up. I just drank it all, it was absolutely the breath of life to me, I mean to go and look at the cart horse was, well, it was better than going on week's holiday, if he could take me to a farm for half a day. I just didn't want anything else, it was absolute heaven to me, just to go to a farm, stand in a stable and look at a row of cart horses

was ... and just the smell the muck and all the ... and everything else with it was absolute heaven (laughs) ... it was really (Christensen, Hockey and James, 2001: 75).

Similarly the age-based occupational retirement which characterises work in an industrial setting is absent in farming. Older men continue to work alongside younger male relatives on family farms, their work roles changing imperceptibly as they age, constituting 'a source of intimate knowledge of the farm and the land' (Christensen, Hockey and James, 1998: 21).

As argued in Chapter 8, postmodernity can be characterised as a form of double coding, a hybrid cross-category process within which traditional, modern and postmodern patterns of social organisation unfold in tandem. Thus, in the sphere of work, we find the persistence of traditional family and age-based work practices alongside a whole set of radical shifts in the very nature of work itself. These include the increasing importance of patterns of consumption, rather than simply production, which now play a central role in marking age-based category membership. In contrast, therefore, with the sociological significance which Weber attributes to the Protestant work ethic – the internally self-perpetuating, ideal type model of profit-making – postmodern culture is associated with the notion of playfulness. Featherstone, for example, describes postmodern culture as 'a playful, youthful and emotional exploratory approach to culture' (1991: 375). Work and leisure may no longer be clearly differentiated from one another.

While many ways of working have features of postmodern hybridity and are indistinguishable from leisure pursuits, these 'leisure' activities may nonetheless include more modernist aspects by being age-specific, whilst simultaneously blurring the boundaries of public and private space: a conspicuous mixing of codes. For example, within the personal spaces of children's bedrooms internet access simultaneously connects them to virtual space, a heterotopia which is theirs to 'play' in (McNamee, 2000). Yet the formation of dot.com companies, however ephemeral, has provided a sizeable income for some teenagers, a play/work activity which, in turn, has produced a subsequent postmodern reshuffling of age-based social categories. As Haynes observes, the failure of many companies to realise their anticipated profits has meant that 'in California, B2C now means "back to college" as disillusioned twenty-somethings who skipped university to make dot-com millions rethink their options' (*Guardian*, 16 January, 2001). He goes on to note that the growth area of internet economic activity is now the 'adult' industry of selling of sex. When the young enter this 'adult' market, as was the case with a group of Edinburgh undergraduates, they then tend to be castigated for illicitly entering a domain set apart for a different age-based social category.

Similarly, young women's seclusion in the home as a result of childcare commitments often leads to the 'relaxation' zone of the lounge becoming a hybrid work/leisure environment which in many respects resembles the heterotopic spaces of children's bedrooms. Here underwear, sex toys and plastic food containers are sold at parties where friends and family gather together. The pyramid selling of toiletries and household cleaning products also takes place within the context of social interchange of this kind; and institutional fundraising accomplishes its goals through informal parental participation in sponsorships related to their children's sporting activities. Among older, retired people, a social life of coffee mornings, tombola, jumble sales and fêtes, represents a similarly hybrid form of activity, important charitable fundraising work taking place under the guise of gentle sociality.

Alongside economically productive forms of leisure such as these, which blur a supposedly clear-cut, chronologised work/leisure distinction, we need also to consider the implications of consumerism for ageing. As Willis argues (1990), consumption is an active rather than reactive process, which reflects the agency of the individual rather than the blandishments of a capitalist hard-sell. As such, it constitutes a site for identification. As Clarke argues in relation to catalogue shopping:

> Material culture, its acquisition and appropriation, is integral to the construction and negotiation of social worlds and identities. The myriad decisions and complexities of household provisioning embody consumption as an arena of power in which social relations and knowledge are constantly rehearsed, rearranged and challenged (1998: 73).

Much of the work on consumption makes social differentiation along class and gender lines its primary focus, yet age and life course stage are also key markers of difference within patterns of consumption as is widely recognised within the market intelligence industry. Thus Mintel, the market research organisation, uses the concept of 'lifestages' in its consumer research (see *The Funeral Business*, Mintel Market Intelligence, September 1999), defining these quite specifically, as follows:

Pre-family	those aged under 35 who are not parents
Family	those aged 15–54 with at least one child aged under 16 still at home.
Empty nesters	no family/empty nesters aged 35–54 with no children under 16.
Post family	post family/retired over 55/not working

These 'lifestages' reflect an overwhelmingly modernist concern with clear boundaries and the chronologisation of ageing. However, the linking of life course with family is a measure of ageing which persists from the pre-modern era. But here it is being made to play an important role within the 'myriad decisions and complexities of household provisioning' around consumption practices held to be 'characteristic of postmodernity' (Clarke, 1998: 73).

Mintel use household income as a further filter which intersects with family lifestage to produce other forms of categorisation, or market segments, such as the following: benefit dependents, families on a tight budget, better-off families, better-off empty nesters, working managers, and working women. In addition, a set of spatialised lifestage distinctions are used and Mintel claim that, 'this classification is a more powerful differentiator of consumer behaviour than traditional socio-economic and demographic indicators' (see *The Funeral Business*, Mintel Market Intelligence, September 1999).

Thriving	Wealthy achievers, suburban areas.
	Affluent greys, rural communities.
	Prosperous pensioners, retirement areas.
Expanding	Affluent executives, family areas.
	Well off workers, family areas.
Rising	Affluent urbanites, towns and city areas.
	Prosperous professionals, metropolitan areas.
	Better off executives, inner city areas.
Settling	Comfortable middle agers, mature home owning areas.
	Skilled workers, home owning areas.
Aspiring	New homeowners, mature communities.
	White collar workers, better off multi-ethnic areas.
Striving	Older people, less prosperous areas.
	Council estate residents, better off homes.
	Council estate residents, high unemployment.
	Council estate residents, greatest hardship.
	People in multi-ethnic, low income areas.

The modernist specificity of these forms of categorisation casts doubt, therefore, on the notion that consumerism is an empowering postmodern site for the creation of personal identity. Used as a guide for economic activity on the part of producers, age and family lifestage remain inextricably tied to markers of economic difference, identified as occupational status and place of residence.

Age-based distinctions of this kind are reflected widely in the niche marketing which characterises contemporary systems of production. Recognition of the importance of consumer items as markers of status and difference among children though appearing as early as the 1930s in Disney merchandising, for example, has developed recently into a significant market. And, once recognised, the centrality of this role within children's processes of identification is ruthlessly exploited. Particular toys are promoted at key points in the selling calendar such as Christmas, their unavailability serving merely to enhance their desirability: Cabbage Patch dolls, Buzz Lightyear and the Telly Tubbies are memorable examples here. Often defined as trash and in poor taste, such children's toys, along with the highly costly labelled items of clothing and personal accessories – trainers, sports clothes, mobile phones – desired by teenagers, have attracted censure from many quarters. This is often on the grounds that young people are economically innocent, unable to make rational judgments as to the value of money and are therefore in need of protection from consumer organisations.

However, as Buckingham (2000) argues, this perspective ignores young people's own insightfulness and overrides the fact that they *do* discriminate in the choices they make as consumers. Just as in the adult world of marketing, some products fail miserably to appeal to children and young people. This perspective also ignores young people's capacity not only to recognise the cultural capital among their peer group, embodied within desired toys and clothing, but also to effectively target the economic resource of parents, grandparents and older relatives. Noteworthy within patterns of child consumerism, therefore, is the relationship between childhood and adulthood where the

> commercial emphasis on satisfying children's *wants* is ... rejected in favour of a renewed insistence on their *needs* ... defined, of course, by well-meaning adults (Buckingham, 2000: 166).

Young people's desire for technological or sexually-oriented items, such as motorised vehicles, make-up and disco clothing is a pattern of consumerism which points towards self-generated life-course transitions: young people are constructing an 'adult' identity through their consumer choices (Hebdige, 1979; Cohen, 1997).

Growing up is, therefore, in part achieved, individually and on a personal basis, via goods, clothing and patterns of leisure, such as being seen in the right pubs and clubs. Growing old is similarly mediated by consumerism. Older adults often successfully resist the life-course transition into old age through clothing and particularly through leisure choices more in keeping with the lifestyles of younger adults. And having choice is, in itself, a positive re-framing of later life for those who albeit briefly have considerable access to the two resources which rarely coincide for younger adults: time and money (Bauman, 1997).

This perspective is fundamental to the magazine *Choice*, formerly named *Retirement Choice*, which is aimed specifically at older adults. Featherstone and Hepworth (1995) show how the hitherto unexploited market segment of affluent over-50s has been drawn into processes of identification via consumerism. For example, comparing the front covers across a period of about thirty years, they show how the word 'retirement' which once dominated the space has gradually retreated, the word 'choice' subsequently being writ large to the gradual, but eventual, exclusion of the word 'retirement'. Featherstone and Hepworth note that in the course of the 1970s the magazine also underwent shifts in its orientation, changing its title to *Pre-retirement Choice*. Its front cover profiled the faces of exemplary older people such as Margaret Thatcher, Vera Lynn and Eric Morecambe, all of whom belied their age through their looks and their refusal to give up work. The magazine seemingly sets out to deconstruct the category retirement, freeing it from its associations with 'useless and passive old age' by allowing men and women to escape 'from their chronological bonds' (1995: 34–7). In December 1972, for example, it carried the following message:

> Generations of older people were expected to conform to a rigid age pattern, today we are trying to let in a healthy gust of air to blow these wretched cobwebs away (Featherstone and Hepworth, 1995: 37).

In this endeavour the body provided a key focus. Mid-life-style clothing, modelled by younger women was inserted into articles which reminded older women in the 1970s that 'time was when, once you were forty or so, you could climb into a 'uniform' of long black skirt, severe blouse and sensible shoes, sit back and officially enter old age for ever', but now, 'Yes, You Can Wear These Clothes' (1995: 34). At a press conference to mark the magazine's first anniversary, an enormous plastic 'gold' pocket watch was ceremonially destroyed with a hammer, an event which the magazine reported as 'breaking a golden spell'. The watch, a traditional reward for a lifetime of work, but also symbolising possibly the intractable pressure of a diminishing life 'time', was thus symbolically rejected.

The magazine's focus on the agency of older people is unmistakable. Extending their market to the pre-retirement age-group, it represents later life as a time when people 'fashion their lives afresh' (1995: 38). Yet as the authors note, letters from subscribers in some cases queried these exhortations, bluntly accusing the magazine of targeting its audience more on the basis of their social class than their age.

The magazine has spawned a whole series of similar magazines and indeed consumerist practices such as off-peak holidays and reduced-price pensioners' lunches at times when the pub and hotel trade is slow. All these have to be recognised as examples of the agency of older people who set out to resist the imposition of negative constructions of later life. Nonetheless, the divisions among older people, on the basis of class, gender and ethnicity, remain deep and the blandishments of consumer magazines are not just shallow but also unachievable for many people. As Featherstone and Hepworth note, alongside the images of politicians and celebrities, still actively pursuing power, fame and wealth, the magazine retains its imagery of retirement as a time of retreat and tranquillity through references to the garden and the countryside. These sustain notions of later life which can be traced back to nineteenth-century representations (Hepworth, 1999). While the ceremonial smashing of the plastic watch in the mid 1970s might have been an attempt to break the 'golden spell', the positive associations of the colour gold with secure forms of maturity and mellow warmth at the end of the day continue to hold sway.

The colour gold's associations with late-life affluence and wellbeing are sufficiently persuasive to also make them a resource for the prepaid funeral planning business. This recently developed aspect of funeral directing is an attempt to rescue an industry shown by the market research company Mintel to be losing profit as a result of advances in medicine: 'Certain forms of cancer, even, no longer inevitably lead to death', it notes gloomily, 'None of this is beneficial to the funeral business' (see *The Funeral Business*, Mintel Market Intelligence, September 1999: 7). And so what we find as a pick-me-up for this depressing prospect are companies such as 'Golden Charter'. These allow clients to 'secure the funeral of their choice', monies being paid ahead of time, competition from other firms thus being staved off.

In the marketing practices which clearly – scientifically – target quite specific age-based consumer groups we find, therefore, a persistence of a modernist chronologisation of the life course. In the name of profit, the market, nonetheless, *does* also provide scope for the individual to negotiate their process of ageing. Younger people often buy items which will secure them the sophisticated status of single, sexually available adulthood: alcohol, mobile phones and fast cars. As the magazine 'Choice' reveals, older people too strive to resist the curtailing of the period of mid-life and respond to images of an active, couple-oriented leisure in old age.

Conclusion

Work, which has been central to this chapter, has been shown to be a site which has been and still is central to the chronologisation of the life course. Nonetheless, by examining evidence from more local-ised, micro-level studies we rapidly discover the agency of the ageing individual. In so doing, we gain insight into the complex processes through which the apparently rigid temporal and spatial boundaries which supported age-based divisions during the modern period are persistently subverted, transgressed and potentially destabilised. As ageing, embodied selves, individuals move between the age-segre-gated spaces of 'home', 'factory' and age-specific sites such as sin-gles chat-lines and retirement magazines. In this process, we find an instability of age-based categorical membership, a hybrid conjoining and manipulation of work/leisure/family, the ageing body being managed in ways which allow for the pursuit of personal agendas and the maximising of goals within social interaction.

As argued in the second half of this chapter, the sociology which explained class-based differences as both the outcome as well as the grounding of relations of production has given way to a much greater focus on consumption and identity-making. This has featured particularly within postmodern theorisations of the life course which highlight the potentiality of consumerist practices for transcending a modernist chronology of age. However, what the sociology of con-sumption highlights is the agency of the individual – and, as the data discussed here indicate, this can involve choices which both affirm as well as dissolve age-based difference. This focus on ageing has been central to the current chapter where we have been at pains to privilege the experiential dimensions of what are often represented simply as the top-down, deterministic influences of industrialisation and urbanisation. As we argue throughout this book, the frozen-moment which 'structure' represents is problematically limited as a theoretical framework for apprehending the processual, contingent experience of ageing across the life course.

11

Time, Memory and the Life Course

Introduction

This book has explored a core tension: the tension between the individual's capacity to make and re-make themselves, to resist the penalties, constraints and imperatives of 'social structure' and the ageing body, and their dependence upon 'the social' as the source of who they experience themselves to be. It is through this tension, we argue, that we come to know that we are ageing. As we explored in earlier chapters, work on rites of passage, by early twentieth-century theorists such as Van Gennep, described the mechanisms through which individuals make transitions between social categories. Later, developed in the work of Turner, these rituals of transition – baptism, initiation, marriage, childbirth, healing and funerals – were seen as a social mechanism which could contain and control the ebb and flow of embodied human ageing. In that it threatened the continuity and therefore stability of 'society', the transitory nature of flesh was seen as dangerous. Much of this work on rites of passage thus emphasises the danger which the ageing person moving between social statuses, or in transition, poses – and the threats to which they are exposed.

According to this model of society, therefore, the biological unfolding and demise of the lives of individual members of society is problematic, in that individual bodies change radically across time and with them, their competencies. However, seeing society in terms of distinctive, fixed and enduring collective identities, the literature on rites of passage still needed to explain the paradox of how these are sustained by an embodied and *changing* membership of individuals, who are themselves in a state of constant flux – being born, growing up, growing old and dying.

Individual and collective identity

One approach to the problem of ageing and the life course, as we have explored in this book, is to see collective entities such as childhood and old age as having distinctive features which are shared and which endure recognisably across time. Indeed, Jenkins notes that one of the meanings of the word identity is 'distinctiveness which presumes consistency or continuity over time' (1996: 3). Collective identity, he argues, is about similarity. It involves the highlighting of common features such as British sangfroid and insularity. This is a point echoed by other recent theorists of identity (Cohen, 1994; Rapport, 1995) who understand differences *between* collective identities – being English and being Scottish, for example – as key to their distinctiveness and continuity. Thus, even if we question the sustainability of collective models of social identity because they mask the agency of individuals, it remains possible to suggest that, at the collectivity's boundary, aspects of more overarching social identities are nonetheless produced and made meaningful – for example, British conceptions of 'unsophisticated northerners', as perceived from the North; and 'cold unfriendly' southerners, as perceived from the North.

But, as this book has also demonstrated, a life course perspective which dealt with aged identities solely in terms of such collectives would not allow us to answer our question: how is it that we know that we are ageing? As we have shown, nominal categories – be they 'child', 'adult' or 'old person' – do not map easily onto the experience of the individual. In memory or imagination, or in some bodily difference, people often fail to live up to the requirements of the category to which they might seem belong on the basis of age and generation. The social structuring and chronologisation of age, by whatever means, is thus insufficient as an account of how the individual – whether child or adult – identifies themself as age-d or ageing. As Cohen argues, 'ritual is a necessary means of dealing with intractable difficulties and otherwise unresolvable tensions and contradictions of everyday social life' but 'to mistake them as state-ments of facts or as descriptions of social reality would be naive' (1994: 92). It is therefore the case that to simply work at the level of categorical identities is to fail to get to grips with the *process* of identification itself – that is, the way it is that social *and* individual identities are inhabited and come into being.

Thus, models which posit movement between static categories tend to emphasise the power of the social structures among and between which the individual is moved, a cognitive privileging which is highly problematic. Categorical or nominal identities – such as that of child, youth, middle-aged person, elderly person – can only ever be virtual identities for the individual. That is to say, they do not have 'life' outside of the person. These identities only become meaningful in terms of the individual's response to them. Thus, though people may share the same nominal identity they may have very different experiences of it, for it is in and through social interaction with others that the individual comes to an understanding of the social identity which he or she inhabits. Thus, across the life course, there is a continual process of tacking back and forth. This ensures that the embodiment of social identity is at one and the same time a 'referent for individual continuity, an index of collective similarity and differentiation and a canvas upon which identification can play' (Jenkins, 1996: 21). And this process is eminently social – indeed it *is* the social – for 'social identity is never unilateral' and must always be validated by others (Jenkins, 1996: 21).

A second approach is to investigate how it is that age-based categories themselves change in nature across time and whether 'age', as a concept, has any bearing on identity. A key contribution to this debate has been the ethnographic evidence that categories such as 'child' or 'adult' are not simply biologically based but are instead the product of particular culturally located historical moments. This is not, however, to argue for the preeminence of purely discursive models of ageing or for identity as infinitely variable. Thus, Giddens' insistence that 'the reflexive project of the self, which consists of the sustaining of coherent, yet continuously revised, biographical narratives, takes place in the context of multiple choice as filtered through abstract systems' is not an argument which we find wholly sustainable (1991: 5). The cultural diversity of the 'natural' categories of age are not an identity pick-and-mix selection standing outside the self as a source of lifestyle choice. Rather, they are in some ways, the reverse. As we have explored in this volume, a less often remarked aspect of the dialectic of identification is that, through their embodiment of the nominal identities of 'child' or 'old person', individuals themselves help re-make and reconstitute in a recursive pattern the very nature of that nominal identity. In other words, it is through experiences of a 'critical lack of fit' that individuals come to contribute to the process of identity formation which constitutes the social world. To give a recent example from Britain, the James Bulger case (1993), whereby one small boy was murdered by two others, is said to have changed the nature of childhood, the actions of these two others radically altering public perceptions of childhood criminality (see James and Jenks, 1996).

And this is not a new phenomenon. While Giddens (1991) identifies the breakdown of the old certainties of tradition and religion, coupled with the provisional nature of scientific 'truths', as the 'risky' environment within which the project of self is now conducted, Jenkins draws attention to the 'crises of identity' which have characterised European history from the early modern period onwards: witch-hunts and the persecution of 'heretics, Jews, lepers and homosexuals' (1996: 9). Pointing out that 'reflexive self-identity is one of the social phenomena which are hailed as diagnostically modern by many sociological commentators', Jenkins then retorts with a robustly critical statement: 'This is at least an overstatement which tells us more about the conceits of Western modernity than about anything else' (1996: 9–10).

Therefore in sum: to fully understand not only what social identity is, but also how the process of identification takes place in society, requires us to adopt an approach which favours neither the individual nor society in terms of the ways in which identity is assigned, achieved or experienced. The identity which is seen as unique to the individual and the identity which is seen as shared, collective and social both have to be understood not only as 'intrinsically social' but also as 'routinely related' to one another, such that the processes 'by which they are produced, reproduced and changed are analogous' (Jenkins, 1996: 19). And, as we have argued, intrinsic to such a view is, therefore, the embodied nature of identity. It is primarily the process of embodiment which enables and facilitates the links between social and individual identities and which is the key process through which we may come to know that we are ageing.

In this final chapter, therefore, we explore some further implications of this perspective by considering other ways – those of memory and imagination – through with we might tap into and access experiential aspects of the embodiment of aged identities across the life course, so overcoming the artificial separation of 'inner' and 'outer' social worlds and their relegation to different disciplines (Cohen and Rapport, 1995).

Integral to the question of how we know we are ageing is the issue of how we experience the passage of time, a point discussed at length in Chapter 3. However, in coming to terms with ageing, we need to consider not just time's passage in the moment, but also the mechanisms through which we surveille a temporal landscape made up of both past and present. It is here, therefore, that the twin realms of the memory and the imagination come into play. Intersecting in the present, it is the conjoining of our remembered and projected selves which produces our current, age-based identity. When we consider the process of ageing across the life course, however, it becomes apparent that the relationship between our past and our future *in* the present can take on different qualities at different times in our lives. In youth, for example, we may seek to shake off childish ways and to create a new and therefore discontinuous future self; in mid-life, past and present may appear remarkably similar and our 'ageing' may become less perceptible to us. However, at times of crisis, loss or extreme old age, the self we know and remember threatens to founder and a new and *un*welcome future self takes shape in our imaginations. This may be a self abandoned by a partner in divorce or death; a self robbed of an occupational identity; or indeed a self bereft of mobility, continence and even the ability to think coherently.

The future self

Giddens (1991) privileges continuity as an important aspect of self-hood. Within western societies, or those where identity is not ascribed through formalised ritual practices, however, this continuity is only achieved through work carried out by the individual. Thus, though he does not explicitly say so, his argument rests on an unacknowledged view of this as an embodied process:

> ... self identity ... is not something that is just given, as a result of continuities of the individual's *action* system, but something that has to be routinely created and sustained in the reflexive *activities* of the individual (Giddens, 1991: 52, our emphasis).

In this account, therefore, Giddens attributes identification with the status of a project. As such it is continuous across time – never abandoned or neglected – yet, as a focus for reflexive effort, it paradoxically involves *change* in that it involves a steady process of self perfection or 'personal growth'. Giddens' model of identity is therefore predicated upon both continuity *and* mutability – the capacity to adapt to changing circumstances in order to create a coherent and durable individual/ social identity. Only through this work does the individual sustain a recognisable self which endures across time. It is for this reason that bodily change must be coped with and personal losses overcome, for fear that they might otherwise derail the continuity of the self. To get 'back on track' requires work on the self. Indeed, it could be argued that managing change is becoming refined as a practice, almost to the degree that it is envisaged as a bodily and mental skill which can be learned in job centres and career development agencies.

For example, counsellors are increasingly available to help individuals 'move forward' through life crises of every description: teenage self-mutilation, post-natal depression, marital instability, redundancy, retirement, bereavement and terminal illness. Growth and change are the watchwords here. Thus for example, in a textbook for bereavement counsellors, Worden says:

> People come for mental health treatment feeling stuck in their grieving. They come believing that they are not passing through the experience, that mourning is not coming to an end, and that they need help to get through it and get back to living (1991: 1).

Within a modernist frame, grief becomes a form of work which requires embodied human effort and Worden schematises it into 'the four tasks of mourning' whose aim is is to 're-establish equilibrium', without which 'further growth and development may be impaired' (1991: 10–18).

Thus, Worden aligns his model of grief with a kind of life course transition and, indeed, draws explicitly on Havighurst's task-oriented model of childhood:

> there are certain developmental tasks that occur as the child grows. If the child does not complete a task on a particular level, then that child's adaptation is impaired when trying to complete tasks on higher levels (1991: 10).

For Worden, in grief and mourning, biographical *continuity*, rather than rupture, is therefore achieved through self-reflexive *practices* which involve growth, change and adjustment to one's social context.

This 'growth and change' orientation towards life takes little account of the temporal positioning of the individual within the life course, however. Rooted in developmental studies of childhood, it is targeted towards the desirable future self of the imagination and fails to address the significance of the remembered self of the past. Yet, if we stay with the example of grief counselling, what the 1990s have seen is a sustained challenge to the notion that the dead should be left behind and survivors helped to 'move on' into an unwelcome solo future. Under the title *Continuing Bonds*, Klass *et al*. open their edited collection as follows:

> this book reexamines the idea that the purpose of grief is to sever the bonds with the deceased in order to free the survivor to make new attachments. We offer an alternative model based on the mourner's continuing bonds with the deceased (1996: 3).

Data from Howarth's study of the experiences of elderly bereaved women reinforce this challenge. She shows that after the biographical rupture of widowhood 'older widows and widowers ... may continue to enjoy significant social relationships with their 'dead' spouse' (Hallam, Hockey and Howarth, 1999: 143). With regard to identification therefore, these are individuals who resist 'growth' into an unwelcome future identity. Continuity is achieved not as an aspect of any project of self perfection; rather it is the outcome of memory practices which project the remembered past into the imagined future:

> When a partner dies, especially after a relationship that has spanned many years, the world of the survivor maybe thrown into turmoil. In order to regain ontological security the individual must construct a biographical narrative which not only restores a sense of meaning but also provides continuity. In order to move forward to the future, they must have a clear sense of who they are in the present and of how the past has led them to the present (Hallam, Hockey and Howarth, 1999: 155).

Such opposed models of grief are instructive. They underscore further the need identified in this volume to draw attention to life-course transitions as arising in and through the engagement and effort of *individuals*. Identities are brought into being through embodied action; they are recollected, enacted and imagined by people. And, it is through such practices, we suggest, that ageing is primarily understood, experienced and, finally, known.

This brings us to one last question – and one which gives a final twist to our argument. Throughout this volume our orientation to the question – how do we know that we are ageing? – has been largely directed toward the present and the future. Its primary focus has been the ongoing, active embodiment of the process of identification. In this last chapter, we turn now to the past, to consider in more detail the specific contribution of memory to our understanding of ageing. Is it perhaps by looking back cross the life course, rather than to the present or the future, that we really get to know that ageing has happened; and, if this is the case, what part does memory play in the reconstruction of our ageing selves?

Reconstructing the past

That there are other ways in which we might apprehend ageing becomes apparent once we reverse our temporal orientation, away from the future toward the past. Memories and mementos fix for us moments in time past. They reveal to us the time that has elapsed and, as we think of that time, so it seems possible that we might, through memory, come to appreciate and understand the temporal flow of the life course. The seaside souvenir made of shells, gathering dust on the shelf, focuses our attention. It recalls a time *then* – that beach holiday in Brighton with the children – and reminds us of the temporal distance between then and *now* – the time when our youngest child is about to embark on a university career.

Drawing on the work of the French sociologist Violette Morin, Hoskins asks about the relationship we have to such objects. She makes the distinction between biographical objects – those which are centred on the person – and public commodities – those objects which have a more generalised public significance. The difference between them, as she points out, is not however intrinsic to the object. More important is what we, as individuals, do with the object and how the object figures in our lives. Thus, the shell souvenir of Brighton was, until bought by the child, simply a publicly available commodity. By bringing it home gleefully, keeping it for many years on a bedroom shelf until finally forgetting and disregarding it, the impersonal and tacky souvenir was transformed into an important biographical object, an object through which a life can be recalled and changing identities recorded. As Hoskins notes, 'biographical objects share our lives with us and if they gradually deteriorate and fade with the years, we recognise our own aging in the mirror of these personal possessions' (1998: 8).

However, more public commodities can also chart the ageing process for us. Even though we might not possess an object and make it integral to the private world of our home and family, we may nonetheless still recognise our ageing selves through our memory of a long-forgotten object or a place. Thus, pictures of the Rotunda Tower and Snow Hill station in Birmingham, push-button telephone boxes in museums and 45-inch records in second-hand shops, memories of frozen Jubbly drinks in triangular wax cartons, platform cork-soled shoes and midi-skirts, all remind the 46-year old woman of a childhood and adolescence spent in the Midlands in the 1960s. It underscores for her the ageing process by reminding her of the passage of time between then and now. And as Zonabend (1984) describes, rose cuttings, swapped between households and then nurtured into mature bushes, map out in their blooms whole sets of close-knit generational identities within a small French village.

Thus, it is in line with such views that Antze and Lambek (1996) argue that 'memory serves as both a phenomenological ground of identity...and the means for explicit identity construction' (1996: xvi). However, as they go on to point out, the role of memory in identity construction is always ambiguous for unconscious processes of selectivity, besides those of simple memory loss, work to shape particular 'truths' about ourselves. These truths are devised to both fit, or indeed contrast, with who we now think we are:

> If I am constituted by what I remember, what about all that I do not remember but that I know, because of other sources including my common sense tell me, must have been mine? Or what about that which I remember but would prefer to forget? Was that awkward adolescent really me? Can I still be him? (Antze and Lambek, 1996: xvi).

For them, 'the past and its retrieval in memory hold a curious place in our identities, one that simultaneously stabilises those identities in continuity and threatens to disrupt them' (Antze and Lambek, 1996: xvi).

Central to the argument put forward by Antze and Lambek (1996) is, then, that memory is a discourse of identity, serving to construct and reconstruct notions of ageing and identity. In this view, memory, therefore, becomes more than a way of accessing the past. It is also fundamental to the present, and by implication to the future, for memory has an important part to play in the subjective experience of the here and now: 'who people are is closely linked to what they think about memory, what they remember, and what they can can claim to remember' (Antze and Lambek, 1996: xxi).

In relation to questions of ageing and identity across the life course, this is a critical insight for it helps explain the wide variety of subjective experiences of ageing that can be found in the literature.

It also helps to demolish arguments which still claim some utility for static ageing categories for an understanding of the life course and its transitions. Finally, it lends further support to the argument we have been advancing in this volume, that is, that social identities across the life course have to be understood in terms of the particular embodied experiences of individuals in particular social and cultural contexts. If our present knowledge of our 'selves' as aged beings is, in part, a function of our memory of ourselves at previous ages then, clearly, it matters a great deal both *how* and *what* we remember about those life-course moments. It is *this* which is significant for our understanding of our present 20-40- or 60-year old selves.

Steedman (1986) makes this point explicitly in her autobiographical account of a working-class childhood. She explores her own and her mother's lives in parallel to argue against those who have generalised about working-class childhood (in a way that is never done for middle-class childhood) and for the importance of working with the complexity of the life course; to see it as it is lived out by individuals in particular moments. In a challenge to the romanticism of remembered accounts such as those offered by Seabrook (1982), which depict working-class life in terms of a heroic story of how material privations can be overcome by the consolation gained from shared discomfort, Steedman describes her mother as 'born into the old working class' yet, as a woman, failing to fit into this life style. On the contrary, she was a working-class Conservative, a woman who took up the ideas of the Food Reform, 'wanted a New Look skirt, a timbered country cottage, to marry a prince' (1986: 9). In recalling her own childhood, as the child of such a mother, Steedman says that,

> it seems now to have been a joyless childhood. There were neighbours who fed us meat and sweets, sorry for us, tea parties we went to that we were never allowed to return (1986: 44).

However, though as an adult it appears thus, Steedman insists that she does not '*remember* the oddness' (1986: 44, emphasis in original). The oddness is an adult reconstruction of the bare facts of a past; in her *memories* however, she is 'playing Annie Oakley by myself all summer long in the recreation ground, running up and down the hill in my brown gingham dress, wearing a cowboy hat and carrying a rifle' (1986: 44). Only as an adult has she learned to see her past as odd; as a child it seemed normal. It was the way life was. Memory thus serves to bolster self identity in different ways through the telling and retelling of particular kinds of narratives. This is not so much fiction perhaps as a set of particular and particularising rememberings. As Steedman observes: 'memory alone cannot resurrect past time because it is memory itself that shapes it, long after historical time has passed' (1986: 29).

This raises questions, therefore, about the salience of memories of the life course for our experience and understanding of the ageing process. As the cornerstone of psychotherapeutic regimes of governance and control of the 'self' (Rose, 1989) the life course is understood as essentially unidirectional – 'childhood' experiences shape those of 'adulthood'. Thus, present adult identity is deemed to have its foundations in a childish past. However, what work on memory reveals, and accounts such as Steedman make clear, is that, although by looking back to the past we do *know* that we have aged, understanding that as an experiential process involves more than simply memory. It includes making comparisons between then and now; it involves using our present knowledge and standpoint to make sense of and interpret past events. The process and experience of ageing is not *remembered*, then, as an orderly transition or rite of passage between a series of aged social identities across the life course, however much we like to think of it in this way. Moreover, this knowledge is only accessed by a *constructed* narrative of comparison. This continually tacks back and forth, between memories of the past and our present lives, between who one was and who one now is. This suggests therefore that, in the last analysis, the *experience* of ageing – like that of time passing – is essentially imperceptible; all that we can know about ageing are its effects on the mind and body, its identity outcomes and social consequences.

Biography, autobiography and the ageing process

Critical writing on the life history method, autobiography and biographical writing makes these processes even more explicit. As Stanley notes, the very act of writing biographically or autobiographically is ideological, rather than factual. As she points out 'both are by nature artful enterprises which select, shape and produce a very unnatural product, for no life is lived quite so much under a single spot-light as the conventional form of written autobiographies suggests' (1992: 4). It is an ideological process in the sense that biographies and autobiographies present a set of ideas about a person. These are not only inevitably partial, being dependent upon memory and scattered evidence, but also socially constructed in the sense that they are authored into being, either by the self or another. This explains why, as Stanley notes, that 'biography tells us, variously, that Virginia Woolf was entirely apolitical or was a quintessentially political writer; was supported by Leonard Woolf or had her life ruined by him' (1992: 11). The presentation of one's own life or that of another becomes bound not only by the implicit, or indeed explicit, biases and persuasions of the author, by the fragmentary and selective nature of memory or the scanty evidence of a life which survives. It is also constrained by the process of presentation itself. This insists that the story of life is, in fact, a story. Thus a coherent and explanatory narrative is carved out of a set of diverse experiences and a set of past identities are assembled to account for a present identity. Nowhere is this more clear than in the *Bildungsroman* tradition of biography, described by Samuel and Thompson as follows:

> Anticipatory moments are seized on which appear retrospectively momentous. The woman who prides herself on being a 'born rebel' retraces her earliest steps towards independence (1990: 9).

As in the novel form, a *Bildungsroman* biography thus traces a heroic life through the stages of the life course: from the early learning years of childhood, through the struggles of youth to the pinnacle and wisdom of adulthood (Gullestad, 1996).

However, although new postmodernist modes of auto/biographical writing often reject such a format and readily acknowledge the socially constructed character of present identities, what remains largely untheorised is the role of the ageing process itself to this endeavour. Like the body in social theory, it is an absent presence. Unacknowledged yet fundamental and inescapable, ageing is the vehicle for transition between identities of all kinds across the life course, *however* they are accounted for.

Though not explicitly stated by Gullestad, it is in fact this link between the relentlessness of the ageing process and its role in shaping identity which sustains her analysis that the current populist and academic fascination with auto/biography is a sign of the emergence of identity politics in modernity. For example, Gullestad describes the 'popular urge to create distinct identities through autobiographical practice' as a response to the accelerated pace of modern life which, through intensive bureaucratisation, has led people to experience the self as fragmented (1996: 14). Looking back at the ageing process via auto/biography, she argues, allows the self to be reconstituted as whole. She sums her position up as follows:

> ... for several hundred years now, bureaucratisation has resulted in both the nostalgic longing for an assumed former wholeness *and* the development of distinct genres of subjectivity and reflection about the continuity of a self *behind* various roles. Individual people integrate more or less disparate roles in their everyday lives. Autobiography – written or told – is a means of constructing a unified self out of a fragmented life. It is precisely the accelerated change in, and fragmentation of, present-day society that turns identity and self-creation into such crucial and central issues (1996: 16).

This is illustrated well in Lorna Sage's account of her own experience of writing *Bad Blood*. Sage (2001) describes the project as like 'opening a door on to the past', and for her, it is in her grandfather that she finds her 'self':

> My bitter, theatrical vicar-grandfather, stagnating in the remote rural parish of Hanmer in North Wales for his sins (women and drink, mostly) was my reference point, my black flag on the map of the past, my arrow pointing – 'you were here', this is where you begin (*Guardian*, 2001).

This bad blood of her grandfather, which entitles the memoir, is revealed by Sage to run through the veins of her own past. His identity lives on through her, signalling various transition points in her life and aspects of her identity. Her early ability to read, her bookishness and skill at passing exams, though grudgingly approved of by the rest of her family, was also seen to have a 'sinister, Grandpa side to them'. Later, conceiving a child and marrying shotgun at 16 was regarded as irrefutable proof that Grandpa's peccadilloes lived on in her. Sage herself, writing as a successful academic, reflects that, although she was unwilling to take on his deviousness, self-pity and self-dramatisation, she nonetheless sees her own identity as she has aged as being inextricably linked with his:

> There were moments when he seemed to reach a skinny hand out of the past to take hold of me, as when he confided to the diary, 'Today' (October 7, 1934) 'I make another resolution to spend my time in journalism and writing. I think I can make good now ...' Well he didn't, but in a strange way he was now doing it through me (*Guardian*, 2001).

Thus, though it might appear that memory and auto/biographical narratives could provide one route to access the experience of ageing, enabling us to locate the transitions we have made between aged identities by fixing them in times past, as we have shown, the partiality and selectivity of memory and the ideological positioning of the authorial voice, renders this as elusive as ever.

Past identities: the body speaks

As noted in Chapters 2 and 3, the process of change which ageing brings to the physical body are, unless through accident or ill health, generally imperceptible on a day-to-day basis. Only once a larger span of time has passed might the body's ageing be consciously registered. At 40-years old, a single grey hair may stay unseen or be slyly removed. Ten years later, a greying head of hair has become resistant to such strategies and is taken as a sure and certain symbol that one has aged. However, individual bodies differ in the ways and the extent to which time and age leave their mark and make their alteration. Age-based rituals of transition – from formal rites of passage through to simple birthday celebrations – therefore mark, first and foremost, changes in social status or position. Simple numerical accounting of time passing tells us little about the physical state of the body. Thus it is that the body both offers *and* denies us access to knowledge of our own ageing.

There is therefore a curious relationship between the physicality of the body and the process of embodiment with regard to the ageing process. This is particularly marked in contemporary industrialised societies. As noted in Chapter 4, in contrast to previous generations, numerical age has become vested with such great bureaucratic and symbolic power that – at all ages – the denotation of a person's age has come to reflect their personhood, permitting and denying access to different kinds of social arenas. Thus, the relentless and irreversible determination of the physical process of ageing, which is calculated in terms of years lived through, would appear to offer a way to cognitively regulate and chart the passage from birth to death. It would seem to link physical progress and decline to the tread of advancing years. And yet, at the start of the twenty-first century, this very physicality of the body's life course is becoming a less and less firm indicator of age-based ability. With better state provision of health and welfare regimes, increases in cosmetic and orthopaedic surgery and a more concentrated concern for individual health and fitness, the ageing body is being made, and literally remade, to resist and challenge the ageing process. As noted in Chapter 6, for many theorists, such developments suggest therefore that the patterning of the life course which ageing brings has no longer the same inevitability as it once had. Instead, personal choice and life strategies are flagged as offering alternative routes and regimes. How far then is it the case, as we have been arguing, that our experience of embodiment does still tell us that we are ageing ? And, if it does, how does this occur?

To answer these questions, we return once more to the questions of structure and agency which have been addressed throughout this volume. Looking at the examples of gender and sexuality, work and family life we have seen empirical illustrations of the ways in which different kinds of social identities across the life course are brought into being and replaced in and across these different domains, both as an ideological structuring of the ageing process and in terms of lives lived. In this sense, these different social identities can be regarded as age-based. They are embodied by people at different points in their lives. They are taken up, taken on and enacted by individuals with the approval – and indeed sometimes disapproval – of others depending upon when – *in the life course* – they appear. Thus, fundamental to our perception of social identities is, we would argue, a primarily bodily-based perception of the ageing process.

In some instances this is clearly and demonstrably evident. Thus, as we have seen in Chapter 8, the demand by a 15-year old girl that she be given breast implants to improve her life-course chances of becoming famous was refused by a surgeon and condemned by the public at large. The possession of big breasts within western culture is symbolic of the sexually active adult woman rather than the teenage girl.

Elsewhere, a body-based perspective remains much more implicit, unconscious and barely articulated. Yet, it is nonetheless as powerful in its symbolic potency to confer age-based identity. For older people, for example, the body as it now is offers a contrast to the body as it was: through photographs of the body at a younger age and through embodied memories of what the body had, at some point in the past, been able to accomplish. Thus it is that, by looking back and recollecting, the present and the future both become framed by a sense of loss – the loss of earlier competences, looks or accomplishments. And it is through such comparisons, between then and now, between what was and what now is, that the time that has elapsed becomes understood and explained in terms of the physical deterioration which the ageing process can bring. For young people, by contrast, the remembered past of the body signals a rather different experience of ageing. Its change in material form is viewed in terms of the welcome loss of unwanted babyish attributes in favour of the gains to be got from the acquisition of the new physical competences which accompany, for example, the transition from childhood to early adolescence. This kind of bodily memory, frequently represented in fulsome detail in the photographic records of families, thus registers this part of the ageing process as a positive, rather than negative, experience.

Conclusion

Our task in this volume has been to build on existing theories of identity, and develop them within the hitherto neglected context of ageing across the life course. Core to this, we have argued, is the triangular relationship between the body, the self and society which is based on three propositions. First, that ageing can only take place at the site of the body. Second, that embodiment necessarily brings with it the social experience of ageing. Third, the biological fact of ageing means that individuals move, inexorably, from birth to death across the life course. Thus, our argument does incorporate what Nicholson (1995) terms a biological foundationalist perspective in that, at some level, it acknowledges a grounding in the 'given' of the ageing body. This is not the same, however, as giving biology a determining role. Rather, we have taken the ageing of the body into proper account in our recognition of the three fundamental issues outlined above. Our argument has been, therefore, that embodiment across the life course has to be understood in terms of an active self, inhabiting a body within particular social structures, producing and reproducing those structures as a set of particular cultural understandings of the ageing process.

It is our focus on the modern era which has made us ask why it is that age and identity meet in the body in the way they appear to in the West. After all, there is no necessity, as we have shown, for the ageing body to confer identity. Throughout this book, we have identified individuals who transgress age-based categorical boundaries and have pointed to societies and histories where age does not count. Thus, though as middle-aged women we are supposedly completing this book within a postmodern context which has seen a withering away of age-based identities, the transcendence of age, as we know from our own experience, requires constant vigilance over bodies which nonetheless persist in ageing.

References

Adam, B. (1990) *Time and Social Theory*. Cambridge: Polity Press.

Adam, B. (1995) *Timewatch: The Social Analysis of Time*. Cambridge: Polity Press.

Alderson, P. (1993) *Children's Consent to Surgery*. Milton Keynes: Open University.

Alderson, P. (1995) *Listening to Children: Children Ethics and Social Research*. London: Barnardos.

Allan, G. and Crow, G. (eds) (1989) *Home and Family: Creating the Domestic Space*. London: Macmillan – now Palgrave Macmillan.

Allat, P. (1996) 'Conceptualizing parenting from the standpoint of children: relationship and transition in the life course' in J. Brannen and M. O'Brien (eds) *Children and Families: Research and Policy*. London: Falmer Press.

Antze, P. and Lambek, M. (1996) (eds) *Tense Past: Cultural Essays in Trauma and Memory*. London: Routledge.

Arber, S. and Ginn, J. (1991) 'The invisibility of age: gender and social class in later life', *Sociological Review*, 39: 260–91.

Arber, S. and Ginn, J. (1995) *Connecting Gender and Age*. Buckingham: Open University Press.

Armstrong, D. (1981) 'Pathological life and death: medical spatialisation and geriatrics', *Social Science and Medicine*, 15(A): 253–7.

Armstrong, D. (1983) *Political Anatomy of the Body: Medical Knowledge in Britain in the Twentieth Century*. Cambridge: Cambridge University Press.

Armstrong, D. (1983b) 'The invention of infant mortality', *Sociology of Health and Illness*, 8: 211–32.

Armstrong, D. (1987) 'Bodies of knowledge: Foucault and the problem of human anatomy', in G. Scambler (ed.) *Sociological Theory and Medical Sociology*. London: Tavistock.

Bachelard, G. ([1958] 1994) *The Poetics of Space: The Classic Look at How We Experience Intimate Spaces*. Boston: Beacon Press.

Barth, F. (1969) 'Introduction', in F. Barth (ed.) *Ethnic Groups and Boundaries: The Social Organisation of Culture Difference*. Oslo: Universitetsforlaget.

Battersby, C. (1993) 'Her body/her boundaries: gender and the metaphysics of containment', in A. E. Benjamin (ed.) *The Body*, Special Issue of *Journal of Philosophy and the Visual Arts*, 4: 30–9.

Bauby, J. (1998) *The Diving-Bell and the Butterfly*. London: Fourth Estate.

Bauman, Z. (1992) *Mortality, Immortality and Other Life Strategies*. Cambridge: Polity.

Bauman, Z. (1997) Plenary paper, BSA Conference, *Power and Resistance*, University of York.

Baxter, P. T. W. and Almagor, V. (eds) (1978) *Age, Generation and Time*. London: Hurst.

Becker, A. (1995) *Body, Self and Society: A View from Fiji*. Philadelphia: University of Pennsylvania.

Belmont, N. ([1974] 1979) *Arnold Van Gennep: The Creator of French Ethnography*. Chicago: University of Chicago Press.

Berkeman, O. (1999) 'Basically, we're pleased' *Guardian*, 15 December.

Bernardes, J. (1986) 'Multidimensional developmental pathways: a proposal to faciliate the conceptualisation of "Family Diversity"', *The Sociological Review*, 34(3): 590–610

Bernades, J. (1997) *Family Studies: An Introduction*. London: Routledge.

Berteaux, D. and Kohli, M. (1984) 'The life story approach: a continental view', *Annual Review of Sociology*, 10: 215–37.

Billington, R., Hockey, J. and Strawbridge, S. (1998) *Exploring Self and Society*. Basingstoke: Macmillan – now Palgrave Macmillan.

Blaikie, A. (1997) 'Age consciousness and modernity: the social reconstruction of retirement', *Self, Agency and Society*, 1(1): 9–26.

Bloch, M. and Parry, J. (1982) *Death and the Regeneration of Life*. Cambridge: Cambridge University Press.

Bloor, M., Monaghan, L., Dobash, R. P. and Dobash, R. E. (1998) 'The body as a chemistry experiment: steroid use among South Wales body builders', in S. Nettleton and J. Watson (eds) *The Body in Everyday Life*. London: Routledge.

Brannen, J., Hepinstall, E. and Bhopal, K. (2000) *Connecting Children: Care and Family Life in Later Childhood*. London: Routledge/Falmer.

Bromley, R. (1988) *Lost Narratives: Popular Fictions, Politics and Recent History*. London: Routledge.

Bryder, L. (1992) 'Wonderlands of buttercups, clover and daisies: tuberculosis and the open-air school movement' in R. Cooter (ed.) (1992) *In the Name of the Child: Health and Welfare 1880–1940*. London: Routledge.

Buckingham, D. (2000) *After the Death of Childhood: Growing up in the Age of Electronic Media*. Cambridge: Polity Press.

Bytheway, B. (1995) *Ageism*. Buckingham: Open University Press.

Bytheway, B. and Johnson, J. (1996) 'Valuing lives? Obituaries and the life course', *Mortality* 1 (2): 219–34.

Callan, H. and Ardener, S. (eds) (1984) *The Incorporated Wife*. London: Croom Helm.

Carsten, J. (ed.) (2000) *Cultures of Relatedness: New Approaches to the Study of Kinship*. Cambridge: Cambridge University Press.

Cavan, R. S., Burgess, E. W., Havighurst, R. J. and Goldhamer, H. (1949) *Personal Adjustment in Old Age*. Chicago: Research Associates Inc.

Chapman, T. (1999) 'Stage sets for ideal lives: images of home in contemporary show homes', in T. Chapman and J. Hockey (eds) *Ideal Homes? Social Change and Domestic Life*. London: Routledge.

Christensen, P. (1993) 'The social construction of help among Danish children', *Sociology of Health and Illness*, 15(4): 488–502.

Christensen, P. (2000) 'Childhood and the cultural constitution of vulnerable bodies' in A. Prout (ed.) *The Body, Childhood and Society*, London: Macmillan – now Palgrave Macmillan.

Christensen, P., Hockey, J. and James, A. (1997) '"You have neither neighbours nor privacy": ambiguities in the experience of emotional well-being of women in farming families', *The Sociological Review*, 45 (4): 621–44.

Christensen, P., Hockey, J. and James, A. (1998) '"You just get on with it": questioning models of welfare dependency in a rural community', in I. A. Edgar and A. Russel (eds) *The Anthropology of Welfare*. London: Routledge.

Christensen, P., Hockey, J. and James, A. (1999) '"That's farming Rosie...." Power and familial relations in an agricultural community', in J. Seymour and P. Bagguley (eds) *Relating Intimacies: Power and Resistance*. London: Macmillan – now Palgrave Macmillan.

Christensen, P., Hockey, J. and James, A. (2001) 'Talk, silence and the material world: patterns of indirect communication among agricultural families in Northern England' in J. Hendry and C. W. Watson (eds) *An Anthropology of Indirect Communication*. London: Routledge.

Christensen, P. and James, A. (2000) 'Children's and parents' negotiations over children's time use'. Unpublished paper presented at ESRC Children 5–16 Final Conference, London House.

Clarke, A. J. (1998) 'Window shopping at home: classifides, catalogues and new consumer skills', in D. Miller (ed.) *Material Cultures. Why some things matter*. London: UCL Press.

Coffield, F. (1987) 'From the celebration to the marginalization of youth', in G. Cohen (ed.) *Social Change and the Life Course*. London: Tavistock.

Cohen, A. P. (1994) *Self Consciousness*. London: Routledge.

Cohen, A. P. and Rapport, N. (1995) *Questions of Consciousness*. London: Routledge.

Cohen, P. (1997) *Rethinking the Youth Question*. London: Macmillan – now Palgrave Macmillan.

Connolly, P. (1998) *Racism, Gender Identities and Young Children*. London: Routledge.

Conway, S. (2000) *'I'd be unhealthy if nobody wanted me anymore': A Sociological Analysis of the Relationship between Ageing and Health Beliefs*, unpublished PhD thesis, University of Hull.

Cooley, C. H. ([1902] 1964) *Human Nature and the Social Order*. New York: Scribner's.

Cooter, R. (ed) (1992) *In the Name of the Child: Health and Welfare 1880–1940*. London: Routledge.

Craib, I. (1998) *Experiencing Identity*. London: Sage.

Crapanzano, V. (1984) 'Life histories', *American Anthropologist*, 86: 953–60.

Cumming, E. and Henry, W. E. (1961) *Growing Old: The Process of Disengagement*. New York: Basic Books.

Dalley, G. (1988) *Ideologies of Caring: Rethinking, Community and Collectivism*. London: Macmillan – now Palgrave Macmillan.

Daniel, P. and Ivatts, J. (1998) *Children and Social Policy*. London: Macmillan – now Palgrave Macmillan.

Davidoff, L., L'Esperance, J. and Newby, H. (1976) 'Landscape with figures: home and community in English society', in J. Mitchell and A. Oakley (eds) *The Rights and Wrongs of Women*. London: Penguin.

Davis, K. (1995) *Reshaping the Female Body*. London: Routledge.

Dennis, B., Henriques, F. and Slaughter, C. (1956) *Coal is our Life*. London: Tavistock.

Denzin, N. (1989)'Interpretive interactionism', *Applied Social Research Methods Series*, 16. Newbury Park, CA: Sage.

Department of Health (1990) Abortion Act (1967) amended 1990, London: HMSO.

Dreitzel, H. P. (ed.) (1973) *Childhood and Socialization*. London: Collier-Macmillan.

du Gay, P., Evans, J. and Redman, P. (2000) *Identity: A Reader*. London: Sage.

Duncan, G. J. (1991) 'The changing economic environment of childhood' in A. C. Huston (ed.) *Children in Poverty*. Cambridge: Cambridge University Press.

Durkheim, E. ([1895] 1964) *The Division of Labour in Society*. New York: Free Press.

Durkheim, E. ([1897] 1966) *Suicide*. New York: Free Press.

Dyer, R. (1997) *White*. London: Routledge.

Eisenstadt, S. N. (1956) *From Generation to Generation*. New York: Free Press of Glencoe.

Elkin, F. (1960) *The Child and Society*. New York: Random House.

Elkind, D. (1981) *The Hurried Child: Growing Up Too Fast Too Soon*. Reading, MA: Addison Wesley.

Elliot, B. J. (1991) 'Demographic trends in domestic life, 1945–87', in D. Clark (ed.) *Marriage, Domestic Life and Social Change*. London: Routledge.

Erikson, E. (1950) *Childhood and Society*. New York: Norton.

Fairhurst, E. (1998) 'Growing old gracefully' as opposed to 'mutton dressed as lamb': the social construction of recognising older women', in

S. Nettleton and J. Watson (eds) *The Body in Everyday Life*. London: Routledge.

Farmer, P. (2001) 'I didn't have a clue', *Guardian*, January 18.

Featherstone, M. (1991) 'The Body in Consumer Culture', in M. Featherstone, M. Hepworth and B. S. Turner (eds) *The Body, Social Process and Cultural Theory*. London: Sage.

Featherstone, M. and Hepworth. M. (1985) 'The male menopause: lifestyle and sexuality', *Maturitas, 7*: 235–46.

Featherstone, M. and Hepworth, M. (1989) 'Ageing and old age: reflections on the postmodern lifecourse', in B. Bytheway, T. Keil, P. Allat and A. Bryman (eds) *Becoming and Being Old: Sociological Approaches to Later Life*. London: Sage.

Featherstone, M. and Hepworth, M. (1991) 'The mask of ageing and the postmodern lifecourse', in M. Featherstone, M. Hepworth and B.S. Turner (eds) *The Body, Social Process and Cultural Theory*. London: Sage.

Featherstone, M. and Hepworth. M. (1995) 'Images of positive aging: a case study of *Retirement Choice* magazine', in M. Featherstone and A. Wernick (eds) *Images of Aging: Cultural Representations of Later Life*. London: Routledge.

Featherstone, M. and Wernick, A. (eds) (1995) *Images of Aging: Cultural Representations of Later Life*. London: Routledge.

Finch, J. (1989) *Family Obligations and Social Change*. London: Polity.

Finch, J. and Mason, J. (1993) *Negotiating Family Responsibilities*. London: Routledge.

Flint, J. (1994) 'The First Cut', *Guardian, 25* April.

Foster, P. (1995) *Women and the Health Care Industry: An Unhealthy Relationship?* Buckingham: Open University Press.

Foucault, M. (1975) *The Birth of the Clinic: An Archaeology of Medical Perception*. New York: Vintage Books.

Frank, A. (1991) 'For a sociology of the body: an analytical review', in M. Featherstone, M. Hepworth and B. S. Turner (eds) *The Body: Social Process and Cultural Theory*. London: Sage.

Franklin, S. (1997) *Embodied Progress*. London: Routledge.

Furman, F. K. (1997) *Facing the Mirror. Older Women and Beauty Shop Culture*. New York: Routledge.

Fyfe, A. (1989) *Child Labour*. Cambridge: Polity Press.

Giddens, A. (1979) *Central Problems in Social Theory*. London: Macmillan – now Palgrave Macmillan.

Giddens, A. (1989) *Sociology*. Cambridge: Polity Press.

Giddens, A. (1991) *Modernity and Self-Identity*. Oxford: Polity.

Giddens, A. (1992) *The Transformation of Intimacy: Sexuality, Love and Eroticism*. Cambridge: Polity.

Gillis, J. R. (1996) *A World of their Own Making*. Oxford: Oxford University Press.

Gillis, J. R. (1999) 'A world of their own making: families and the modern culture of aging', in J. Povlsen, S. Mellemgaard and N. de Connick-Smith (eds) *Childhood and Old Age: Equals or Opposites*. Odense: Odense University Press.

Giroux, H. A. (1998) 'Stealing innocence: the politics of child beauty pageants', in H. Jenkins (ed.) *The Children's Culture Reader*. New York: New York University Press.

Goffman, E. (1963) *Stigma: Notes on the Management of Spoiled Identity*. Englewood Cliffs, NJ: Prentice Hall.

Goffman, E. (1968) *Asylums: Essays on the Social Situation of Mental Patients and Other Inmates*. Harmondsworth: Penguin.

Goffman, E. (1971) *The Presentation of Self in Everyday Life*. Harmondsworth: Penguin.

Goffman, E. (1974) *Frame Analysis*. New York: Harper Row.

Goldsack, L. (1999) 'A haven in a heartless world? Women and domestic violence', in T. Chapman and J. Hockey (eds) *Ideal Homes? Social Change and Domestic Life*. London: Routledge.

Goody, J. (1972) 'The evolution of the family' in P. Laslett (ed.) *Household and Family in Past Time*. Cambridge: Cambridge University Press.

Gullestad, M. (1996) *Everyday Life Philosophers: Modernity, Morality and Autobiography in Norway*, Oslo: Scandinavian University Press.

Hall, S. (1996) 'Introduction: who needs 'identity'?' in S. Hall and P. du Gay (eds) *Questions of Cultural Identity*. London: Sage.

Hall, S. (2000) 'Who needs "identity?", in P. du Gay, J. Evans and P. Redman (eds) *Identity: A Reader*. London: Sage.

Hallam, E., Hockey, J. and Howarth, G. (1999) *Beyond the Body: Death and Social Identity*. London: Routledge.

Hareven, T. (ed.) (1978) *Transitions: The Family and the Life Course in Historical Perspective*, London: Academic Press.

Hareven, T. K. (1978) 'Introduction: the historical study of the life course', in T. K. Hareven (ed.) *Transitions: The Family and the Life course in Historical Perspective*, London: Academic Press.

Hareven, T. K. (1982) *Family Time and Industrial* Time. Cambridge: Cambridge University Press.

Hareven, T. K. (1986) 'Historical changes in the social construction of the life course', in M. Kohli and J. W. Meyer (eds) Social Structure and Social Construction of Life Stages (Proceedings), *Human Development*, 29: 145–80.

Hareven, T. K. (1995) 'Changing images of aging and the social construction of the life course' in M. Featherstone and Wernick, A. (eds) (1995) *Images of Aging: Cultural Representations of Later Life*. London: Routledge.

Hareven. T. K. (2000) *Families, History and Social Change: Life-course and Cross-cultural Perspectives*. Colorado: Westerview Press.

Harper, S. and Laws, G. (1995) 'Rethinking the geography of ageing', *Progress in Human Geography*, 19 (2): 199–221.

Harris, C. (1987) 'The individual and society: a processual approach', in A. Bryman, B. Bytheway, P. Allat and T. Keil (eds) *Rethinking the Life Cycle*, Basingstoke: Macmillan – now Palgrave Macmillan.

Havighurst, R. J., Neugarten, B. L. and Tobin, S. S. (1964) 'Disengagement, personality and life satisfaction in later years', in P. F. Hansen (ed.) *Age with a Future*. Philadelphia: Davis.

Hazan, H. (1994) *Old Age: Constructions and Deconstructions*. Cambridge: Cambridge University Press.

Hebdige, D. (1979) *Subculture: The Meaning of Style*. London: Methuen.

Held, T. (1986) 'Institutionalization and Deinstitutionalization of the Life Course', in M. Kohli and J. W. Meyer (eds) Social Structure and Social Construction of Life Stages (Proceedings), *Human Development*, 29: 145–80.

Helman, H. (1990) *Culture, Health and Illness*. Oxford: Butterworth Heinemann.

Hendrick, H. (1997) 'Constructions and reconstructions of British childhood: an interpretative survey, 1800 to the present', in A. James and A. Prout (eds) *Constructing and Reconstructing Childhood*. London: Falmer Press.

Hendry, J. (1999) *An Introduction to Social Anthropology: Other People's Worlds*. Basingstoke: Macmillan – now Palgrave Macmillan.

Hepworth, M. (1987) 'The mid life phase', in G. Cohen (ed.) (1987) *Social Change and the Life Course*. London: Tavistock.

Hepworth, M. (1999) 'Privacy, security and respectability: the ideal Victorian home', in T. Chapman and J. Hockey (eds) *Ideal Homes? Social Change and Domestic Life*. London: Routledge.

Hepworth, M. and Featherstone, M. (1982) *Surviving Middle Age*. Oxford: Basil Blackwell.

Hertz, R. ([1907] 1960) *Death and the Right Hand*. New York: Free Press.

Higgs, P. (1995) 'Citizenship and old age: the end of the road?', *Ageing and Society*, 15: 535–50.

Hockey, J. (1992) *Making the Most of a Funeral*. London: Cruse-Bereavement Care.

Hockey, J. and James, A. (1993) *Growing Up and Growing Old*. London: Sage.

Holland, J., Ramazanoglu, C., Sharpe, S. and Thomson, R. (1998) *The Male in the Head*. London: The Tufnell Press.

Holstein, J. A. and Gubrium, J. F. (2000) *The Self We Live By*, New York: Oxford University Press.

Hoskins, J. (1998) *Biographical Objects: How Things Tell the Stories of Peoples Lives*. London: Routledge.

Howkins, A. (1981) 'The taming of Whitsun: the changing face of a nineteenth-century rural holiday', in E. Yeo and S. Yeo (eds) *Popular Culture and Class Conflict 1590–1914*. London: Harvester.

Hummel, C., Rey, J., Lalive d'Epinay, C. J. (1995) 'Children's drawings of grandparents', in M. Featherstone and A. Wernick (eds) (1995) *Images of Aging: Cultural Representations of Later Life*. London: Routledge.

Huston, A. C. (ed.) (1991) *Children in Poverty*. Cambridge: Cambridge University Press.

Irvine, J. M. (1995) 'Regulated passions: the invention of inhibited sexual desire and sexual addiction', in J. Terry and J. Urla (eds) *Deviant Bodies*. Bloomington: Indiana Press.

James, A. (1986) 'Leaning to belong: the boundaries of adolescence', in A. P. Cohen (ed.) *Symbolising Boundaries: Identity and Diversity in British Cultures*. Manchester: Manchester University Press.

James, A. (1993) *Childhood Identities*. Edinburgh: Edinburgh University Press.

James, A. (1998) 'Imaging children 'at home', 'in the family' and 'at school': movement between the spatial and temporal markers of childhood identity in Britain' in N. Rapport and A. Dawson (eds) *Migrants of Identity*. Oxford: Berg.

James, A. (1999) 'Parents: a children's perspective', in A. Bainham, S. Day Sclater and M. Richards (eds) *What is a Parent? A Socio-legal Analysis*. Oxford: Hart Publishing.

James, A. (2000) 'Embodied being(s): understanding the self and the body in childhood' in A. Prout (ed.) *The Body, Childhood and Society*. London: Macmillan – now Palgrave Macmillan.

James, A. L. and James, A. (2001) 'Tightening the net: children, community and control', *British Journal of Sociology* 52(2): 211–28.

James, A. and Jenks, C. (1996) 'Public perceptions of childhood criminality' *British Journal of Sociology*, 47 (2): 315–31.

James, A. and Prout, A. (1997) 'Re-presenting childhood: time and transition in the study of childhood', in A. James and A. Prout (eds) *Constructing and Reconstructing Childhood*. London: Falmer Press.

Jenkins, R. (1996) *Social Identity*. London: Routledge.

Jenkins, S. and Jarvis, S. (1999) 'Marital splits and income changes: evidence from the British Household Survey Panel', *Population Studies*, 53(2), 237–54.

Jenks, C. (1996) *Childhood*. London: Routledge.

Jordanova, L. (1989) *Sexual Visions: Images of Gender in Science and Medicine between the Eighteenth and Twentieth Centuries*. London: Harvester Wheatsheaf.

Katz, C. (1993) 'Growing girls/closing circles: limits on the spaces of knowing in rural Sudan and US cities', in C. Katz and J. Monk (eds) *Full Circles: Geographies of Women over the Life Course*. London: Routledge.

Kelley, P., Buckingham, D. and Davies, H. (1999) 'Talking dirty: children, sexual knowledge and television' in *Childhood*, 6(2): 221–43.

Kenyon, L. (1999) 'A home from home: students' transitional experience of home', in T. Chapman and J. Hockey (eds) *Ideal Homes? Social Change and Domestic Life*. London: Routledge.

Kenyon, L. (2000) *In their own words: a biographical approach to the study of young adults' household formation*, Paper presented at the BSA Annual Conference: Making Time/Marking Time, University of York.

Kimball, S. T. (1960) 'Introduction', in A. Van Gennep, *The Rites of Passage*. London: Routledge and Kegan Paul.

Kitzinger, J. (1997) 'Who are you kidding? Children, power and the struggle against sexual abuse', in A. James and A. Prout (eds) *Constructing and Reconstructing Childhood*. London: Falmer Press.

Klass, D., Silverman, P. R. and Nickman, S. L. (1996) *Continuing Bonds: New Understandings of Grief*. Washington D.C.: Taylor and Francis.

Kohli, M. and Meyer, J. W. (1986) 'Social structure and social construction of the life stages' (Proceedings), *Human Development*, 29: 145–80.

Kondo, D. K. (1990) *Crafting Selves: Power, Gender and Discourses of Identity*. London and Chicago: University of Chicago Press.

Komaromy, C. and Hockey, J. (2001) '"Naturalizing" death among older adults in residential care', in J. Hockey, J. Katz and N. Small (eds) *Grief, Mourning and Death Ritual*. Buckingham: Open University Press.

Lakoff, G. and Johnson, M. (1980) *Metaphors We Live By*. Chicago: University of Chicago Press.

Laws, S. (1990) *Issues of Blood: The Politics of Menstruation*. London: Macmillan – now Palgrave Macmillan.

Layder, D. (1994) *Understanding Social Theory*. London: Sage.

Layne, L. (2000) '"He was a real baby with real things": a material culture analysis of personhood, parenthood and pregnancy loss', *Journal of Material Culture*, 5(3): 321–47.

Le Vine, R. Dixon, S., LeVine, S., Richman, A., Leiderman, P. H. Keefer, C. H. and Brazelton, T. B. (eds) (1994) *Child Care and Culture: Lessons from Africa* Cambridge: Cambridge University Press.

Leach, E. (1966) 'Two essays concerning the symbolic representation of time', in E.R. Leach *Rethinking Anthropology*. London: Athlone Press.

Lees, S. (1986) *Losing Out: Sexuality and Adolescent Girls*. London: Hutchinson.

Lyon, C. (1995) 'Representing children – towards 2000 and beyond', *Representing Children*, 8 (2): 8–18.

Lyon, M. L. and Barbalet, J. M. (1994) 'Society's body: emotion and the "somatization" of social theory', in T. J. Csordas (ed.) *Embodiment and Experience: The Existential Ground of Culture and Self*. Cambridge: Cambridge University Press.

Marshall, T. H, (1950) *Citizenship and Social Change*. London: Pluto.

Martin, E. (1987) *The Woman in the Body*. Milton Keynes: Open University Press.

Mauss, M. ([1934] 1976) 'Techniques of the body', *Economy and Society*, 2: 70–88.

Mayall, B. (1996) *Children, Health and the Social Order*. Buckingham: Open University Press.

Mayer, P. and Mayer, I. (1990) 'A dangerous age: from boy to young man in Red Xhosa youth organisations', in P. Spencer (ed.) *Anthropology and the Riddle of the Sphinx: Paradoxes of Change in the Lifecourse*. London: Routledge.

McNamee, S. (2000) 'Foucault's heterotopia and children's everyday lives' in *Childhood*, 7 (4): 479–93.

McRobbie, A. and Thornton, S. (1995) 'Rethinking "moral panic" for a multi-mediated world', *British Journal of Sociology*, 46 (4): 559–74.

Mead, G. H. (1934) *Mind, Self and Society: From the Standpoint of a Social Behaviourist*. Chicago: Chicago University Press.

Meyrowitz, J. (1985) *No sense of Place: The Impact of Electronic Media on Social Behavior*. Oxford: Oxford University Press.

Ministerial Group on the Family (1998) *Supporting Families: A Consultation Document*. TSO: London.

Morgan, D. (1996) *Family Connections*. Cambridge: Polity Press.

Morrow, V. (1998) *Understanding Families: Children's Perspectives*. London: National Children's Bureau.

Mulkay, M. (1993) 'Social death in Britain', in D. Clark (ed.) *The Sociology of Death*. Oxford: Blackwell Publishers/The Sociological Review.

Murch, M. (1995) 'Listening to the voice of the child – critical transitions, support and representation for children' *Representing Children*, 8 (2): 19–27.

Murphy, M. (1987) 'Measuring the family life cycle: concepts, data and methods', in A. Bryman, B. Bytheway, P. Allat and T. Keil (eds) *Rethinking the Life Cycle*, Basingstoke: Macmillan – now Palgrave Macmillan.

National Family and Parenting Institute (1999) *The Millennial Family*. London: MORI.

Neale, B., Wade, A. and Smart, C. (1998) *'I just get on with it': Children's Experiences of Family Life following Parental Separation and Divorce*. Leeds University: Centre for Research on Family Kinship and Childhood.

Nettleton, S. (1996) 'Women and the new paradigm of health and medicine', *Critical Social Policy*, 48: 33–53

Nettleton, S. (1998) *The Body in Everyday Life*. London: Routledge.

Nicholson, L. (1995) 'Interpreting gender' in L. Nicholson and S. Seidman (eds) *Social Postmodernism: Beyond Identity Politics*. Cambridge: Cambridge University Press.

Nyambedha, E. (2001) '"Children changing places" – intergenerational dynamics and orphans' movement in a high HIV/AIDS prevalence community among the Luo in Western Kenya' (Unpublished paper given to Children, Generation and Place workshop, Institute for Anthropology, Copenhagen)

Oakley, A. (1974) *The Sociology of Housework*. Oxford: Martin Robertson.

Oakley, A. (1979) *Becoming a Mother*. New York: Schocken.

O'Donnell, M. (1985) *Age and Generation*. London: Tavistock Publications.

Office of National Statistics (1997) *Living in Britain: Preliminary Results from the 1995 General Household Survey*, London: The Stationery Office.

Oliver, M. (1989) 'Disability and dependency: a creation of industrial societies' in. L. Barton (ed.) *Disability and Dependency*. Lewes: Falmer Press.

Pahl, J. (2000) 'Our changing lives' in G. Dench (ed.) *Grandmothers of the Revolution*. London: Hera Trust with Institute of Community Studies.

Parry, M. (1994) 'Children's welfare and the law: The Children Act 1989 and recent developments', *Panel News*, 7:3: 4–11.

Parsons, T. (1951) *The Social System*. London: Routledge and Kegan Paul.

Petchesky, R. P. (1987) 'Foetal images: the power of visual culture in the politics of reproduction', in M. Stanworth (ed.) *Reproductive Technologies. Gender, Motherhood and Medicine*. Minneapolis: University of Minnesota Press.

Plummer, K. (1983) *Documents of Life*. London: Allen and Unwin.

Plummer, K. (1995) *Telling Sexual Stories*. London: Routledge.

Porter, R. and Teich, M. (1994) (eds) *Sexual Knowledge, Sexual Science*. Cambridge: Cambridge University Press.

Postman, N. (1983) *The Disappearance of Childhood*. New York: Delacotte Press.

Prendergast, S. (1995) 'The spaces of childhood: psyche, soma and the social existence: menstruation and embodiement at adolescence', in J. Brannen and M. O'Brien (eds) *Childhood and Parenthood*. London: London Institute of Education.

Qvortrup, J. (1994) 'Childhood matters: an introduction', in J. Qvortrup, B. Bardy, S. Sgritta and H. Wintersberger (eds) *Childhood Matters*. Aldershot: Avebury.

Radcliffe-Brown, A. (1929) 'Age organisation terminology', *Man*, 29: 21.

Rapport, N. (1993) *Diverse World-views in an English Village*. Edinburgh: Edinburgh University Press.

Rapport, N. (1995) 'Migrant selves and stereotypes: personal context in a postmodern world', in S. Pile and N. Thrift (eds) *Mapping the Subject: Geographies of Transformation*. London: Routledge.

Rapport, N. (1997) *Transcendent Individual: Towards a Literary and Liberal Anthropology*. London: Routledge.

Rapport, N. and Dawson, A. (eds) (1998) *Migrants of Identity. Perceptions of Home in a World of Movement*. Oxford: Berg.

Richards, A. (1956) *Chisungu: A Girls' Initiation Ceremony among the Bemba of Northern Rhodesia*. London: Faber.

Richardson, R. (1987) *Death, Dissection and the Destitute*. London: Routledge & Kegan Paul.

Roebuck, J. (1978) 'When does "Old Age" begin?: the evolution of the English definition', *Journal of Social History*, 12: 416–28.

Rose, N. (1989) *Governing the Soul*. London: Routledge.

Roseneil, S. and Seymour, J. (1999) *Practicising Identities: Power and Resistance*. London: Macmillan – now Palgrave Macmillan.

Sage, L. (2000) *Bad Blood. A Memoir*. London: Fourth Estate.

Said, E. (1999) *Out of Place: A Memoir*, London: Granta Books.

Samuel, R. and Thompson, P. (eds) (1990) *The Myths we Live By*. London: Routledge.

Sawchuck, K. A. (1995) 'From gloom to boom: age, identity and target marketing', in M. Featherstone and A. Wernick (eds) *Images of Aging*. London: Routledge.

Schuller, T. (1989) 'Work-ending: employment and ambiguity in later life', in B. Bytheway, T. Keil, P. Allat and A. Bryman (eds) *Becoming and Being Old*. London: Sage.

Scott, S., Jackson, S. and Backett-Milburn, K. (1998) 'Swings and round-abouts: risk anxiety and the everyday worlds of children', *Sociology*, 32(4): 665–89.

Seabrook, J. (1982) *Working Class Childhood*. London: Gollancz.

Serematakis, C. N. (1991) *The Last Word: Women, Death and Divination in Inner Mani*. Chicago: University of Chicago Press.

Sharpe, S. (1994) *Fathers and Daughters*. London: Routledge.

Shaughnessy, L. (1998) 'Female genital mutilation: beyond mutilating mothers and foreign feminists', *Women's Studies Review*, 5: 123–34.

Shilling, C. (1993) *The Body and Social Theory*. London: Sage.

Showalter, E. (1987) *The Female Malady: Women, Madness and English Culture, 1830–1980*. London: Virago.

Shostak, M. (1981) *Nisa: The Life and Words of a !Kung Woman*. Cambridge Mass: Harvard University Press.

Sibley, D. (1995) 'Families and domestic routines: constructing the boundaries of childhood', in S. Pile and N. Thrift (eds) *Mapping the Subject: Geographies of Cultural Transformation*. London: Routledge.

Simons, J. (2001) 'The child death helpline', in J. Hockey, J. Katz and N. Small (eds) *Grief, Mourning and Death Ritual*. Buckingham: Open University Press.

Simpson, B. (1998) *Changing Families*. Oxford: Berg.

Simpson, B. (1999) *The Kinship Consequences of Posthumous Reproduction: Diane Blood versus the Human Fertilisation and Embryology Authority*. Leeds: Centre for Research on Family, Kinship and Childhood, Working Paper, 17.

Slater, D. (1998) 'Work/leisure', in C. Jenks (ed.) *Core Sociological Dichotomies*. London: Sage.

Sontag, S. (1978) 'The double standard of ageing', in V. Carver and P. Liddiard (eds) *An Ageing Population*. Milton Keynes: Open University Press.

Spence, J. (1986) *Putting Myself in the Picture: A Political Persona and Photographic Autobiography*. Seattle: The Real Comet Press.

Spencer, P. (1990) 'The riddled course: theories of age and its transformations', in P. Spencer (ed.) *Anthropology and the Riddle of the Sphinx: Paradoxes of Change in the Lifecourse*. London: Routledge.

Stainton-Rogers, R. and Stainton-Rogers, W. (1992) *Stories of Childhood: Shifting Agendas of Child Concern*. London: Harvester Wheatsheaf.

Stamp, P. (1999) 'Power to the elders: the politics of ageing amongst the Kikuyu women of Kenya', in J. Poulsen, S. Mellemgaard, N. de Coninck-Smith (eds) *Childhood and Old Age: Equals or Opposites?* Odense: Odense University Press.

Stanley, L. (1992) *The Auto/biographical I: The Theory and Practice of Feminist Auto-biography*. Manchester: Manchester University Press.

Steedman, C. (1986) *Landscape for a Good Woman*. London: Virago.

Steedman, C. (1990) *Childhood, Culture and Class in Britain: Margaret McMillan 1860–1931*. London: Virago.

Steedman, C. (1992) 'Bodies, figures and physiology: Margaret McMillan and the late nineteenth-century remaking of working-class childhood', in R. Cooter (ed.) *In the Name of the Child: Health and Welfare, 1880–1940*. London: Routledge.

Steedman, C. (1995) *Strange Dislocations: Childhood and the Idea of Human Interiority, 1780–1930*. London: Virago.

Strathern, M. (1992) *After Nature: English Kinship in the Late Twentieth Century* Cambridge: Cambridge University Press.

Talle, A. (1993) 'Transforming women into "pure" agnates: aspects of female infibulation in Somalia' in V. Broche-Due, I. Rudie and T. Bleie (eds) *Carved Flesh Cast Selves*. Oxford: Berg.

Taylor, L. (1982) 'Preface', in M. Hepworth and M. Featherstone, *Surviving Middle Age*. Oxford: Basil Blackwell.

Thane, P. (1983) 'The history of the provision for the elderly to 1929', in D. Jerrome (ed.) *Ageing in Modern Society*. London: Croom Helm.

Thomas, W. I and Znaniecki, F. (1918–1920) *The Polish Peasant in Europe and America*. New York: Dover Publications (1st edn, 5 vols).

Thompson, E. P. (1968) *The Making of the English Working Class*. London: Pelican Books.

Thorne, B. (1993) *Gender Play*. New Jersey: Rutgers University Press.

Townsend, P. (1981) 'The structural dependency of the elderly: a creation of social policy in the twentieth century', *Ageing and Society*, 1: 5–28.

Turner, B. S. (1987) *Medical Power and Social Knowledge*. London: Sage

Turner, B. S. (1992) *Regulating Bodies: Essays in Medical Sociology*. London: Routledge.

Turner, B. S. (1993) 'Contemporary problems in the theory of citizenship' in B. S. Turner (ed.) *Citizenship and Social Theory*. London: Sage.

Turner, B. S. (1995) 'Aging and identity: some reflections on the somatization of the self', in M. Featherstone and A. Wernick (eds) (1995) *Images of Aging: Cultural Representations of Later Life*. London: Routledge.

Turner, B. S. (1998) Plenary paper given at the After the Body Conference, University of Manchester.

Turner, V. (1967) *The Forest of Symbols: Aspects of Ndembu Ritual*. Ithaca: Cornell University Press.

Turner, V. (1969) *The Ritual Process*. Harmondsworth: Penguin Books Ltd.

Turner, V. (1974) *Dramas, Fields and Metaphors: Symbolic Action in Human Society*. Ithaca: Cornell University Press.

Twine, F. (1994) *Citizenship and Social Rights*. London: Sage.

Urwin, K. and Sharland, E. (1992) 'From bodies to minds in childcare literature: advice to parents in interwar Britain', in R. Cooter (ed.) *In the Name of the Child: Health and Welfare, 1880–1940*. London: Routledge.

Valentine, G., Holloway, S. and Bingham, N. (2000) 'Transforming cyberspace: children's interventions in the new public sphere' in S. L. Holloway and G. Valentine (eds) *Children's Geographies*. London: Routledge.

Van Gennep, A. ([1908] 1960) *The Rites of Passage*. London: Routledge & Kegan Paul.

Vincent, J. (1995) *Inequality and Old Age*. London: UCL Press.

Walter, T. (1994) *The Revival of Death*. London: Routledge.

Wasoff, F. and Dey, I. (2000) *Family Policy*. Eastbourne: Gildredge Press Ltd.

Watson, J. (2000) *Male Bodies: Health, Culture and Identity*. Buckingham: Open University Press.

Weeks, J., Donovan, C. and Heaphy, B. (1999) 'Everyday experiments: narratives of non-heterosexual relationships', in E. B. Silva and C. Smart (eds) *The New Family?* London: Sage.

Westwood, S. (1984) *All Day Every Day: Factory and Family in the Making of Women's Lives*. London: Pluto Press.

White Riley, M. (1986) 'The dynamisms of life stages: roles, people and age', in M. Kohli and J. W. Meyer (eds) Social Structure and Social Construction of Life Stages (Proceedings), *Human Development*, 29, 145–80.

Williamson, B. (1982) *Class, Culture and Community: A Biographical Study of Social Change in Mining*. London: Routledge and Kegan Paul.

Willis, P. (1977) *Learning to Labour*. Farnborough: Saxon House.

Willis, P. (1990) 'Symbolic work at play in everyday cultures of the young', in P. Willis *et al.* (eds) *Common Culture*. Milton Keynes: Open University Press.

Winn, M. (1984) *Children Without Childhood*. Harmondsworth: Penguin.

Worden, J. W. (1991) *Grief Counselling and Grief Therapy*. London: Routledge.

Wright, P. (1987) 'The social construction of babyhood: the definition of infant care as a medical problem', in A. Bryman, B. Bytheway, P. Allat and T. Keil (eds) *Rethinking the Life Cycle*, Basingstoke: Macmillan – now Palgrave Macmillan.

Woodroffe, C. *et al.* (1993) *Children, Teenagers and Health: The Key Data*. Buckingham: Open University Press.

Zeilig, H. (1997) 'The uses of literature in the study of older people', in A. Jamieson, S. Harper and C. Victor (eds) *Critical Approaches to Ageing and Later Life*. Buckingham: Open University Press.

Zonabend, F. (1984) *The Enduring Memory: Time and History in a French Village*. Manchester: Manchester University Press.

Index